THE
SOVIET CHALLENGE
IN THE 1990s

THE SOVIET CHALLENGE IN THE 1990S

Edited by
STEPHEN J. CIMBALA

PRAEGER

New York
Westport, Connecticut
London

Library of Congress Cataloging-in-Publication Data

The Soviet challenge in the 1990s / edited by Stephen J. Cimbala.
    p.   cm.
    Includes bibliographical references.
    ISBN 0-275-92788-1 (alk. paper)
    1. Soviet Union— Military policy. 2. United States— Military
policy. I. Cimbala, Stephen J.
UA770.S6578   1989
355'.033547— dc20   89-16128

Library of Congress Catalog Card Number: 89-16128
ISBN: 0-275-92788-1

First published in 1989

Praeger Publishers, One Madison Avenue, New York, NY 10010
A division of Greenwood Press, Inc.

Printed in the United States of America

∞

The paper used in this book complies with the Permanent
Paper Standard issued by the National Information Standards
Organization (Z39.48— 1984).

10 9 8 7 6 5 4 3 2 1

Contents

Introduction

Stephen J. Cimbala

The proverbial Soviet riddle, mystery, and enigma have never seemed more elusive to Western analysts than now. General Secretary Gorbachev has set in motion an ideological bow wave termed "reasonable sufficiency" or "defensive sufficiency," which may have profound implications for U.S.-Soviet relations. Soviet academician Georgi Arbatov has been declared that defensive sufficiency will apply to Soviet relations with the Third World, perhaps leading to the moderation or cancellation of Soviet fraternal assistance to wars of national liberation. Prudent observers are taking a wait and see attitude toward all this. On the one hand, defensive sufficiency is nothing new as a general orientation to the world outside the USSR or to the politico-military aspects of the Soviet military doctrine. The "military-technical" aspect of that doctrine may not change as rapidly as the sociopolitical content does. Soviet armed forces may retain their offensively oriented cast because the Kremlin leadership sees no other option in the near term, relative to the perceived encirclement of the USSR by the United States and its NATO allies, the People's Republic of China, and Japan. Soviet memories of World War II and the surprise inflicted on Stalin by Operation Barbarossa are still living wounds.

On the other hand, defensive sufficiency is one indicator among many that Gorbachev is intent upon reallocating resource sin the short term and upon the redefinition of strategic investment in the long run. The Soviet leadership has reached the conclusion, not unreasonable for Marxists, that their economic strength is the basis of their military power. Nor is this the only reason for Soviet concern. In Afghanistan Soviet leaders also discovered the frustration of unwinnable wars. By the spring of 1988 they were prepared to begin recalling their combat forces that had propped up the Afghan government since December 1979. From the Soviet perspective, the utility of military power, of the traditional sort, seemed to wane in the face of the probable escalation of any major conventional war into nuclear war. And nuclear war seemed self-evidently inopportune.

Further pressures were placed on the Soviet leadership to choose among modernization strategies by the Reagan administration's pursuit of the Strategic Defense Initiative (SDI) and the president's declaratory objective of removing the threat of ballistic missiles. The Soviets did not fear suddenly finding a U.S. space armada over their heads that nullified unexpectedly their deterrent. The more realistic fear was the longer-run one, losing the competition in high technology innovation. Trailing the United States, Europe, and Japan in this competition could prove fatal to Soviet major power status by the twenty-first century. Indeed, by the 1990s the high technology competition might very well have come down to earth in the form of conventional deep strike operations by NATO or, if technology permitted, the Warsaw pact against NATO. Thus the previous bases of deterrence in Europe could be undermined deliberately or inadvertently by the combination of SDI (from above) and high technology conventional warfare (from below).

Even "traditional" nuclear weapons in the superpower inventories were becoming very nontraditional. Greater accuracies and lower yields offered the possibility of more selective and discriminating attacks against a variety of time urgent and militarily important targets, while minimizing collateral damage to civilians and property. The U.S. Commission on Integrated Long Term Strategy, in its report *Discriminate Deterrence*, recognized that the available new technologies for remote sensing, data analysis in real time, and precision guidance of weapons could raise the probability of selective and politically limited nuclear and conventional conflicts.[1] This could be viewed as either more or less stabilizing of the U.S.-Soviet deterrence relationship. The possibility of smart conventional weapons and force multipliers might raise the nuclear threshold in Europe, which was desirable from the standpoint of crisis stability. However, the matter of crisis stability could not be pushed too far in the direction of corrupting deterrence stability. The Soviets should not be made to feel that because the nuclear threat had been pushed too far offstage, they could write a plausible plan for conventional war in Europe. In addition, conventional high technology weapons, such as cruise missiles or short- and medium-range ballistic missiles, could find their way into the hand of Third World adversaries of the

United States or Soviet Union. The war in the Falkland Islands demonstrated some of the potential for conventional high technology warfare, of a very early generation, to corrupt preconflict expectations about the outcome of force engagements. The Iran-Iraq war offered other evidence that uncontrollable forces of nationalism and sectarianism could be mated to high technology warfare with unexpected consequences for superpower bystanders.

The global spread of high technology might also allow various states to bypass the superpowers' restrictions on the proliferation of nuclear weapons. Wars of highly destructive nature, such as the Iran-Iraq one, would be made possible by the consequences of the high technology diffusion into military systems could be different for the arena of superpower relations, compared to the arena outside that relationship. Within the framework of U.S.-Soviet and NATO-Pact relations, conventional high technology might allow for more discrimination in warfighting if deterrence failed. Outside the superpower relationship, it could contribute to a greater willingness of states to resort to war and to the destructiveness of regional wars outside the Eastern or Western bloc.

Inside or outside the superpower relationship, most discussions of the near-term prospects for war have emphasized conflicts of short duration. Military strategists in the Reagan administration also indicated unusual interest in the possibility of extended war, perhaps global in nature, without the use of nuclear weapons. Soviet military strategists have shown apparent interest in this issue in recent years. The inability of U.S. or Soviet planners to see a feasible outcome for any nuclear war, beyond the most limited, has increased planners' interest in preparing for wars without nuclear weapons, including superpower conflicts that might occur throughout several theaters of operation simultaneously.

The serious U.S. study of extended war was impeded early in the Reagan administration by two related issues that received undue press coverage: protracted nuclear war and the problem of "horizontal escalation" from one theater of operation to another. The first of these, protracted nuclear war, quickly degenerated into a debate whether Armageddon was desirable. The second, horizontal escalation, was perceived by Reagan spokesmen as a plausible planning contingency and by Reagan critics as a blueprint for multitheater conventional military preemption. Extricating the issue of extended war from either of these bedfellows would not be easy. There was, beyond the question of extended war, the question of conflict termination. War termination seemed self-deciding or irrelevant in a short, intense, and highly destructive nuclear or conventional war in Europe. But in the context of a longer and global conflict, perhaps beginning with war between superpower allies and clients, the matter of war termination might be higher on policy makers' agendas. The Reagan administration gave lip service to the importance of war termination but did little more than its predecessors to move the concept into the operational planning stage. As for the Soviets, there was little evidence suggesting how the doctrinal shift to defensive sufficiency might affect their previously understood approaches to conflict termination, which preferred avoiding war if possible, not losing if war was unavoidable, and stalemating to losing — if the past is any indication.

The impact of defensive sufficiency on the ability of the USSR to support its objectives in the Third World was unclear. The Soviet tendency before Gorbachev had been to invest in revolutionary movements that seemed likely to topple pro-Western governments and to replace them with fraternal socialist ones. However, the Soviet experience in the 1970s in this regard was not so one-sidedly successful as Reagan officials supposed. Moreover, the Soviets, against the recommendations of their military leadership, got themselves mired in Afghanistan and could extricate their forces only in the latter 1980s with U.S. diplomatic cooperation. The reversals in Afghanistan were small consolation to the U.S. defense and intelligence communities. Despite harsher rhetoric, the U.S. record of intelligence incapacity continued into the Reagan administration from the Carter era. The assignment of strategic bomber aircraft to the mission of attacks on Quaddafi's desert headquarters testified to the weakness of U.S. covert action capabilities as much as it did to the wrath of President Reagan over allegations of Libyan responsibility for the bombing of a discotheque in Germany. The United States had a three-ring circus in the 1970s under several CIA directors and Congressional investigatory bodies that accomplished several remarkable feats. These accomplishments included making the subject of political assassination front page news, compiling a comprehensive account of CIA "misdeeds" and selectively leaking it to the press, and throttling U.S. covert operations and counterintelligence capabilities.[2] The solution, of course, was to step up the tempo of investigations. The Reagan administration was more interested in getting the CIA into covert operations than was its predecessors. But key policy issues could not be deemed candidates for overt or covert action, such as aid to the Contras, and they finally fell between two stools.

The U.S. professional armed forces were no more inclined in the 1980s to enter wars in the Third World than formerly. With good reason they were suspicious of presidential and Congressional staying power once forces were committed. Nor were U.S. allies always of the sort who encouraged U.S. public sympathy, as in the cases of Ferdinand Marcs and "Baby Doc" Duvalier, whom the Reagan administration belatedly, and justifiably, abandoned. U.S. Secretary of Defense Caspar Weinberger was the most dovish on the issue of use of force in low-intensity wars outside Europe, and the Pentagon resisted strenuously when the United States joined three Western allies in an expeditionary force in Lebanon. The tragic deaths of 241 U.S. marines in the subsequent truck bombing of their barracks in October 1983 subjected the Reagan administration to its worst crisis among its military involvements in the Third World. U.S. public consternation was partly alleviated by the invasion of Grenada shortly thereafter. But common to both cases, and to other Reagan uses of force or offers of military assistance, was the suspicion on the part of the U.S. Congress, media, and public that another Vietnam was being hatched in the White House. The Reagan administration claimed with some justification that the United States had aided the Afghan resistance, which appeared ultimately successful in its objective of driving the Soviet armies from that country. It also claimed a successful holding operation in El Salvador in the form of military technical and economic assistance to the Duarte government. And Reagan advocates would also claim that, despite the embarrassment of the Iran-Contra scandal, the United States had raised the costs for the Sandinistas to remain in power and had forced them to negotiate with the Contras over the future of Nicaragua.

The issue whether the Third World was any longer an East-West playground, or something *sui generis* where both sides would find that gains balanced losses, was unsettled as the second Reagan term ended. The Reagan defense program claimed a substantial buildup of U.S. force structure, especially the navy. This was thought to have deterred the soviet Union from otherwise contemplated adventurism. Yet the actual uses of U.S. military force and clandestine warfare occurred in the developing societies in which the primary issues were social and political, not military. The global confrontation with the Soviet Union that the Reagan administration had envisioned in the early 1980s was occurring in areas where the superpowers had limited reach and flaccid staying power. Perhaps defensive sufficiency is in part the Soviet acknowledgment of this limitation in the reach of firepower compared to ideological competition, although even the latter is supposedly going to be muted in the "new military thinking" of Moscow. The possibility cannot be dismissed that the Cold War has actually ended and that it has now moved into a phase of protracted coexistence. Protracted coexistence implies that competition within certain clearly defined boundaries is permissible but that both superpowers have a sufficient stake in the status quo not to attack its essence. This implies that nuclear war and major conventional war between superpower forces are highly improbably but that below that threshold the situation becomes more unpredictable.

There is an old saying that the more things change the more they stay the same. Whether the emergence of what we are calling "protracted coexistence" is epiphenomenal or enduring remains to be seen. Brezhnev reminded his audiences in the 1970s that detente was not the end of the class struggle. The Soviet Union in the 1990s cannot renounce its self-defined identity. It does have remarkable leeway to use the instruments of diplomacy, intelligence, and military power for stabilization, or destabilization, of the superpower relationship. So, too, do U.S. leaders.

NOTES

1. Commission on Integrated Long-Term Strategy, *Discriminate Deterrence* (Washington, D.C.: January 1988). The commission was chaired by Fred C. Ikle and Albert Wohlstetter.

2. Stephen J. Cimbala, ed., *Intelligence and Intelligence Policy in a Democratic Society* (Ardsley on Hudson, N.Y.: Transnational Publishers, 1987).

I

Nuclear Deterrence and Major Conventional Wars: Policy and Strategy Options

1

The Soviet Strategic Triad in the 1990s

Daniel Gouré

The 1990s is likely to be a period of flux in Soviet strategic thought and force planning. The Soviets have spent decades and hundreds of billions of dollars to develop their current ICBM-dominated triad of strategic nuclear forces. By the late 1980s, this process had all but been completed with the deployment of the fourth-generation ICBMs, the introduction of the first fifth-generation ICBMs, improved SSBNs with longer-range MIRVed ballistic missiles, and a revitalized strategic bomber program. It was decidedly fortuitous, to say the least, that Soviet strategic offensive acquisition programs reached this stage when they did, that is in time to meet the agenda of the new Soviet leadership on arms control and stable defense budgets. Progress toward the completion of long-standing Soviet acquisition programs provided the necessary planning base on which to integrate future acquisition plans with arms control.

A number of new conditions militate against the continuation of the relatively stable strategic planning environment that the United States and the Soviet Union enjoyed in the 1970s and early 1980s. Rapid progress in arms control may constrain Soviet offensive force options while simultaneously altering the threat against which they are directed. Advances in weapons technology are creating the prospects for new forms of strategic combat. The possible introduction of strategic defenses by either or both sides could undercut the utility of ballistic missiles and simultaneously require new offensive systems. Budget constraints and the apparent desire of the new Soviet leadership to limit the seemingly uncontrolled growth in Soviet strategic forces challenge the ability of Soviet military planners to meet the requirements and constraints of a new strategic environment.

Even in the face of these challenges, Soviet strategic forces and plans will change only slowly. Systems originally developed under the old strategic environment such as the SS-24 and SS-25 ICBMs are just beginning to come into the Soviet force. Thus, much of the character of the Soviet strategic force triad of the 1990s is set in stone. However, even if the systems to be deployed can be predicted, the character of the overall triad of Soviet strategic forces and their mission structure may be different. Moreover, as the Soviets plan now for the systems of the late 1990s and beyond, they will do so with a recognition that the old ways of doing business are changing. How they resolve the current doctrinal and planning debates and the extent of change from current concepts and practices will affect the future character and missions of the Soviet strategic forces triad.

THE DOCTRINAL CONTEXT FOR
SOVIET FORCE PLANNING

The Western understanding of Soviet military doctrine and strategy has been largely conditioned by the role that nuclear weapons have appeared to play in Moscow's management of its external relations and national security policy. The West has come to accept the Soviet contentions that the latter's acquisition of nuclear weapons in the late 1940s and its attainment of strategic parity in the early 1970s sharply shifted the political relationship between East and West. At the same time that the United States and its principal allies were struggling to deal with the political effects of the changing strategic balance, they were forced to confront evidence suggesting that Moscow, or at least the Soviet military, held a fundamentally different view of the role of nuclear weapons in any future war.

Soviet military writings since the late 1950s asserted that there had been a revolution in military affairs created by the introduction of nuclear weapons and long-range, high-speed delivery systems. This revolution, Soviet military theory declared, fundamentally altered the expected character of any future war should it involve nuclear-armed adversaries. This revolution removed the distinction between front and rear, altered the tempo of anticipated operations, increased the emphasis on initial actions — including preemptive strikes — and changed the relationship between strategic and nonstrategic forces. This revolution, Soviet military planners argued, created requirements for a new force posture, one geared to the new tempo, scope, and scale of nuclear operations at continental and intercontinental ranges and in keeping with the Soviet view on the purposes of and methods for waging war.

The essence of this force posture and associated doctrine were developed during the 1960s and recorded in a series of military theoretical writings, the most noteworthy of which were Marshal Sokolovsky's three editions of *Military Strategy.* Sokolovsky and his contemporaries spelled out the requirement for a force posture perceptually equal to opposing Western forces, sufficiently robust to deter Western aggression with the promise of massive retaliation and, should the Soviet deterrent fail, able to provide the basis for successful warwaging.[1] Given the Soviet view that the threat of war was imminent in the class-oriented structure of the international system, only a greater more certain threat of its own destruction would deter the Western imperialist camp from initiating counterrevolutionary military actions and, if they saw a possibility to substantially alter the class struggle, from direct military action against the Socialism community and the USSR. Although Soviet doctrinal writings of this period did not advocate preventive war, it did direct Soviet military planners to develop a strategy that could respond to the failure of deterrence by destroying hostile forces, defeating opposing political-military coalitions, and limiting damage to the Soviet Union. It also required Soviet military planners to develop the capability to control escalation and ensure that should homeland exchanges become inevitable the USSR would have some prospect for dominating the course and outcome of the unfolding conflict.

The Soviets concluded that their political objectives and view on war dictated the requirements for a force posture enabling them to take the offensive from the outset of a future war, thereby setting the conditions in the so-called "initial period," which would determine the course and outcome of the conflict. This requirement also had the additional advantage of promising some level of damage limitation if hostile offensive forces could be destroyed before the enemy had a chance to employ them. As a result, the Soviets required reliable forces, able to reach distant targets with extreme rapidity and capable of destroying those targets. The ballistic missile possessed a unique combination of range, speed, accuracy, reliability, controllability, and in-flight invulnerability. This combination made it the ideal weapon around which to build a strategic and long-range continental strike capability and military strategy.

The first formal Soviet doctrine for the nuclear age was that of Khrushchev's "one-variant war." According to this view, a future war would be extremely short and swift, would emphasize only forces in being, and would have an initial period that would decide the course and outcome. Consequently, Soviet nuclear strategy emphasized initial mass nuclear strikes and dismissed Western notions of escalation thresholds or limitations to the character or size of nuclear operations. Because an advantage would accrue to the side that struck first and because Soviet strategic offensive forces in the 1960s were relatively inflexible, vulnerable, and somewhat unreliable, Soviet nuclear strategy focused on the rapid detection of enemy preparations for war and enemy attack and on launch-on-warning. The intent of Soviet strategy, it appears, was not to win the war in any qualitative sense but to ensure that the opponent was also incapable of further war effort. Soviet superiority in conventional forces, even after Khrushchev's demobilization efforts, meant that Soviet Ground Forces, supported by nuclear strikes in the theater, could conceivably have occupied Western Europe. Given the uncertainties of strategic warning indicators, the relative weakness of Soviet tactical warning systems, and the need to make rapid strikes against intercontinental and continental targets, emphasis was placed on the ballistic missile and the Strategic Rocket Forces as "the basic means of conducting modern war." Other strategic forces occupied lesser, supportive roles but did not make a decisive contribution either to the initial period or during the course of a war; they could, however, help achieve the outcomes the Soviets desired.

The drawbacks to the one-variant war concept soon became apparent to Soviet political and military leaders. The threat of massive retaliation served only to deter direct, massive attacks on the Soviet homeland but was of doubtful utility in responding to either less-than-all-out attacks or the employment of U.S. or NATO nuclear weapons outside the Soviet homeland. Moreover, the Khrushchevian strategy offered no prospect for Soviet survival in the event of a general nuclear war.

In the late 1960s, the Soviet military conducted a review of its military doctrine and force acquisition policy. From this review came a number of extremely important decisions respecting the purposes and nature of Soviet military doctrine and forces. The first of these appears to have been agreement on the need to develop a strategic nuclear capability of sufficient size and robustness to permit the Soviet Union to engage in nuclear warwaging within the United States. In the debate on the role of nuclear weapons in Soviet national security policy, those who argued that nuclear weapons were not useful in the event of a general nuclear war except to deter similar forces on the other side appear to have lost to the side arguing that, for political as well as military reasons, it was wrong to deny the possibility of victory in a general nuclear war or to develop capabilities that would destroy the opponent's means of warwaging and limit damage to the Soviet Union.[2]

Another decision was to change the extant formulation on the inevitability of mass use of nuclear weapons. Soviet military writings began to acknowledge the possibility of a conventional phase during the initial period of a war between the nuclear-armed coalitions.[3] Moreover, Soviet military writings admitted the possibility that higher-level strategic and political considerations might color the character of initial nuclear operations. Selective destruction in support of the furtherance of specific military or political goals was preferred over wholesale destruction. Colonel Shirokov, writing in the classified military journal, *Military Thought*, in 1966 argued that the objective of Soviet nuclear strategy was not

> to turn large economic and industrial regions into a heap of ruins ... but to deliver strikes which will destroy strategic combat means, paralyze enemy military production, make it incapable of satisfying the priority needs of the front and rear areas and sharply reducing the enemy's capability to conduct strikes.[4]

By the late 1960s, Soviet military writings were considering not only the possibility of a conventional phase in the course of a general war but also different types of war, ones in which the use of nuclear weapons was limited for its duration. Marshal Sokolovsky, among others, appeared to be modifying the tenets of the Khrushchevian doctrine to reflect the change in military technology and to recognize that NATO, under MC 14/3, was committed to a strategy of Flexible Response, which rejected the notion of immediate all-out use of theater and strategic nuclear forces in favor of a strategy based on deliberate and controlled escalation. Such a doctrinal shift opened the door for a Soviet strategy that entailed more controlled use of nuclear weapons.

> The possibility is not excluded of wars occurring with the use of conventional weapons, as well as the limited use of nuclear means in one or several theaters of military operations, or of a relatively protracted nuclear war with the use of capabilities of all types of armed forces.[5]

Soviet military writings in this period went even further, acknowledging that the political leadership could determine the character and scale of nuclear strikes and might even require withholds from certain targets or even countries.[6] These writings suggested that the Soviet military was considering the problems posed by the need to develop a spectrum of capabilities with which to engage in hostilities at whatever level might be dictated by circumstances or the political leadership.

As a result, there emerged a consensus on the need to create a more robust strategic force posture, one capable of achieving Soviet political and military strategic objectives in wartime under a variety of conditions and limitations. The basic case that drove Soviet strategic and force planning was that of a preemptive nuclear action taken in response to strategic indicators of impending attack. If successful in its efforts to "outguess" its opponent, and if the appropriate means were available, the Soviets could hope to engage in a preemptive counterforce operation that could substantially limit damage to the USSR. A counterforce strategy also presented prospects for limitations in targeting enemy value targets. Primary deterrence could be achieved by threat of objective denial rather than by punitive retaliation. This appears to have fit better the Soviet perspective on the political character of decisions to go to war. Capitalism could best be deterred by a Soviet force posture able to disarm the West should it ever, even in the throes of its death struggle, seek to even the odds by striking at the USSR. Although the means for preemptive counterforce operations were unavailable in the 1960s, the Soviets set about to create the desired force structure.

Preemptive attack on the enemy's nuclear means of attack was considered the most effective way to vitiate an enemy's attempt at a first strike and deny his attaining strategic advantage through initiating a nuclear war. The value of preemption, according to Soviet military theory, was that it could make victory inevitable by establishing a favorable correlation of military forces. Coupled to air and missile defense operations, the preemptive strike gave the Soviet Union an opportunity to deny enemy objectives and achieve their own, including the limitation of damage to critical warwaging assets. Two authors, writing in the classified military journal, *Voyennaya Mysl*, almost 20 years ago argued that for defeating an opponent intent on a surprise counterforce attack the most effective posture combined "powerful and numerous means of destruction maintained in high combat readiness" and "well-developed anti-missile and anti-air defenses (which) can reliably repulse any aero-space attack."[7]

In developing the required force posture and strategy, the Soviets had to recognize that the temporal dimension of any future war had contracted while its spatial scope had expanded greatly. Moreover, and this was critical to the Soviet view of strategic operations, a world war could encompass virtually the entire expanse of the homelands of the warring sides. As a result, Soviet military theory came to argue, the objectives of strikes with nuclear weapons in a future war would be to defeat the enemy's armed forces, to disrupt and destroy his administrative-political and military-industrial centers, and to totally disorganize his rear.[8] The problem for Soviet strategic planners was how to prevent the destruction of the critical targets in the homeland in the course of such a war.

According to one Soviet military theoretician of the late 1960s, although superiority in total numbers of nuclear weapons still constituted the critical measure of the correlation of forces, considerations of how they were used, how they were controlled, and the relationship between offense and defense were important elements of all calculations of relative military capability.

> In the past, in armies of developed states in the main military equipment was identical. Now they have two different types of weapons — conventional and nuclear missiles. Additionally, an army can start a war with mass or limited employment of nuclear weapons or with a non-nuclear variant. As a consequence of this the qualitative determination of the combat capabilities of the armed forces of the sides has become more complex. First and foremost it depends on the presence and distribution of nuclear weapons among the various branches of the armed forces and the combat arms, on the power of the available nuclear warheads, the capabilities of their carriers, and the effectiveness of the systems of air defense and the control of troops.[9]

By the late 1970s, the Soviets began to acknowledge that even successful preemption was unlikely to determine the outcome of the war. The initial strikes by land-based ballistic missiles, it was said repeatedly, would have a decisive impact on the initiation and course of hostilities but not on an outcome.[10] This was a signal that the Soviets believed that more than a single massive nuclear salvo was required for victory. Such formulations also gave an increasing role to other Soviet forces, the SSBN and air force, in determining the course and outcome.[11] The targeting objectives for the SSBN force suggest that although some use of SLBMs in the initial strikes was contemplated, the majority of SLBMs at sea would be withheld to follow strikes that could determine the overall course of the war.[12] The other legs of the Soviet strategic triad were viewed as critical to the destruction of the enemy's overall warwaging potential with particular emphasis on reconstituted strategic forces, nonstrategic military forces, war-supporting industry, and critical administrative-political command and control. The introduction of the idea that systems other than ICBMs would be required in a strategic nuclear war may have reflected Soviet concerns that the number and quality of their SRF assets were not adequate to cover missions beyond counterforce.

The emphasis on offensive nuclear forces in Soviet military planning has often led Western observers to minimize the defensive elements of Soviet military thought and force acquisitions. In the West the widely held image of the armed forces of the Soviet Union has been that of a predominantly offensively oriented military machine relying on speed, maneuver, and long-range striking power to carry war to the enemy, destroy his offensive forces, and seize his territory. The Soviet strategy for damage limitation, or the protection of the Soviet homeland in the event of a nuclear war, is commonly associated with a policy of counterforce preemption that relies on the ability to destroy the opponent's offensive forces before they can be launched as the main "defensive" action. The heavy investment in ballistic missiles, in general, and counterforce capable ICBMs, in particular, is often referenced as incontrovertible evidence of the offensive nature of Soviet military strategy in the nuclear age.

However, this does not mean that strategic defenses do not have an important place in Soviet strategy. Defenses have been critical to the Soviet effort to negate Western offensive threats, particularly in the era before reliable offensive means were available to the Soviets. In the absence of counterforce, the Soviets had to rely heavily on defenses operating close to or within Soviet territory to achieve its strategic goals. Because of this situation, between 1950 and 1970 the Soviets were willing to invest proportionately more of its military resources in strategic defense than strategic offense, recognizing that their capability to achieve effective damage limitation was virtually nonexistent.[13]

It appears that the requirement for more effective air and missile defenses increased after the mid-1960s as the threat evolved and as Soviet military strategy moved away from the concept of a short, spasmodic nuclear war to one that was more protracted in scope in which victory would come to the side with superior enduring warwaging capabilities.[14] Nuclear war, the Soviets argued, might not be total and might involve intrawar and postwar coercion. In this context, defenses had an important role to play in Soviet military strategy, not only in combat but also in determining the correlation of military forces, a prime measure of the competitive strength of the socialist and capitalist camps.

Soviet military commentaries have consistently underscored the dialectical unity between offense and defense. Each type of operation in war, offensive or defensive, must be planned with an appreciation of the requirements and capabilities for the other. According to a recent Soviet military-theoretical work,

> Offense and defense are interrelated. In the offensive there is always included an element of the defense, just as defense is impossible without offensive action. The very conduct of the offensive is impossible to undertake without elements of the defense.[15]

Moreover, even when the Soviets deployed large numbers of counterforce-capable ballistic missiles, they continued to devote attention to defensive systems. The Soviets have always recognized that total success in an initial preemptive strike cannot be guaranteed. As a result, Soviet military planners must under all circumstances address the problem of limiting damage to the homeland and remaining Soviet military forces in the aftermath of a preemptive strike. Even where initial offensive and defensive actions are successful, the Soviets acknowledge that they merely mark the conclusion of the initial phase of hostilities and set the course of the war; further exchanges and strikes are to be expected. Given the inherent destructiveness of nuclear weapons, the Soviets recognize that even a few penetrators can wreak devastation on the Soviet homeland and disrupt critical military operations. Additionally, the Soviets recognize the possibility, albeit remote, that they will not receive timely attack warning and, hence, be forced to withstand an enemy strike before retaliating. Hence, defenses must be capable not only of defeating a surprise attack on the Soviet Union but of continuing to provide the necessary level of defense throughout the course of hostilities and to support a favorable conclusion to the war.

Discussions of the prospects for victory in a strategic nuclear war appeared to turn on judgments regarding the ability of Soviet offensive and defensive forces to successfully avoid being preempted, attrit enemy nuclear forces, and limit damage to the Soviet homeland. Marshal V. Sokolovsky, former chief of the Soviet General Staff, declared that, although offensive action was the best overall method of protecting the rear areas of the country from attack, there is no guarantee that considerable aircraft and rocket forces can be annihilated at their base, particularly at the start of the war with a surprise enemy strike. Therefore, it is required to have the necessary forces and means for destroying great masses of enemy aircraft and rockets in the air in order that there be no nuclear attacks against important objectives within the whole territory of the country.[16]

Even in the late 1960s, some Soviet military writings expressed concerns regarding the degree of success to be expected from preemptive counterforce strikes alone. General Anureyev, long considered one of the most influential Soviet military theoreticians, argued that actions by offensive forces alone would be insufficient for decisively turning the correlation of forces in the Soviet Union's favor, hence the need to also increase strategic defenses.

It would appear that in order to obtain a favorable correlation of forces to one's own advantage, maximum effort must be directed against the nuclear means of the enemy, that is the struggle against active targets. However, the development of modern carriers of nuclear weapons, especially of ballistic missiles, has led to a sharp improvement in the combat readiness of primarily the strategic nuclear forces, as a consequence of which the struggle against them *at the time of launching* becomes even more difficult. . . . A most important factor which makes it possible to accomplish the task of changing the correlation of forces in one's own favor is anti-air defense (emphasis added).[17]

Soviet views on the role of strategic defenses were conditioned in part by the belief that U.S. nuclear strategy would inevitably include strikes against countervalue targets. As the nuclear arsenals of both sides developed qualitatively and quantitatively, the destruction that the Soviet Union would suffer, regardless of who struck first, was clearly unacceptable. Hence, the requirement on the air defense became that of stopping all penetrating nuclear weapons. Often in the 1960s and 1970s this requirement was articulated as a statement of existing capability. Thus, Marshal Sokolovsky, in the third edition of his seminal text, published in 1968, spoke both of the ability of the armed forces to inflict unstoppable and crushing retaliatory blows on an aggressor and of the capability of the PVO to reliably destroy all hostile aircraft.[18] In a more candid comment, Marshall of Aviation G. Zimin, writing in 1976, established the mission requirement for the PVO/S as follows:

> Victory or destruction in a war will be dependent on the state's ability to constantly defend important targets on its own territory from destruction by strikes from the air or from space.
>
> Aero-space will become the basic arena of combat action. Under conditions of the use of rocket-nuclear weapons, the center of the weight of armed combat will be spread across the entire depth of the nation's territory and may lead to the annihilation of the material basis of the state and colossal losses among the peaceful population. *The tremendous destructive force of nuclear explosives engenders the necessity of the destruction, without a single exception, of targets penetrating into the interior of the state from the air or from space* (emphasis added).[19]

These views may, in part, explain why the Soviets chose to deploy their ABM system. It also parallels the Soviet approach at that time to strategic air defense. The critical region to protect was that in which the uppermost echelons of the Soviet national, political, and military command structure were located. This would be particularly important if the Soviets were concerned about ensuring adequate and timely C3 for strategic offensive and defensive forces to respond to a surprise or unanticipated attack. A missile defense located around Moscow also had the capability for limited protection of a portion of the Soviet ballistic missile force and a large number of other OMI and WSI targets.

Concern for the prospects of successful damage limitation and doubts regarding the prospects for absolute preemption may have been reflected in the formulation of a new form of strategic action for Soviet forces, that by strategic nuclear forces and national air defense troops in repelling enemy air and outer space attacks.[20] The expression appears to reflect a change in the Soviet view on the importance of initial nuclear strikes as the determinant of the course *and* outcome of a nuclear war. This formulation was probably phrased in this manner deliberately, its ambiguous quality reflecting the Soviet view that the dividing line between offense and defense, preemption and retaliation, missile and airbreathing components of the offensive and defense forces was increasingly blurred. Another way of interpreting this formulation is that the

Soviets recognized that while offensive preemption could provide only a partial solution to the damage limitation requirement, defensive capabilities were so restricted technically that it could offer only a relatively small contribution in its own right.

At the level of military strategy, the purpose driving Soviet military planning since the late 1960s has remained the development and maintenance of capabilities to repel and defeat hostile forces and to limit damage to the homeland. However, the Soviets have never assigned absolute priority to the offense in their strategic or operational planning for the attainment of these goals. Many factors, such as the correlation of military forces, their disposition, the quality and quantity of armaments, and the training and capabilities of the troops, will influence the choice between offensive and defensive operations. In the nuclear age, the means of destruction, specifically nuclear-armed bombers and ballistic missiles, have held an advantage over the means of defense. Under current circumstances, the Soviets recognize that nuclear-armed ballistic missiles are the most decisive and dangerous instruments of war. According to Soviet military writings, their availability enables the Soviet Armed Forces to meet its strategic requirement in rapid fashion and by means of strikes "to the entire depth of the theaters of military operations and on any continents from which aggression originates, even if they are separated by broad expanses of seas and oceans."[21] Offensive forces, in general, and ballistic missiles, in particular, are judged to be the most effective means for repelling nuclear attack and defeating an aggressor armed with nuclear weapons.[22]

For the past 40 years, the Soviets have struggled to find the proper mix of responsiveness, speed, controllability, and effectiveness in their strategic posture to meet an ever-changing threat. From a largely shell organization in 1960, they built the Strategic Rocket Forces (SRF) into a massive instrumentality for political coercion, deterrence, and warwaging. At the same time, the Soviet political and military leadership has been forced to recognize that there are limits to a purely quantitative buildup in nuclear forces and to the utility of a strategic force posture that is so highly dependent on one service, the SRF, and a single instrumentality, the ballistic missile. As a result, some within the Soviet establishment appear willing to question long-standing doctrinal precepts that have guided Soviet force posture development for the past 20 to 30 years. Should this challenge prove successful, the shape of the Soviet strategic triad in the next decade may be substantially altered.

SOVIET MILITARY DOCTRINE IN A
PERIOD OF FLUX

Recent Soviet military writings have begun to show a decided twist with respect to their views on the character of, and the prospects for conducting, a possible strategic nuclear war. Whereas the writings of the period from 1965 to 1977 emphasized the requirements for superiority in the initial conduct of nuclear strikes and the role such superiority served in enabling Moscow to dominate the course and outcome of a future conflict, later writings evinced a decidedly less optimistic view with respect to the outcome of such initial offensive operations. Strategic war, according to leading Soviet strategic thinkers such as Admiral Kuznetsov and General Gareyev, was becoming increasingly complex. No longer could the Soviets hope to control the course and outcome of such a war, particularly if it involved nuclear weapons use, simply by the expedient use of initial massive offensive operations.

In this regard, General Gareyev, in his prize-winning book on the first Soviet military theoretician, M. V. Frunze, criticizing Marshal Sokolovsky's famous work for its excessive emphasis on the role of mass nuclear strikes as the only determinant of victory in a strategic nuclear war, argued that war had to be viewed as a series of strategic operations. Success could not be determined by a single action, even if it were a massive nuclear counterforce strike. Gareyev emphasized that no set of advantages — superior numbers, weight of attack, or a better strategy — could guarantee complete success. Soviet military planners would have to be satisfied with a series of partial victories leading, they hoped, to overall victory.

> Regardless of the fact that the main, most powerful means of waging war are in the hands of the superior military commands and their employment can have a decisive influence both on the course of the war as a whole and on the conduct of military operations, the principle of a partial victory has still not lost its importance.[23]

Moreover, Gareyev and others argued that the evolution of strategic nuclear forces made it increasingly likely that regardless of the success of initial actions, a strategic nuclear war was likely to be protracted.

> The experience of war shows that under modern-day conditions it has become significantly more complicated to achieve the aims of a war than it was previously. Modern

armies possess colossal viability which is completely linked to the overall state of a nation. Even after the complete destruction of the enemy, the shattered troops still have behind them an economically and politically sound rear.[24]

What appears to lie at the heart of the Soviet drive to reevaluate their national security policy (including military doctrine, strategy, and force acquisition policies) is a recognition that the drive to increase nuclear forces, particularly ballistic missiles, has reached the point of diminishing returns. As early as 1977, one commentator stated publicly, "The time has come when existing weapons systems, one might say, have exhausted themselves, and are only being quantitatively increased. At the same time, the possibility of creating new weapons systems based on new physical principles has arisen."[25] Despite the attainment of strategic parity, termed a historical achievement by many Soviet commentators, the continual production of nuclear weapons by itself is seen as providing no enduring advantages for the Soviet Union. Former Chief of the Soviet General Staff Marshal Ogarkov made a number of provocative statements between 1982 and 1985 about the paradox existing between the continual acquisition of nuclear weapons and their inability to achieve decisive military results against another nuclear-armed opponent.[26] A change in the basic military-technical means around which modern Soviet military art has been built is likely to constitute yet another revolution in military affairs and the start of a new, long cycle. Moreover, Marshal Ogarkov suggested that the Soviets themselves have begun to ask questions regarding the role strategic nuclear forces will play in a future war and, hence, the validity of an acquisition philosophy set in place some 25 years ago.[27]

The intensification of the military-technological competition between East and West over the past several decades only serves to reinforce the Soviets' belief that the introduction of new types of weapons and new forms of combat is inevitable. Some sources have even noted that the current phase of the revolution in military affairs has reached the end in its potential for dynamic growth; for weapons based on current technology, only their quantities can be changed. Marshal Ogarkov, in his 1985 book, goes one step farther, applying the Marxist dialectical principle of negation of the negation to argue that the nuclear revolution in military affairs has produced the basis for destruction precisely because of its tremendous success. The quantitative increase in nuclear weapons is producing a qualitative backlash.

In other words, he argues that more is not better and may be worse.[28]

The Soviets also acknowledge this process of dialectical motion is neither clean nor simple. Current Soviet writers are fond of quoting Engels to the effect that changes in weapons technologies produce, in turn, changes in tactics and after that operations and, ultimately, military strategies. This process can take years. Moreover, the obsolescing technologies and the strategies based on them fade away only slowly over time. Historically, these processes have taken hundreds of years. However, because the rate of technological change is increasing and the evolution in Soviet military theory and policy is occurring in shorter time periods, the dialectical process is moving faster. Thus, existing forces and even forms of warfare could become outmoded and obsolete in extremely short time periods.

The process of change in technology moves in two directions. The first, as noted above, is the replacement of one system for a given role, such as strategic offense, with another. The second, and more complex process, is the dialectical struggle between offense and defense. The Soviets have argued that, *ceterus paribus*, defenses are an inevitable — and correct — response to the development of offensive weapons systems. Interestingly, they have argued that this phenomenon applies equally well to nuclear offense and defense as it does in the traditional arenas of conflict.

> The experience of past wars convincingly demonstrates that the appearance of new offensive weapons has always inevitably led to the creation of means to counter them. . . . This applies fully also to nuclear missile weapons whose creation and rapid development forced military-scientific thought and practice to actively develop means of countering them. In their turn, the appearance of means of defense against weapons of mass destruction caused improvements in means of nuclear-missile attack. All this confirms the conclusion that the constant struggle between means of attack and defense is one of the main sources of development of military affairs as a whole.[29]

The above discussion does not mean that the Soviets have dismissed the possibility of strategic nuclear war or abandoned the desire to prevail in such a conflict. Rather, they are debating the likely character and scope of such a conflict in order to define the desired military strategy and force posture with which to pursue their strategic objectives in the event such a war occurs. In a recent work by senior Soviet military theoreticians from the General Staff Academy written under General Milovidov, it was argued, *inter alia*, that war had not ceased to be an instrument of policy and that such a war, unleashed by imperialism, would still constitute a political struggle conducted by military means (the Clauswitzian dicta is often used in Soviet military debates as a signal that the issue is one which involves fundamental principles of doctrine). This collective work argues that in the event of such a war the central means to be employed would be long-range rocket and missile strike systems. "Massive use of rocket-nuclear weapons and other combat means can bring about sharp changes in the situation."[30] Finally, the authors make the point that nothing in the current strategic situation or military balance has negated the concept of offensive action in a strategic conflict. Rather, they assert, the offensive is the proper most direct route to the solution of the military and political conflicts.

> Extremely important in this connection is the Leninist instruction that the socialist state conducts and will only conduct defensive wars. However, these wars are defensive only in their political goals but not in the means of their conduct. . . . Their offensive is the fundamental type of military activity, and its goal is the full and total destruction of the opponent.[31]

The issue of offensive versus defensive action is also raised by this collective. The attention the authors devoted to this issue and its complexities as a wartime planning consideration suggests that there may be an ongoing debate in the Soviet military, perhaps triggered by the U.S. 1983 decision on SDI, regarding the relative weight to be placed on offensive and defensive operations.

> In modern times, the correlation of offense and defense has become deeper and more complex. Defense, in large measure includes retaliatory strikes, often using means which are also used by offensive forces. Great changes have taken place in the character of the linkages (between the two) itself, in the growing together of forces' offensive and defensive possibilities. Transit from one type of military activity to another is becoming significantly faster and more decisive than in previous wars.[32]

Given past experiences with other revolutions in military affairs, it is likely to take the Soviet Union until approximately

2010 to integrate fully the technologies embodied in the new scientific-technical revolution into the Soviet force posture and to make the appropriate modifications to Soviet military art. Military systems based on new technologies, as distinct from modifications of existing capabilities, have often taken 20 or more years to reach fruition. A critical factor affecting the Soviet Union's military capabilities in the twenty-first century is the success of Gorbachev's program of reform, or restructuring. The Soviets realize that if they are to make the transition from quantity to quality in military forces, they will have to develop the indigenous capability to design, develop, and produce the needed new systems themselves. Gorbachev himself acknowledges that the domestic reform program is likely to take several decades.

Addressing the forces that are pressing toward a new scientific-technical revolution in military affairs will require time and resources at a time when the Soviet leadership is concerned that it will have neither. As a result, the Soviets have begun to introduce new political and military doctrinal concepts that appear directed at both providing that breathing space and resource base for long-term modernization of the Soviet state and military nation and at providing the breathing space necessary to enable the Soviet state and its military forces to make the transition to a new revolution.

NEW POLITICAL THINKING, REASONABLE SUFFICIENCY, AND A DEFENSIVE DOCTRINE

There is strong evidence that an intense struggle is currently underway within the top Soviet political-military leadership on issues of military strategy, force sizing and character, and defense budgets. Evidence of this struggle has emerged in the form of a high-level policy debate on so-called "new political thinking," which has been presented as a new and comprehensive approach to Soviet security policy and to establishing criteria for sizing the Soviet force posture of the future, termed "sufficiency."

An unusual feature of this debate is the participation of a number of senior foreign affairs and defense analysts from the social science institutes attached to the Soviet Academy of Sciences. In particular, members of the Institute for the Study of the USA and Canada (IUSA) and the Institute of World Economics and International Relations (IMEMO) have, over the last year and a half, published extensively in Soviet journals and newspapers. Although members of these institutes have always written on foreign military thought or arms control, the current debate marks the first time that they have become involved publicly in discussions of Soviet military affairs. Their participation suggests that one side in the debate, probably associated with General Secretary Gorbachev, is attempting to counter directly the power and influence of the military theoreticians in the formulation of military strategy and force requirements. Although their access to classified information, at least in the past, was believed to be fairly limited, these political experts can use their experience in describing and analyzing Western military strategy and theory as the basis for articulating a new Soviet military line.

As noted above, two themes have emerged over the past several years in Soviet writings on the strategic balance and East-West relations. The first is a new and extremely innovative national security policy, based on so-called new political thinking (*Novoye Politickeskoye Mishleniye* or NPM). The second is the proper military strategy and force posture requirements under this new security regime. The concepts that have emerged to describe a set of potential responses to this issue are that of a "defensive" military doctrine and "reasonable sufficiency" (*pazumnaya dostatochna*). It is too early to be able to say whether the debate over the content of these terms signals a revolution in Soviet doctrine on national security, but the Soviet discussions about them point the way to basic policy concerns that may drive their military programs and strategic considerations over the next several decades.

The New Political Thinking

What is important to understand, particularly in terms of the possibility of a new, long cycle in Soviet military development, is that the NPM is an effort to redefine the basic national security environment in which the Soviet state will exist. Such a change in the Soviet leadership's answers to questions about the nature and extent of threats to Soviet security, Soviet national security requirements, and the relationship between domestic stability and development and external policy could have a profound effect on the character of Soviet military strategy and force acquisition policy and on the share of national resources devoted to the military.

At the heart of the Soviet argument about the NPM and the case for a new concept of Soviet national security is the contention that the character of the world political system, in general, and that of world capitalism led by the United States, in particular, has changed in the last 15 to 20 years. The slogan that Gorbachev articulated, and that has been employed in innumerable subsequent commentaries is that the modern world is integrated and interdependent and that security for one must mean security for all.[33]

The Soviets assert that the creation of this interdependent world and an interdependence of security interests has led to powerful political pressures on ruling circles in the capitalist countries to accommodate their class interests to the desires of their citizens for peace and security from the threat of war. Although such formulations have a stilted, propagandistic quality, they, nevertheless, reflect a considered Soviet judgment of the balance of political forces in the overall correlation of world forces and the vulnerability of Western governments to disarmament and pacifistic tendencies in their own countries.

The assertion that capitalism is becoming a less threatening competitor to the USSR is an essential element of the argument put forward by Gorbachev and his allies in the internal Soviet policy debates. Based on this thesis, Gorbachev could argue that the USSR can afford to enter into arms control agreements — including those such as the INF Treaty, which calls for a four-to-one ratio in Soviet to U.S./NATO nuclear warheads — which would reduce expenditures on defense and potentially disrupt its internal solidarity with social and economic reforms. To support this thesis, Soviet political theorists have had to perform some strenuous mental and ideological gymnastics. In an article in *Pravda*, one Soviet political commentator chastised "certain left-wing theorists" who argued that capitalism was constitutionally incapable of giving up its aggressive ways. This author went on to dispute one of the fundamental tenets of Leninist theory, that the intensification of the crisis of capitalism would increase its reliance on military production as a means of stimulating its economy and that this would lead to greater military adventurism. The author concludes by insisting that capitalism can reform itself and evolve to peaceful economic development.[34]

NPM theorists also argue that this peaceful transition, the convergence of capitalism and socialism, is made inevitable by the absence of militaristic alternatives as outlets for capitalist antipathy toward socialism. In the nuclear age, they argue, there can be no meaningful resort to the use of force to solve the historic class conflict between East and West. Indeed, some Soviet civilian commentators have declared that Clausewitz's often cited dictum that war is a continuation of politics is no longer true in the nuclear age. According to one senior Soviet political commentator, the presence of nuclear weapons in the hands of the superpowers has fundamentally changed the relationship of war and politics and eliminated the choice of war as a tool of international politics.

Here Clausewitz has become outdated. In contemporary politics, involving the proliferation of nuclear weapons, there is no such choice (between war and politics). Also, there is not and cannot be a political objective, such that its successful attainment could give rise to the idea to start a nuclear war and to risk the future of humankind.[35]

The basic framework for the NPM is not new; many of the concepts currently being articulated were introduced by the Brezhnev regime in the late 1970s and early 1980s. In the city of Tula in January 1977, General Secretary Brezhnev publicly eschewed a policy of nuclear superiority and a first-strike nuclear strategy. Since that time, the Soviets have developed a general declaratory policy line including the statement that there could be no victors in a nuclear war; the argument that military security required political security in the form of agreements between the opposing sides to limit the sources of friction; a tacit Soviet Union commitment to limit its nuclear force posture to a level consistent with its defensive requirements; a Soviet commitment not to be the first to use nuclear weapons; and the claim that Soviet military doctrine is strictly defensive.

Nevertheless, in scope and character, the current discussion of NPM is distinct from that which occurred under Brezhnev. Those arguing the virtues of the new approach use language and concepts that mirror those of Western integration and convergence theorists of the 1960s and 1970s. NPM advocates focus on such issues as international integration, North-South relations, stability and crisis management, technology policy, and confidence building. There is also a strong positivist note in Soviet writings on NPM. Whereas from the late 1970s to 1985 there was a consistent theme in Soviet writing on East-West relations on the constancy of the threat and on the need for constant vigilance and continual efforts to ensure Soviet military security, the NPM advocates appear to argue that the threat is not as severe as had been described and that realistic forces among imperialism's ruling circles are basically in accord with the Soviet Union's view of the requirements for security in the last quarter of the twentieth century.

The international political-military content to the NPM is reflected in the Soviet approach to arms control under Gorbachev. The goal of his predecessors, that of establishing and maintaining strategic parity with the United States, has been replaced by the more ambitious goal of achieving a single international security regime based on almost complete disarmament. In January 1986, Gorbachev announced a program of comprehensive disarmament that would progressively, between 1987 and 2000, eliminate nuclear weapons, prohibit all nuclear testing, ban new conventional weapons capable of substituting in range of effect for previously existing weapons, and ban — or render irrelevant — strategic defenses.[36]

The Soviets argue that the process of disarmament and arms control is not merely an aspect of traditional international politics but an imperative of the age, driven by considerations of the ultimate security of mankind. The reason for this is the danger posed to all nations by the arsenals of the superpowers. The initiation of a nuclear conflict between the superpowers or their alliances, the Soviets argue, would be a catastrophe of global proportions. This theme has been articulated repeatedly by Gorbachev and echoed even by senior military men, such as Minister of Defense General Yazov in his recent monograph.[37]

The core of the Soviet concept of new political thinking (NPM) as applied in the area of military affairs is a restructuring of international relations in a fashion that will reduce the prospect for East-West conflict and, consequently, reduce the requirement for military forces on both sides. The political argument being made is that a qualitatively new situation exists, one in which the objectives of any political dispute are dwarfed by the risks inherent in confrontation between nuclear-armed adversaries. Security, it is argued, cannot be assured unilaterally. It cannot be secured, the Soviets claim, through the attainment of military-technical superiority, that is, a superior correlation of military forces.

By making the danger of nuclear war the central political and security problem of all states, the very real political and moral differences that have divided East and West for more than 40 years are minimized, and the argument for maintaining Western strength as a deterrent to Soviet aggression is rendered, seemingly, irrelevant. This is the potential within the Soviet arguments supporting NPM.

Sufficiency and a Defensive Doctrine

Beginning in 1987, the Soviet press began to publish articles suggesting that a debate had begun over Soviet force planning and resource allocation to the defense sector. This debate centers on two themes. The first of these is the proper use of the concept of sufficiency as a criterion for force planning. Related to such discussions, the Soviets also introduced the idea of a new "defensive" military doctrine.

Although they have not yet presented an authoritative definition, in general Soviet usages of the term "sufficiency" do not mean minimum deterrence or the elimination of all nuclear weapons. Rather, at one level it is similar to the way sufficiency was defined during the Nixon administration — that level of forces necessary to maintain the perception of equality, to deter direct aggression, to deter coercion, and to enable the United States to meet its military objectives in the event of war. Because those objectives were not defined in terms of warwaging and victory, they amounted to a rationalization of a force posture that neither matched that of the USSR in all categories nor established a basis for military superiority, but, nonetheless, was sufficient to achieve military objectives. Some Soviet military experts have attempted to relate the ideas of sufficiency, arms reductions, and restructuring of the Soviet Armed Forces, employing sufficiency either as an argument for more efficient use of resources or as a way of defining the criteria for arms reduction. Still others have rejected any notion of sufficiency that does not correspond to specified military requirements.

At another level the concept of sufficiency may be part of the argument by some in the Soviet civilian decision-making hierarchy on the need to transfer resources from the military to the civilian sector. A few Soviet political analysts and economists have argued for the necessity of using military production facilities and the management skills of the military-industrial sector to bolster the efficiency and productivity of the civilian economy.[38] One Soviet economist, Krivosheyev, writing in the relatively liberal journal *Literaturnaya Gazeta*, argued that the unilateral reduction in the Soviet army of 1.2 million men in the late 1950s was a net benefit to the USSR and resulted in additional funds for housing construction and old-age pensions.[39] One signal that the economists may be winning their argument was the recent elevation of the head of the Military-Industrial Commission, which oversees military industrial planning, to the position of chairman of Gosplan, the central planning agency for the entire Soviet economy. An amusing example of theory put into practice was the Soviet announcement that the factory that formerly produced the SS-20 intermediate-range ballistic missile would be converted to the production of baby carriages.

As in the case of NPM, the concept of sufficiency, per se, is not new. Soviet spokesmen have long asserted that the policy of the Soviet state was to maintain only that level of forces and weapons necessary to defend the Soviet state and its allies. Moreover, the Soviets have insisted that the 1972 SALT agreements established the basic framework by which to define a stable balance of strategic forces.

In keeping with this theme, the current chief of the Soviet General Staff, marshal Akhromeyev, declared in a newspaper article on February 22, 1987, that

> The defensive character of Soviet military doctrine is based on the USSR's support for a balance (ravnovesiye) of forces at the lowest possible level, the reduction of military potentials to the limits of sufficiency such as is necessary for defense.[40]

The crux of the debate within the Soviet leadership is over the criterion for judging military sufficiency. Civilian analysts and commentators use the term "reasonable sufficiency," which appears to have become a code word for restricting military budgets to a level commensurate with Soviet objectives.

Some within the military, however, take a different tack arguing that sufficiency should be judged by what is deemed necessary or essential to meeting the threat. General Volkogonov, for example, argued that as long as the threat of war existed, it was necessary to use the military to enforce Soviet security and "maintain the military balance of power." He went on to say,

> We would like to do this with a reduced level of armaments — and we have already taken steps in this direction — but, to be able to maintain the strategic balance, we must make use of the new scientific and technological achievements and, relying on the principle of sufficiency, we cannot afford to lag behind our potential enemies. Thus, life itself — including history, logic and dialectics — forces us to increase the technical standard of our armed forces.[41]

Another senior Soviet military official, Deputy Chief of the General Staff General Varennikov, argued that "the development of the Soviet Armed Forces is limited to essential defensive adequacy and to the strengthening of strategic military parity."[42] However, this officer went on to define essential defensive adequacy as that sufficient to deny the West and the United States, in particular, the capability for waging nuclear war under conditions of surprise, preemptive attack. Thus, the general concludes by defining the requirements of Soviet defense as follows:

> In general, all of the preparations of our Armed Forces involves the ability to take responsive, protective measures. At the same time, we are not forgetting the lessons of history. We remember that imperialism is a treacherous and ruthless enemy. If it senses weakness, it will stop at nothing. It is necessary, therefore, today as never before to maintain the Army and the Navy at the highest level of combat readiness.[43]

A senior Soviet arms control and foreign policy expert defined sufficiency in the context of NPM, saying: "What characterizes sufficiency? The Soviet Union proceeds from the fact that in the arms sphere it is determined primarily by the requirements of defense against aggression."[44]

A similar comment was made by the head of the Main Political Administration, General Lizichev. Although tending to echo the Gorbachev line in most respects, on the issue of sufficiency and resource allocation, Lizichev appears to move away from Gorbachev's position and hew more to the line established by the military.

> And today, expenditures on defense, the number of personnel in the Army and Navy, the quantity and quality of weapons and military equipment are defined exclusively by the demands of the Fatherland and the collective defense of the gains of socialism. In our country, nothing more is being done than is necessary.[45]

Against these arguments by the military, a small set of Soviet political analysts has begun to develop a different view of sufficiency and to take the almost unprecedented step of arguing military doctrine. Zhurkin, Karaganov, and Kortunov, writing in the January 1988 issue of the authoritative journal of the Communist party, *Kommunist,* suggest that the existing parity between the two sides does not serve the interests of the Soviet Union but, rather, continues to stimulate an arms race. They suggest that as long as the USSR can maintain a secure capability to inflict unacceptable damage, it is secure.[46] In essence the authors reject the standard Soviet view of the importance of the correlation of forces and of the parity principle in Soviet international relations.

The concept of NPM was reflected in the newly formulated Warsaw pact "military doctrine." Rather than a formulation on military policy and the guiding principles for development of strategy and forces, it is a political tract that asserts the primacy of changes in political relation between the two sides as a basis for resolving the military competition. This doctrinal statement asserted that the Warsaw Pact's goal was no longer a reliable defense of the socialist community but, rather, the prevention of wars of any kind.[47] In the interest of attaining this objective, the Warsaw Pact advocated the reduction of forces on both sides, strategic as well as those in the theater, to the lowest possible level of strategic equilibrium.[48] The issue of sufficiency reemerges with respect to what level of force is consistent with Soviet national security objectives. According to a senior foreign policy spokesman, the answer is that

> Security becomes reliable when balance exists at the lowest possible level. In this connection, the task of military means for the prevention of war is, in particular, oriented towards maintaining the sides' military potential at a level sufficient for defense only.[49]

A more authoritative source, First Deputy Minister of Defense General Lushev, made a more sweeping statement about the relationship between the new doctrine and the sufficiency criterion, declaring that the requirement existed for both East and West to reduce their military potentials "to limits that are necessary only for the defense and not for attack."[50]

The discussion of nonoffensive defense and sufficiency for defense as arms control arguments is being buttressed by new efforts to develop defensive strategies and strategic principles. While rejecting Clausewitz's wisdom on war and politics, Soviet theorists are embracing his commentaries on the superiority of defensive over offensive combat.[51] One such effort by Kokoshin and Larionov argued that the example for future Soviet military strategy should be the battle of Kursk in 1943. Here, they claim, the superiority of the defense over the offense was proven. They assert that "in the history of war and military art this was the first instance in which the stronger side went over to the defense." However, the authors go even farther in criticizing the tendency of the Soviet military to emphasize offensive action above all other forms of combat.[52]

One interesting view was expressed by Kokoshin, who recently has become one of the leading Soviet theorists on new political and military strategies. In an article for the journal of the Institute of World Economics and International Relations, he suggests that the key to the problem of the arms race and to a stable balance is the struggle between offense and defense.

Although this is nothing novel, Kokoshin's conclusion is. He suggests the problem rests not with the defense but with the offense and with continual efforts by military and scientific experts to find new ways to overcome the defense. Kokoshin makes reference to the offense-defense dialectic, citing former Chief of the General Staff Marshal Ogarkov. Kokoshin argues that even the destabilizing aspects of the offense-defense dynamic could be mitigated if efforts were made to ensure the nonoffensive character of strategic and theater forces. He argues that instability is a product of the increasing destructiveness of offensive systems and their increased cost.

> In examining the cyclic alternation of the prevalence of either offense or defense in major wars on the European Continent, including World War II, one cannot fail to note the presence of one stable, long-term trend that seemingly permeates all these phases; namely, there was a constant increase in the destructive capability of the weapons used and a growth in the intensity of combat operations and in the depth of operations and the territorial area encompassed by military events. There was also an increase in resources used for warfare and in the level of their mobilization and military-economic strain that each state experienced during a war.[53]

The Soviet military literature, however, provides quite a different perspective on military attitudes toward the new doctrine. While paying lip service to the defensive character of Soviet military doctrine, Soviet military leaders indicate that they have not abandoned the idea of the offensive or the goal of the destruction of the enemy as part of their wartime strategy. Minister of Defense Yazov, in his recent monograph, asserted that "Soviet military doctrine regards *defense* as the main type of military operation for repelling aggression." He went on to say, "It is impossible to route an aggressor with defense alone, however. After an attack has been repelled, the troops and naval forces must be able to conduct a *decisive offensive*." Yazov resolves the seeming contradiction between these two statements by resorting to a legalist sleight-of-hand that confuses military actions with political intent.

> The Soviet Armed Forces used a combination of defense and offense to rout the aggressor during the civil war and the Great Patriotic War. This in no way contradicts the defensive nature of Soviet military doctrine, since, I would stress once again, it was an issue of offensive actions against an aggressor which had attacked our country.[54]

General Gareyev took a similar approach in addressing the new Soviet military doctrine. Soviet military doctrine, he states, is defensive because it is drawn from the political principles of the Soviet state that, at least by assertion, are defensive and nonaggressive. Confronted with aggression, however, Gareyev asserts that the Soviet Armed Forces would undertake those operations necessary both to defend the Soviet homeland and to deal the opponent an annihilating responsive strike. Defense and offense are operationally linked.

> In correspondence with the defensive character of military doctrine, military art starts from the premise that at the start of the war in the repulse of enemy aggression the basic form of combat action by our army will be defensive operations and battles. However, it is impossible to achieve the full destruction of the enemy by defense alone. For this reason, in the course of the war (following the repulse of the enemy aggression) the basic form of combat action will be by the transition in the counteroffensive to decisive counteroffensive actions in conjunction with defense, depending on the circumstances.[55]

Many Soviet military leaders are unwilling to make the future force posture a tool for either foreign or domestic policy. In an interview with a Radio Moscow correspondent, General Tretyak, recently made commander in chief of the national Air Defense Forces and a long-time associate of General Yazov, asserted that significant reductions in the Soviet Armed Forces could come about only if the security of the Soviet state was guaranteed. "Any problem, however, must be solved without forgetting the most important thing: the country's defense must be absolute." Tretyak also argued against those Soviet economists who hope to achieve additional resources for the domestic economy from reductions in military spending. He directly challenged the contentions put forward by Krivosheyev (cited above) asserting that unilateral actions by the Soviet leadership in the 1950s, regardless of their benefit to the civilian economy, "dealt a colossal blow at our defense potential, the officer corps included."[56]

The debate regarding the criterion for sufficiency and the operational and force posture implications of the new Soviet military doctrine is likely to continue. In the context of the trends in Soviet military thought regarding Soviet views on a new, long cycle in military developments, this debate may provide signals regarding Soviet strategic choices over the next decade. If, as some Soviets have alleged, strategic nuclear offensive forces can no longer hold forth the promise of a reduction in the opponent's retaliatory potential, even if employed in a first strike, and the scientific-technical revolution threatens to render irrelevant — or at least complicate — Soviet military strategy and force acquisition planning, then radical changes in the current Soviet approach to strategic forces and their uses may be in the offing. Certainly, the implementation of proposed START reductions would alter the character of the Soviet strategic offensive force posture (but not necessarily its effectiveness). Moreover, the discussion of defensive actions as the centerpiece of Soviet military doctrine might suggest an increasing Soviet interest in strategic defenses, even a preference for enhancement of existing limited strategic defensive over offensive force improvements in the next decade, with or without arms control.

In either case, the Soviet strategic force posture by the end of the 1990s may look substantially different from what it is today. Moreover, its missions and tactics may have changed even more substantially.

THE CHARACTER AND COMPOSITION OF THE SOVIET STRATEGIC FORCE POSTURE BY 1999

As noted above, barring radical moves by either superpower toward strategic arms reductions or the introduction of qualitatively new forms of strategic defense (such as SDI) the character of the Soviet strategic forces triad for the 1990s has already been set. The Soviets already are committed to specific modernization programs involving all three legs of the Soviet triad and Soviet strategic defenses. The character and timing of these programs suggest that Soviet military planners in the early 1970s anticipated the changes that occurred in the threat to the Soviet homeland, the evolution in the mission structure for Soviet strategic forces, and their targeting requirements. As a result, the systems available to be deployed in the 1990s are, in many respects, potentially highly effective responses to these changes. Even with a START agreement the Soviets are likely to be able to complete their qualitative modernization program and to protect their employment options for strategic offensive forces.

The Soviet Strategic Rocket Forces consist of a combination of third-, fourth-, and fifth-generation ICBMs. With the completion of the deployment of the fourth-generation systems in 1983 the SRF consisted of some 308 SS-18s, 360 SS-19s, 150 SS-17s, 500 SS-11s, and 60 SS-13s silo-based ICBMs. This force, able to deliver some 5,800 RVs against intercontinental targets, was judged by Western analysts to be more than capable of providing the Soviet Union with both a first-strike capability against fixed U.S. strategic forces and the means to cover all other time-urgent targets.[57]

The principal weakness in this force, as it would have been perceived by Moscow, was the potential vulnerability of Soviet reserve ICBMs to a U.S. retaliatory strike. At about the time that development decisions were required for the fifth-generation Soviet ICBMs, the United States was in the process of upgrading the accuracy of some of its existing ICBMs and was also considering deployment of a new, hard-target capable ICBM, the MX, upgrading the SLBM force with the Trident II D-5 SLBM, and deploying highly accurate cruise missiles on its bomber force. Announcement of a new U.S. targeting strategy, PD-59 or the "countervailing strategy," which sought to hold Soviet strategic forces and leadership at risk, must have confirmed Soviet concerns regarding the threat to their fixed land-based strategic assets. If sufficient numbers of U.S. hard-target ballistic missiles were deployed, the Soviets could also have expected to face a first-strike threat.

In response to this need to maintain the viability of the land-based portion of its strategic offensive force posture, the Soviets sought to incorporate survivability enhancements in their fifth-generation ICBMs. Given the expectation that ICBM accuracies would continue to improve, the Soviets made the decision to seek survivability primarily through mobility.

Beginning in 1985, the Soviets began deploying the first of these ICBMs, the SS-25, a small, single warhead missile, although as yet deployed only in silos, capable of being deployed in a road-mobile mode, on a transporter-erector-launch vehicle (TEL) similar to that used by the SS-20 IRBM. It is believed that a modified SS-25 system is already in development; this system would deploy several RVs instead of only one. Deployment of the SS-24, capable of carrying ten warheads in both a silo and rail-mobile mode is underway in 1989. In addition, the Soviets are now in the final stages of testing a follow-on heavy ICBM to replace the SS-18. By the end of the decade, if the Soviets continue to adhere to SALT constraints and no reductions were implemented, the SRF could consist of some 300 SS-18 follow-on ICBMs, 400 SS-24s with about one-half each in silo and mobile-basing modes, approximately 300 to 500 silo and road-mobile SS-25s, of which 100 or so would be MIRVed. Each of these systems is expected to also have improved performance characteristics, including higher delivery accuracies. This force would be capable of delivering about 8,000 RVs.

As in the case of the SRF, the Soviet strategic submarine force is beginning a generational change, which should be completed in the mid-1990s. This process will involve replacing old and obsolescing SBNs, specifically the Yankees and DELTA Is and IIs with the newer Delta IV and Typhoon. Currently, the Soviet SBN fleet consists of some 62 SSBNs in six classes with approximately 960 SLBMs carrying about 2,700 RVs. Half the Yankee force has been retired over the past ten years, replaced first by the Delta IIs and IIIs and since 1983 by Delta IVs and Typhoons. The remainder of the Yankee force will probably disappear by the end of the 1990s as will a number of the older Delta Is and IIs. In addition to the expected deployments of new Delta IVs and Typhoons, possibly a new SSBN will appear, starting in the early 1990s.[58] Overall, the Soviet SSBN fleet is not expected to grow much beyond its current number of 62, but the number of missiles carried is likely to increase somewhat, and the number of RVs disposed by this force will grow substantially.

The main drive in the modernization program is to increase the range, warhead capability, and endurance of the Soviet SSBN fleet. This means replacing older, noisy submarines armed with short-range, single warhead weapons. The newest SSBNs are armed with improved, longer-range, MIRVed SLBMs that greatly enhance the potential effectiveness of this portion of the Soviet strategic force posture. The Delta IV is armed with the SS-N-23, a liquid-fueled missile carrying up to ten MIRVed warheads. The Typhoon carries the SS-N-20 solid-fueled SLBM with between six and nine MIRVed warheads. All the modern Soviet SSBNs, those armed with MIRVed SLBMs, can strike targets in the continental United States from Soviet home waters. Combined with the DELTA III SSBNs, which are armed with the MIRVed SS-N-18, and the older Delta boats, armed with the single warhead SS-N-8 SLBM, the total number of SLBM/RVs deployed in this force could grow to approximately 1,000 missiles and as many as 7,000 RVs.

Introduction of the Typhoon is particularly significant because it is the first modern Soviet SSBN not based on the basic Yankee design. It carries 20 SLBMs and is believed to be configured specifically for operations under Arctic ice.[59] As a result, the Typhoon must be considered to be relatively safe from current U.S. active ASW capabilities. Because of the characteristics of both the platform and its missile system, Western analysts have tended to ascribe a strategic reserve role to the Typhoon, and perhaps to the other newer SSBNs. This notion is supported by the deployment of the first of a class of ocean-going submarine tenders capable of at-sea missile replenishment.[60]

The Soviet Navy is also deploying long-range, nuclear-capable cruise missiles on both dedicated and multipurpose submarines. The Soviets have employed tactical cruise missiles on surface ships and submarines for many years; however, they are only now completing development of a set of strategic cruise missiles. The SS-NX-21 is a nuclear-armed, long-range (3,000 km.), subsonic cruise missile capable of being launched from a standard submarine torpedo tube or from special launch tubes. Some Soviet SSNs are expected to carry this weapon. The SS-NX-24 is a larger, possibly supersonic, nuclear-armed cruise missile with similar or greater range than the SS-NX-21. It has been filght-tested from a specially converted Yankee class SSBN. It is likely that this system would be deployed either on convert-ed SSBNs or on a new class of cruise missile-firing submarines (SSGNs), which would enter the Soviet inventory in the mid-1990s. Although the numbers of such weapons, as a percentage of the Soviet nuclear arsenal, are likely to remain relatively small, their effectiveness, particularly if employed with surprise, could be quite high. It should be remembered that virtually three-fourths of all potential Soviet targets in the United States are within 1,000 kilometers of the ocean. A 3,000-kilometer cruise missile provides plenty of ocean room in which to hide.

The third element in the offensive side of the Soviet strategic force posture, the strategic bomber force, also is undergoing a transformation, even a renaissance. Once considered, at least in the West, to be all but irrelevant as a threat, the current planned modernization of the Soviet strategic bomber force will, by the mid-1990s, pose a formidable intercontinental threat.

Currently, Soviet strategic aviation consists of some 300 Bear, Bison, and Backfire bombers. The majority of this force is able to carry only a few gravity bombs or cruise missiles. The total delivery capability of this force is approximately 1,000 weapons. Portions of it, particularly the remaining Bisons and the early model Bears, are rapidly aging. Moreover, the Bear, while possessing long-range and endurance, is a propeller-driven aircraft and, hence, relatively slow.

The Soviet air offense upgrade program involves improve-ments to existing platforms, introduction of one and possibly two new strategic bombers, and development of long-range cruise missiles.[61] The most modern portion of this force is the 50 Bear-H, an upgraded version of the basic model, capable of carrying up to eight long-range (2,500 kilometer) AS-15 cruise missiles. The Blackjack, which is now undergoing developmental testing, would be a large, supersonic bomber able to carry gravity bombs, short-range missiles, the AS-15, and an advanced air-launched cruise missile similar to that currently deployed on U.S. B-52s and B-1s. Some evidence suggests that the Soviets are also developing a dedicated cruise missile-carrying strategic bomber that might carry 20 or more cruise missiles.[62] Improvements in the strike portion of the Soviet strategic air arm are being matched by the deployment of the Midas jet tanker. Aerial refueling would permit the Blackjack, and even the Backfire, to conduct round-trip missions against the United States. By the late 1990s Soviet strategic aviation could consist of more than 100 Bear-Hs, a similar number of Blackjacks, and a relatively small number of dedicated cruise missile carriers. This force could, potentially, be capable of delivering as many as 4,000 weapons.

The modernization program described above is a logical extension of the long-term Soviet acquisition strategy, set down in the early 1960s, for the attainment of a secure strategic deterrent and a meaningful nuclear warwaging capability. Changes in Soviet military strategy have not led to the abandonment of Soviet interests in perfecting their strategic posture but merely levied new requirements such as those offensive forces useful for fighting controlled nuclear conflicts, for exercising control over near-Earth space, and for establishing a secure strategic reserve force.

However, the quantitative expansion of the Soviet strategic force posture and the introduction of the next generations of marginally improved systems may prove insufficient in themselves in the 1990s to provide the Soviet Union with a high-confidence strategic warwaging/warwinning capability. As Soviet forces have improved and become more survivable and flexible, so too have those of their potential adversaries. As a result, the old Soviet notion that more is better may no longer be relevant. The Soviets will have to exploit successfully a wide range of those force-enhancement and force-support technologies in the areas of real-time surveillance and targeting, automated troop control, ballistic missile and anti-air defenses, and "exotic" weapons technologies if they are to have any expectation of being able to best the United States in a strategic conflict.

The Soviets recognize that the means of targeting, weapons delivery, and target destruction will continue to change over the next decade. For this reason it is possible to envision the beginnings of a movement toward a Soviet strategic offensive force posture that does not rely nearly so much on the ICBM or on massive nuclear strikes to achieve a warwinning position. There is reason to believe that the Soviets may already have recognized this change, downgrading the role of the ICBM as the decisive warwaging instrument and according greater value in strategic planning to the SLBM and strategic bomber forces.[63]

The proposed START treaty would reduce the overall size of the U.S. and Soviet strategic arsenals, albeit not by anything approaching 50 percent. However, it may have the perverse effect of increasing the Soviet commitment to the ICBM at the expense of SLBMs. It is likely that under the current proposals both sides will be able to deploy between 7,000 and 10,000 strategic weapons. The Soviets will be able to maintain virtually all their current targeting objectives under a START agreement. A Soviet START triad will probably consist of some 3,300 ICBM

RVs, 1,600 SLBM RVs, and 2,000 to 5,000 airbreathing weapons (gravity bombs and cruise missiles).

NOTES

1. Marshal V. D. Sokolovsky, *Voyennaya Strategiya* [*Military Strategy*] (Moscow: Voyenizdat, 1962, 1963, 1968).

2. Stephen Meyer, *Soviet Theater Nuclear Forces, Part I*, Adelphi Paper No. 187 (London: International Institute for Strategic Studies, 1983).

3. Daniel Gouré, "The Impact of an INF Agreement on Soviet Nuclear Strategy and Forces for Europe," in *Nuclear and Conventional Forces in Europe: Implications for Arms Control and Security*, ed. W. Thomas Wander (Washington, D.C.: American Association for the Advancement of Science, 1987), pp. 145–68.

4. Colonel M. Shirokov, "On the Question of Influencing the Military and Economic Potential of Warring States," *Voyennaya Mysl* [*Military Thought*] 4 (April 1968), FPD 0052/59, May 27, 1969, p. 38.

5. Marshal of the Soviet Union N. Ogarkov, "Strategy," *Sovetskaya Voyennaya Entsiklopediya* [*Soviet Military Encyclopedia*] Vol. 7 (Moscow: Voyenizdat, 1979), p. 564.

6. Shirokov, op. cit., p. 39.

7. Major General N. Vasendin and Colonel N. Kuznetsov, "Modern Warfare and Surprise Attack," *Voyennaya Mysl* [*Military Thought*] 6 (June 1968), FPD 0015/69, January 16, 1969, p. 22.

8. Sokolovsky, op. cit., 1968, p. 360.

9. Major General I. Anureyev, "Determining the Correlation of Forces in Terms of Nuclear Weapons," *Voyennaya Mysl* [*Military Thought*] 7 (July 1968), FPD 0112/68, August 11, 1968, p. 38.

10. James M. McConnell, *The Soviet Shift Towards and Away from Nuclear Warwaging*, Working Paper 84–0690, Center for Naval Analyses, pp. 112–24; Marshal of the Soviet Union A. Grechko, *Vooruzhenniye Sili Sovetskovo Gosudarstvo* [*The Armed Forces of the Soviet State*] (Moscow: Voyenizdat, 1974), p. 353.

11. William T. Lee and Richard F. Staar, *Soviet Military Policy since World War II* (Stanford, Calif.: Hoover Institution, Stanford University, 1986), pp. 45–46.

12. McConnell, op. cit., pp. 85–86.

13. Robert Berman, *Soviet Airpower in Transition* (Washington, D.C.: The Brookings Institution, 1975); Lee and Staar, op. cit., pp. 106–7.

14. John Hines, Phillip Petersen, and Notra Trulock III, "Soviet Military Theory 1945–2000: Implications for NATO," *Washington Quarterly*, Fall 1986, pp. 124–25.

15. Major-General A. S. Milovidov, ed., *Voyenno-Teoreticheskoye Naslediye V. I. Lenin i Problemi Sovremennoi Voini* [*The Military Theoretical Heritage of V. I. Lenin and Problems of Modern War*] (Moscow: Voyenizdat, 1987), p. 252.

16. Sokolovsky, op. cit., p. 361.

17. Anureyev, op. cit., p. 39.

18. Sokolovsky, op. cit., p. 365.

19. Marshal of Aviation G. Zimin, *Razvitiye Frotivovozdushnoi Oboroni* [*Development of the Air Defense*] (Moscow: Voyenizdat, 1976), pp. 191–92.

20. General M. Cherednichenko, "The Strategic Operation," *Sovetskaya Voyennaya Entsiklopediya* [*Soviet Military Encyclopedia*] Vol. 7 (Moscow: Voyenizdat, 1979), p. 552.

21. General P. Zhilin, ed., *Istoriya Voyennogo Isskustva* [*The History of Military Art*] (Moscow: Voyenizdat, 1986), p. 30.

22. General M. Kir'yan, *Voyenno-Tekhnichesky Progress i Vooruzhenniye Sili SSSR* [*Military-Technical Progress and the Armed Forces of the USSR*] (Moscow: Voyenizdat, 1982), p. 330.

23. General M. A. Gareyev, *M. V. Frunze — Voenniy Teorik* [*M. V. Frunze — Military Theoretician*] (Moscow: Voyenizdat, 1985), pp. 330–31.

24. Ibid., p. 340.

25. G. Nekrasov, "Observer," Radio Moscow Report, February 6, 1977, cited in *Foreign Broadcast Information Service* (Soviet Union), February 17, 1977, p. AA-2.

26. Marshal N. V. Ogarkov, "The Defense of Socialism: Experience of History and the Present Day," *Krasnaya zvezda* [*Red Star*], May 9, 1984, p. 2; Marshal N. V. Ogarkov, *Istoriya Uchit Bditelnost* [*History Teaches Vigilance*] (Moscow: Voyenizdat, 1985), pp. 51–54.

27. Ogarkov, *Istoriya*, p. 51.

28. Ibid., p. 89.

29. Marshal N. V. Ogarkov, *Vsegda v Gotovnosti k Zaschite Otechestva* [*Always in Readiness to Defend the Fatherland*] (Moscow: Voyenizdat, 1982), p. 36.

30. Milovidov, op. cit., p. 249.

31. Ibid., p. 251.

32. Ibid., p. 252.

33. Deputy Foreign Minister V. Petrovsky, "Trust and the Survival of Mankind," *Mirovaya Ekonomika i Mezhdunarodniye Otnosheniye* [*World Economics and International Relations*] 11 (November 1987): 15–26; A. Novin and V. Lukin, "On the Threshhold of a New Century," *Mirovaya Ekonomika i Mezhdunarodniye Otnosheniye* [*World Economics and International Relations*] 12 (December 1987): 50–62; "Dialectic of New Thinking," *Kommunist* 12 (December 1987): 3–12.

34. Yu. Krasin. "Life without Militarism. Can Capitalism Adapt to a Non-Nuclear World?" *Pravda*, January 27, 1988, p. 4.

35. D. Proektor, "On Politics, Clausewitz and Victory in a Nuclear War," *Mezhdunarodnaya Zhizn* [*International Affairs*], April 1988, p. 82.

36. M. Gorbachev, "Speech to the Twenty-Seventh CPSU Congress," *Pravda*, February 26, 1986; M. Gorbachev, "Speech to the Moscow Peace Forum," *Pravda*, February 17, 1987.

37. Ye. Primakov, "New Philosophy of Foreign Policy," *Pravda*, July 10, 1987, p. 4.

38. M. Ponomarev, "Ready to Repel the Aggressor," *Krasnaya zvezda* [*Red Star*], June 17, 1987, p. 3; L. Semeyko, "Instead of Mountains of Arms — On the Principle of Reasonable Sufficiency," *Izvestiya*, August 13, 1987, p. 5; V. Petrovsky, "Security through Disarmament," *Mirovaya Ekonomika i Mezhdunarodniye Otnosheniye* [*World Economics and International Relations*] 1 (January 1987): 6–9.

39. V. Krivosheyev, "Expert Opinion: The Economics of Disarmament," *Literaturnaya Gazeta* [*Literature Newspaper*], February 3, 1988, p. 9.

40. Marshal of the Soviet Union S. Akhromeyev, *Sovetskaya Rossiya* [*Soviet Russia*], February 16, 1987, p. 1.

41. General D. Volkogonov, "Restructuring in the Armed Forces," *Nepszabadsag*, February 20, 1988, p. 9, cited in *Foreign Broadcast Information Service* (Soviet Union), February 20, 1988, p. 89.

42. General V. Varennikov, "Guarding the Peace and Security of Peoples," *Partinaya Zhizn* [*Party Life*] 5 (March 1987): 9.

43. Ibid., p. 11.

44. Ye. Primakov, "A New Philosophy of Foreign Policy," *Pravda*, July 10, 1987, p. 3.

45. General A. Lizichev, "October and Leninist Teaching on Defense of the Revolution," *Kommunist* 3 (1987): 90.

46. V. Zhurkin, S. Karaganov, and A. Kortunov, "Views on Security — Old and New," *Kommunist*, January 1988, pp. 42–50.

47. Minister of Defense General D. Yazov, "The Military Doctrine of the Warsaw Pact Is the Doctrine of Peace and Socialism," *Pravda*, July 27, 1987, p. 5; Marshal of the Soviet Union S. Akhromeyev, "The Doctrine of Preventing War, Defending Peace and Socialism," *Problemy Mir i Sotsializma* [*Problems of Peace and Socialism*] 12 (December 1987): 23–28.

48. General A. Gribkov, "Doctrine of Maintaining Peace," *Krasnaya zvezda* [*Red Star*], September 28, 1987, p. 4; Rear Admiral G. Kostyev, "Our Military Doctrine in Light of the New Political Thinking," *Kommunist Vooruzhennyk Sil* [*Communist of the Armed Forces*] 17 (September 1987): 9–15.

49. Deputy Foreign Minister V. Petrovsky, Radio Moscow News Conference, June 22, 1987, cited in *Foreign Broadcast Information Service* (Soviet Union), June 23, 1987, p. AA2.

50. General P. Lushev, "High Combat Readiness of the Soviet Armed Forces — An Important Factor in the Defense of Socialism," *Voyenno-Istorichesky Zhurnal* [*Military History Journal*] 6 (June 1987): 8.

51. Colonel R. Savushkin, "Origins and Development of Soviet Military Doctrine," *Voyenno-Istorichesky Zhurnal* [*Military History Journal*] 2 (February 1988): 2–26; General M. Gareyev, "Sovetskaya Voyennaya Nauka (Soviet Military Science)," *Zashchita Otechestva* [*Defense of the Fatherland*] 11 (November 1987): 33–34.

52. A. Kokoshin and B. Larionov, "The Kursk Battle in Light of the Contemporary Defensive Doctrine," *Mirovaya Ekonomika i Mezhdunarodniye Otnosheniye* [*World Economics and International Relations*] 8 (August 1987): 32–40.

53. A. Kokoshin, "The Development of Military Thought and the Limitation of Armed Forces and Conventional Arms," *Mirovaya Ekonomika i Mezhdunarodniye Otnosheniye* [*World Economics and International Relations*] 1 (January 1987): 25.

54. Minister of Defense General D. Yazov, *Na Strazhe Sotsializma i Mira* [*On Guard over Socialism and Peace*] (Moscow: Voyenizdat, 1987), p. 33.

55. Gareyev, "Sovetskaya Voyennaya Nauka," op. cit., p. 36.

56. General I. Tret'yak, "Interview with TASS Correspondent," *Radio Moscow*, February 17, 1987, cited in *Foreign Broadcast Information Service* (Soviet Union), February 18, 1987, p. B9.

57. Lee and Starr, op. cit., Chapter 8.

58. U.S. Department of Defense, *Soviet Military Power* (Washington, D.C.: U.S. Government Printing Office, 1988), p. 34.

59. The configuration of the sail on the Typhoon makes it capable of forcing a hole in thin ice through which it can launch its missiles.

60. *Soviet Military Power*, op. cit., p. 95.

61. Ibid., pp. 36–38.

62. Ibid., p. 39.

63. Daniel Gouré, "C3 for the New Soviet Nuclear Forces," *Signal* 41 (December 1986): 61–63.

2

Soviet Strategic Defense

Carnes Lord

Since the late 1960s little effort has been devoted to understanding the Soviet doctrinal and programmatic commitment to strategic defense and its implications for the strategic posture of the United States. This is owing in part to the doctrinal disfavor in which strategic defense has come to be held in the United States, in part to the stringent limitations on ballistic missile defense created by the Antiballistic Missile (ABM) Treaty of 1972 and the curtailing or elimination of ballistic missile defense (BMD) forces on both sides, and in part to the lack of good information concerning Soviet activities and intentions in this area. The assumption that the ballistic missile "will always get through" has become a virtual fixture of U.S. strategic analysis. Even when some attention is given to possible offense-defense interactions, analysts tend to think in terms of purely notional ballistic missile defenses, with little reference to the actual doctrine, posture, and operational characteristics of the defensive forces the Soviets possess now or are likely to acquire in the future.[1]

A number of relatively recent developments suggest the desirability of a comprehensive reassessment of the Soviet strategic defense posture and its implications for the United States. Soviet activity at and beyond the margins of the ABM Treaty has raised troubling questions concerning Soviet intentions in this area. Improved air defense technologies are increasingly blurring distinctions between surface-to-air missile (SAM) and BMD systems, with potentially significant implications for the penetrativity of U.S. ballistic missiles and for operational nuclear planning. Shifts in Soviet doctrinal thinking in the 1970s may have led to altered and increased requirements for strategic defenses. And the Strategic Defense Initiative (SDI) enunciated by President Reagan in March 1983 has almost certainly provided an additional impetus for intensification of Soviet efforts both in pursuing current-generation defensive systems and in research and development of exotic defensive technologies.

The Soviets have long recognized the importance of active (as well as passive) defenses as an element of a balanced strategic posture. Soviet military doctrine provides an essential backdrop to the problem addressed here, and the history of Soviet programs sheds important light on the current situation. Accordingly, these matters are treated at the outset in some detail. A brief discussion of the current Soviet strategic defense posture and possible future directions follows. Then, the implications for the U.S. strategic posture are explored, with particular attention to the prospects for penetration of U.S. ballistic missiles under a variety of circumstances, the problems posed by Soviet defenses for U.S. nuclear attack planning, and related issues.

Although an attempt is made to assess broadly the capability of current and programmed U.S. strategic forces against Soviet defenses, the assessment is qualitative rather than quantitative, basing itself primarily on doctrinal and historical data and inferences from the Soviet force posture and related Soviet activities (such as the Soviet compliance record under the ABM Treaty). The focus is on active as distinct from passive defenses although some attention is given to the relationship between them. The discussion limits itself to air and ballistic missile defense, with no attempt to assess the role of Soviet antisubmarine and antispace warfare doctrine and capabilities. The primary aim is to elucidate the strategic significance in Soviet thinking and practice of the capabilities controlled by the Troops of Anti-air Defense (*Voiska PVO*), and to examine implications for the basic posture and strategy of the United States.

THE DIALECTIC OF OFFENSE AND DEFENSE

Any analysis of Soviet thinking on the question of strategic defense must begin by considering basic Soviet views or attitudes toward the defense as a form of warfare. The Soviet view of defense is a complex one, shaped in part by Russian geography and history, in part by the ideology of Marxism-Leninism, and in part by the nineteenth-century military tradition deriving from Clausewitz. At the most fundamental level — the level that is sometimes referred to as "strategic culture" — the Soviet strategic outlook (in sharp contrast to that of the United States) may be said to be essentially offensive.[2] Both traditional Russian imperialism and Communist ideology rest on an offensive dynamic, and Soviet military doctrine takes its overall orientation from a Clausewitzian understanding of victory in war and the role of the offensive in securing it. The Soviets regard the offensive as the "basic type of military operation," to which defensive operations of all kinds are and must be essentially subordinate.[3]

At the same time, the geographical exposure of the Soviet homeland and the historical experience of invasion have made the Russians sensitive to the importance of defenses, both for the sake of protecting the population and governing apparatus of the nation and for the sake of maintaining a secure "rear" for the support of offensive military operations. Yet defense for them is more than a mere adjunct or supplement to the offense. Soviet military writers regularly emphasize the reciprocal interaction of offense and defense, which is sometimes characterized as a "dialectical unity of opposites."[4] This is so in two senses. The defense is at once a form of the offense, just as the offense can and necessarily does serve defensive purposes. And because defense is fundamental and integral to warfare generally, the development of defensive countermeasures to new offensive means and methods of war is an inevitable feature of the dialectical movement of history.

The "revolution in military affairs" created by the appearance in the 1950s of large numbers of nuclear weapons in the arsenals of the major powers seems to have caused some questioning of traditional views of offense and defense within the Soviet ruling hierarchy. When the Soviets completed revision of their fundamental military doctrines in the early 1960s, however, they emphatically reaffirmed the validity of these views. Although admitting and even emphasizing the central role of nuclear weapons in modern offensive military operations, Soviet theorists insisted that the atomic bomb was in no sense an "absolute weapon." In his authoritative work on Soviet military strategy, which appeared in three editions in 1962, 1963, and 1968, Marshal V. D. Sokolovskiy stated that there is a need for a "countermeasure for each new type of weapon developed by the enemy," in order to ensure "continual superiority" over the enemy in the means and methods of warfare, particularly "firepower, mobility and maneuverability."[5] In an important article in 1964, which was intended in large measure as a response to developing Western skepticism concerning the desirability of ballistic missile defense, General Major Nikolay A. Talenskiy argued that "every decisive new means of attack inevitably leads to the development of a new means of defense." According to Talenskiy:

> Every rationally designed arms system tends to be a harmonious combination of the means of attack and the means of defense against it, of offensive and defensive armaments. This law appears to be operating in the age of nuclear rockets as well. It goes without saying that these weapons have worked a radical change in the nature of any possible armed struggle, but the law governing the search for reliable defense against nuclear-rocket attack continues to be in full effect, and antimissile systems will have an important part to play in this respect.[6]

It is often argued or assumed that Soviet attitudes on this score have changed fundamentally since the ABM Treaty of 1972. In fact, however, authoritative Soviet spokesmen have continued to affirm the inevitability and legitimacy of defensive countermeasures to all offensive force developments. In a pamphlet published as recently as 1982, for example, then Chief of the General Staff Marshal Nikolay V. Ogarkov asserted that "the experience of past wars convincingly demonstrates that the appearance of new means of attack has always invariably led to the creation of corresponding means of defense. . . . This applies fully even to the nuclear-missile weapons."[7]

BMD AND STRATEGIC OFFENSIVE FORCES

The dialectical relationship of offense and defense is particularly apparent in Soviet thinking about the role of strategic offensive forces. Soviet doctrine over the years has consistently emphasized the primacy of a damage-limiting, counterforce mission for Soviet nuclear weapons. Although Soviet theorists do not have a term equivalent to "damage limitation," they refer explicitly to a defensive mission of the Strategic Rocket Forces (SRF), and there is every reason to assume their acceptance of the strategic concept underlying this term.[8] Such a view of nuclear missile weapons is also consonant with the Soviet tendency to regard these weapons as an extension of traditional artillery geared to counterbattery and other defense suppression missions in direct support of the battle.

In the early 1960s, the Soviets acknowledged that ballistic missiles were "virtually invulnerable" to existing means of air defense. Accordingly, the requirements of defense of the Soviet homeland — preservation of the vital functions of the government and economy as well as essential support for the armed forces — had to be met primarily by the strategic offensive forces, through "annihilation of the enemy's means of nuclear attack in the regions in which they are based."[9] This mission could be accomplished most effectively in a preemptive strike that took enemy forces by surprise and destroyed them before launch. Numerous Soviet statements through the 1960s suggested that a counterforce first strike, launched on strategic warning of enemy attack, was the approach preferred in Soviet operational nuclear doctrine.

There can be little doubt that this doctrinal preference continues to provide the fundamental framework for Soviet nuclear strategy today even though the tone of more recent treatments of these issues have been much milder than the tone of those in the 1960s and early 1970s.[10] The Soviets recognized from an early point, however, that an approach based on offensive forces had critical limitations and was insufficient by itself to satisfy Soviet defensive requirements. Apart from the possibility of a surprise first strike by the United States, there could be no certainty that a successful surprise attack could be mounted under all circumstances by the Soviet SRF. The second (1963) edition of *Military Strategy* already acknowledges the decreasing opportunities for strategic surprise resulting from improved intelligence and warning on both sides.[11] Enhanced capabilities for timely tactical warning of ballistic missile attack created the possibility of launch-on-warning (LOW) as an important option for nuclear planners. There is evidence of serious Soviet interest in the LOW option for their own forces beginning in the late 1960s, and it is not impossible that the renunciation of first use of nuclear weapons by Soviet General Secretary Brezhnev in 1982 had some operational consequences in reducing the scope for preemption in nuclear contingency planning.[12]

Although the United States has never endorsed a nuclear posture based on LOW, official statements have cultivated a degree of ambiguity on this score. This fact, in combination with aspects of the U.S. posture such as high alert rates and C3 vulnerability, is likely to have discouraged any Soviet tendency to discount the possibility of U.S. recourse to LOW. In addition, the Soviets admitted that the survivability of nuclear forces could be considerably enhanced by measures such as camouflage and hardening of missile launchers. In any event, Soviet doctrine soon recognized that active defenses would be necessary as insurance against the failure of a damage-limiting offensive nuclear strike.

In the period 1963–1968, ballistic missile defense emerged in Soviet military doctrine as a critical element in the overall military relationship between the Soviet Union and its Western adversaries. At the end of this period, a Soviet writer noted that a nuclear balance had been established that could be disrupted only by a "sharp change" in offensive capabilities or by "the creation by one of the sides of highly effective means of anti-ballistic missile defense while the other side lags considerably in solution of these tasks."[13] Throughout much of this period, a number of authoritative Soviet spokesmen discussed the technical progress of the Soviet Union in antiballistic missile systems in such a way as to assert or suggest that the Soviets had achieved a decisive advantage in this realm over the United States. In the light of evidence which has since become public concerning the actual state of Soviet ABM developments at this time, it is clear that these Soviet claims formed part of a systematic campaign of strategic deception designed to mislead the West about Soviet capabilities in a number of areas. This unavoidably complicates interpretation of the statements about BMD — in any event, never very abundant — that were made by Soviet officials during these years. But it confirms the basic importance assigned BMD in Soviet thinking about nuclear war.

Perhaps the most interesting discussion of the role of ballistic missile defenses in Soviet strategy occurs in the Talenskiy article cited earlier. This article is free of deceptive exaggeration of Soviet BMD capabilities, but the involvement of its author in Western strategic and arms control debates indicates that it, too, should be used with caution. Talenskiy is fundamentally concerned to argue for the benign character of ballistic missile defenses in the hands of a peace-loving state (a qualification worth noting) in opposition to advocates of deterrence based on mutual vulnerability to attack by strategic offensive forces. In a remarkable outburst of technological optimism, he says:

> There are no limits to creative human thinking, and the possibilities offered by modern science and technology are tremendous. And I think that it is theoretically and technically quite possible to counterbalance the absolute weapons of attack with equally absolute weapons of defense, thereby objectively eliminating war regardless of the desires of resisting governments.[14]

Talenskiy emphasizes that SBM systems are purely defensive weapons, in the sense that their use would be unambiguously defensive in a "political and international law context." He also makes the intriguing remark that such weapons could be used to protect "the population of one's own country or of allied and neutral states" — possibly a reference to the recently troublesome issue of Soviet "extended deterrence" on behalf of the People's Republic of China. He further argues, against already familiar Western criticisms, that BMD is not "destabilizing" in the sense that it encourages offensive action by the side possessing it and that it is not a fundamental cause of the arms race. He effectively criticizes Western ideas of deterrence by stressing the irrational element in nuclear decision making and the tendency of aggressive regimes to underestimate the strength of the enemy. "In such conditions, the creation of an effective antimissile system enables the state to make its defenses dependent chiefly on its own possibilities, and not only on mutual deterrence, that is, on the goodwill of the other side."[15]

Talenskiy's emphasis on the unambiguously defensive character of BMD systems as well as their potential technical effectiveness can be taken as a response not only to Western arms controllers but also to Soviet strategists who preferred to assign the damage-limiting mission primarily to strategic offensive forces. That Talenskiy may have intended such a doctrinal challenge is not implausible in view of the dissent he was shortly to register against the developing Soviet orthodoxy concerning the meaning of "victory" under conditions of nuclear war, as well as his role in the renovation of Soviet military thought immediately after the death of Stalin.[16] However this may be, there can be little doubt that BMD developed a powerful constituency in the Soviet political-military leadership during the 1960s. The visceral appeal of BMD to Soviet leaders was clearly evident in the spontaneous remarks of Prime Minister Alexei Kosygin, at a news conference in London on February 9, 1967, echoing Talenskiy's view of BMD as a purely defensive system and denying it should be considered a cause of the arms race.[17]

It is sometimes argued that the Soviets underwent a fundamental change in attitude toward ballistic missile defense at the end of the 1960s in connection with their decision to seek negotiated limitations on defensive as well as offensive strategic forces and their eventual adherence to the ABM Treaty.[18] The evidence for such a change in attitude remains, however, highly questionable. It seems more likely that the Soviet decision to accept severe limits on BMD reflected both the technological deficiencies of the Soviet program at this time (together with the development by the United States of MIRVed ICBMs) and progress on the U.S. side toward deployment of a first-generation ABM system. Although the evidence is scanty, there are some indications in Soviet doctrinal writings of the 1970s that BMD continued to play an essential role. Indeed, it would seem that developments in Soviet strategic doctrine in this period support, if anything, an increased requirement for BMD or strategic defenses generally.

STRATEGIC DEFENSE AND PROTRACTED WAR

Modern Soviet military doctrine has consistently stressed the importance of the "initial period" of a global nuclear war while acknowledging the possibility that such a war might be prolonged for a considerable period of time beyond the first exchanges. However, there have been important shifts in emphasis in Soviet thinking concerning the prospects for protracted conflict and the priority to be assigned to preparations for it. As first publicly enunciated by the then Premier Nikita Khrushchev in January 1960, Soviet doctrine for nuclear war heavily stressed the central role of nuclear missile exchanges at the outset of a conflict with the West and served to justify both the creation of a separate service (the Strategic Rocket Forces) for the conduct of missile warfare and dramatic cutbacks in Soviet conventional forces. As early as 1962–1963, however, a marked shift occurred in the direction of protracted war assumptions. There appears to have been renewed debate on this question during the 1970s. The evidence suggests that additional emphasis has since been given to protracted war in Soviet thinking and higher priority given to the operational requirements deriving from it.[19]

The shift toward protracted war in the early 1960s may well have been motivated to some degree by the resistance of military traditionalists to Khrushchev's sharp downgrading of the role and resources assigned to the Soviet ground forces and by Khrushchev's weakened political position following the Cuban missile crisis in October 1962. However, other factors may have been at work as well. It is striking that the period 1962–1963 also witnessed a marked change in Soviet assessments of the prospects for successful surprise missile attack — and in stated Soviet requirements for antimissile defenses as well as evaluations of the potential effectiveness of such defenses. If or to the extent that either side is incapable of delivering a crippling initial nuclear strike, a protracted war is more likely and strategic defenses are more necessary. Strategic defenses are particularly important for protection of the political and military leadership essential to the prosecution of a protracted war. But they are also important for protection of the support structure and mobilization base of the conventional air, naval and ground forces necessary to conduct offensive operations and achieve ultimate victory. The Soviet emphasis on "combined arms" operations under conditions of protracted general war logically entails an emphasis on strategic defense.

Soviet military writings of the 1970s and early 1980s suggest an effort to reinforce and operationalize the turn to protracted war assumptions in the 1960s. At the same time, important new elements make their appearance in Soviet thinking on this subject.

The Soviet commitment to fulfilling the requirements of protracted global conflict was authoritatively reaffirmed in 1979 by Marshal Ogarkov:

> It is considered that with the contemporary means of destruction, world nuclear war will be comparatively short. However, considering the enormous potential military and economic resources of the coalitions of belligerent states, it cannot be excluded that it may also be prolonged. Soviet military strategy proceeds from the view that should the Soviet Union be thrust into a nuclear war, then the Soviet people and their Armed Forces need to be prepared for the most severe and protracted trial. . . . [Victory in such a war requires] timely and comprehensive preparations of the country and the armed forces.[20]

Ogarkov's statement emphasizes the broad continuity in Soviet policy in this area, yet there are nuanced differences with important operational implications. His reference to the economic resources of the combatant states suggests a belief that modern economies could continue to function and produce military equipment under conditions of general war. This belief appears to represent a significant change from the prevalent Soviet view in the 1960s, according to which a new world war would have to be fought with the forces and equipment on hand at the outset. Such optimism seems to reflect an increased Soviet interest in protection of the population and critical economic assets through civil defense measures.[21] But it also suggests an increased requirement for active strategic defenses. Ogarkov's use of the phrase "comprehensive preparations" could also be taken as pointing in this direction.

A recent book by Colonel General M. A. Gareyev represents the clearest challenge to the older Soviet view. Generally speaking, Gareyev is critical of the heavily nuclear emphasis associated with the Sokolovskiy volume and the early literature on the "revolution in military affairs," and returns in important respects to more traditional Soviet military thinking. This is in part a reflection of the increased willingness of Soviet strategists during the 1970s to contemplate the possibility of a prolonged conventional phase in a general war or in a general war that (because of the deterrent effect of the growing Soviet strategic and theater nuclear arsenal) would not escalate to nuclear use. In part, too, it is a reflection of a greater Soviet emphasis on the role of "strategic deployment," "strategic maneuver," and strategic reserve forces in protracted general war.[22]

The emphasis on strategic deployment is new and significant. Gareyev criticizes the lack of attention to this question in Sokolovskiy, arguing that

> The timely strategic deployment of the armed forces before the start of the war, despite its advantage from a military viewpoint, is not always possible for military-political reasons. Mobilization, let alone all the range of measures for strategic deployment, has always been equated with a state of war, and a return from it to a peacetime posture is very difficult to implement. If war, in general, is entirely political, then the political aspects on the eve of the war and during its start are even more predominant.[23]

Gareyev goes on to reaffirm in strong terms the need "to be prepared for a protracted stubborn and fierce armed struggle" and, hence, the continuing validity of the classic military principle of "economy of forces." This implies the need for strong reserve forces and their effective deployment and maneuver in the course of protracted conflict: "The appearance of new means of destruction does not reduce, but rather increases even further, the importance of strategic reserves and the necessity of maneuvering with them in the course of the war."[24]

Of particular importance for present purposes is the immediate sequel to this remark: "In this connection, the question of the dispersal of troops and naval forces, and measures to protect them against the enemy's weapons of mass destruction, cannot be solved in previous ways and must be dealt with by taking new requirements into account." Gareyev may refer here specifically to the role of mobile SAM systems with an antitactical ballistic missile capability. Somewhat later, he says explicitly that "forms of strategic action such as strategic offense and defense" have not lost their importance, "although one must naturally take into account the new methods of their preparation and execution." This may hint at a new strategic-operational approach to protection of reserve ballistic missile forces using some combination of passive defenses (principally concealment and deception) and mobile anti-air and antimissile defenses.[25]

The logic of the Soviet emphasis on protracted war scenarios through the 1970s to the present would thus appear to suggest that Soviet requirements for strategic defense have, if anything, increased since the signing of the ABM Treaty in 1972. Yet available Soviet sources have maintained an almost complete silence on the subject of ballistic missile defense since that time, a fact that would seem difficult to explain if Soviet military literature remains in any real sense an authoritative guide to actual Soviet military thinking and practice.

This silence is less difficult to explain, however, if a plausible case can be made that the Soviet BMD program has long been associated with Soviet strategic deception efforts and if due consideration is given to the evidence for a general tightening of controls over Soviet military literature in the 1970s.

STRATEGIC DEFENSE AND STRATEGIC DECEPTION

Military camouflage, concealment and deception — in Soviet terminology, *maskirovka* — has historically had an important place in the Soviet art of war. Soviet military doctrine calls for the employment of *maskirovka* at the strategic as well as the tactical and operational levels. There is also a Soviet tradition of deception at a political-diplomatic level, including the employment of propaganda and disinformation, which is highly relevant to understanding the Soviet approach to military deception.[26]

Although little systematic study has been given to this topic in the West, there is ample evidence that the Soviets have engaged in deliberate and sustained strategic deception efforts in relatively recent years. Since the mid-1950s, Soviet strategic forces have figured repeatedly in such efforts.[27] Early Soviet attempts to exaggerate the strength of their ICBM force led to the "missile gap" debate of the 1960 U.S. presidential elections.[28] After the exposure of the missile gap by the first generation of U.S. photoreconnaissance satellites and Khrushchev's subsequent failure to compensate for Soviet strategic inferiority by emplacing missiles in Cuba, the Soviets appear to have cast about for other ways to mask the weakness of their strategic forces. They turned initially to antiballistic missile systems and the "global rocket" (subsequently known as the Fractional Orbital Bombardment System), which was presented as a counter to a possible U.S. ABM system. A later and somewhat less extensive campaign was devoted to mobile ICBMs.

It is not necessary to discuss in detail the ABM deception campaign of the 1960s. It began in July 1962 with Khrushchev's declaration that an antimissile missile had been developed that could "hit a fly in outer space" and continued until 1967–1968, when claims by high-level military spokesmen on behalf of the effectiveness of the Soviet ABM system or of Soviet superiority in this sphere began to give way to more realistic appraisals. These early Soviet claims were intended to apply to the missiles associated with the "Leningrad" and later with the "Tallinn" systems for defense of the northern attack corridors into the USSR. Most Western analysts subsequently became convinced that these systems had been designed primarily or exclusively for defense against the air-breathing threat. A case can be made, however, that these missiles and associated radars were initially conceived as a dual-capable air- and ballistic-missile defense system. In either case, the Soviets not only exaggerated but actively misrepresented the characteristics of the system in question.

The strategic environment was fundamentally transformed by the initiation in the late 1960s of serious negotiations between the United States and the Soviet Union on limiting strategic nuclear arms, as well as by the rapid growth of Soviet strategic offensive forces. Under these circumstances, the Soviets had less need to exaggerate the capabilities of any of their strategic forces. Rather, particularly given the relative lead in ABM technology then enjoyed by the United States, the Soviets had a strong incentive to downplay their interest in ballistic missile defense and to seek an agreement that would freeze or narrow the margin of U.S. advantage. It seems hardly coincidental that references to BMD in Soviet doctrinal writings virtually cease after 1969. Following the conclusion of the ABM Treaty in 1972, silence on the subject has been maintained, in spite of (after 1974) the Soviets' having had the only operational BMD system in the world and their maintaining a vigorous program of research and development in this area.

Of particular interest in this connection is the evidence relating to the organizational support for strategic deception in the Soviet Union. According to recent defector sources, a separate directorate for strategic *maskirovka* was established in the Soviet General Staff in 1969, under then General Nikolay Ogarkov (who also served as representative of the General Staff in the SALT I negotiations). Among the responsibilities of this organization are said to be the control of classified and unclassified information on military and economic matters; the dissemination of information on these matters in the Soviet Union and abroad; and coordination of international negotiations on military subjects, military exercises, and measures to defeat or mislead enemy technical intelligence collection in order to create a false picture of Soviet defense capabilities and to enhance the prospects for attaining strategic surprise in any operation.[29]

Although this information is of uncertain reliability, it makes considerable sense in the light of recent changes in Soviet military literature and other official statements as well as in Soviet practices. It is generally admitted that Soviet military doctrinal literature has become much less informative and more propagandistic from the point of view of Western analysts than was the case in the 1950s and 1960s. This is usually traced to Soviet realization of the damage caused by the use of this literature by conservative analysts and political figures in the West. The tightening of controls on military literature and the development by top Soviet officials of a more pacific rhetorical line, however, would seem to predate by several years (it may be traced to at least 1973–1974) the beginning of real debate in the United States over the significance of Soviet military doctrine. Moreover, an expanding pattern of physical concealment and deception relative to Soviet strategic forces began to be observed about the same time and has continued (in spite of the high level of concern expressed by the United States over encryption of telemetry in the testing of Soviet ballistic missiles).[30]

If this view of the role of strategic deception in recent Soviet practice is essentially correct, it raises important questions about the Soviet attitude toward existing strategic arms control agreements and Soviet intentions relative to strategic arms control in the future. The history of Soviet violations or near-violations of the ABM Treaty is highly relevant to understanding Soviet strategic defense planning and programs. Particularly significant in this connection is the Soviets' possible covert upgrading of their air defense capabilities — notably, the SA-5 system — to provide them a significant capability against current-generation U.S. ballistic missiles.

STRATEGIC DEFENSE DOCTRINE IN THE ERA OF SALT

In view of the widespread assumption that Soviet interest in strategic defense declined with the signing of the ABM Treaty in 1972, it is worthwhile emphasizing the evidence for continued, and even increased, Soviet commitment to nationwide civil and air defense in the 1970s. There are also occasional indications in the doctrinal literature of this period that the PVO recognized a continuing military requirement for comprehensive antimissile defense. Indeed, there are very probably important clues to Soviet BMD doctrine and plans to be derived from a close analysis of Soviet air defense doctrinal writings of the last 10 to 15 years. Such an analysis is beyond the scope of the present study, but a few salient points need to be made.

Within several months of the signing of the initial SALT agreements, the Soviet civil defense program was apparently elevated to a status fully coequal with that of the individual military services. In 1973, a thorough review of Soviet efforts in this area was undertaken and a series of sweeping measures were implemented to restructure and improve them.[31] This review seems to have responded in part to the new doctrinal requirement to provide for continued wartime production of military material.

As regards air defense, Soviet spokesmen in the 1970s have typically stressed the strategic importance of the mission of the national air defense forces and suggested that this importance is "growing." A number of spokesmen, particularly but not only from the PVO itself, have indicated that the PVO's mission is not limited to air defense narrowly understood. According to General V. Kulikov, then chief of the General Staff, the PVO "must ensure the protection of the country and armed forces from air and nuclear missile attack, inflict maximum destruction on the air opponent, and prevent his strikes on the most important objectives, force groupings and naval forces."[32] Other high-ranking officers variously stated that the PVO must maintain the "inviolability" of Soviet borders "from even one missile or plane" or be "capable of destroying any modern means of forces of the air opponent."[33]

The most explicit statements along these lines appear in a collection published in 1976 under the signature of Marshal of Aviation G. V. Zimin, chief of the Military Command Academy of the National Air Defense. According to Zimin, "the enormous destructive power of nuclear warheads raises the necessity of destroying all targets without exception, which accomplished a breakthrough into the interior of the country from air or space." Because "the activity of the opponent in contemporary war will be carried out in the form of a unified air-space operation with the use of aviation, ballistic missiles and space equipment," it is necessary to utilize "the coordinated activity by anti-aircraft, anti-missile and anti-space defense."[34] Particularly noteworthy is the reference to the coordination of air defense, BMD, and ASAT activities, the full spectrum of the responsibilities historically assigned to the PVO. The seriousness of the Soviet commitment to such coordination was dramatically illustrated by the comprehensive exercise of Soviet strategic offensive and defensive forces carried out in June 1982.[35]

Two basic points may be made about Soviet air defense doctrine. First, the Soviets appear to assume that any U.S. nuclear attack will be both massive and counterforce. Accordingly, the PVO's mission is often formulated as involving protection of the population, administrative-political and economic centers, and the combat capability of the armed forces. The Soviets do not expect attacks designed to maximize the destruction of their urban population, but they evidently do not expect the U.S. to attempt to avoid counterforce targeting that would entail substantial collateral destruction of urban areas.[36]

Second, it is important to note the emphasis in Soviet air defense doctrine on the ideal of preclusive barrier defense of Soviet territory and the need for nationwide protection.[37] Soviet air and civil defense alike evolved after World War II from a traditional focus on local or area defense to a focus on nationwide defense. While recognizing a continuing need for local or area defense of critical civilian and military assets throughout the country, the Soviets clearly view strategic defense generally within a larger, nationwide framework.[38] This is highly relevant to any evaluation of Soviet intentions relative to ballistic missile defense (as well as the operational characteristics of the ABM system currently deployed around Moscow) and is important to bear in mind in attempting to understand the history of Soviet BMD efforts in the 1960s and subsequently.

HISTORY OF SOVIET PROGRAMS

The early history of Soviet air and ballistic missile defense remains imperfectly understood and controversial in some crucial respects.[39] Construction of an ABM system for the Moscow area began in 1962. This system, subsequently known as the ABM-1b or GALOSH, involved the very long-range exoatmospheric GALOSH interceptor missile, large phased array radars for target acquisition (the HEN HOUSE radars on the periphery of the Soviet Union) and battle management (the DOG HOUSE and CAT HOUSE radars in the Moscow area), and smaller radars (the TRY ADD) for missile tracking and guidance. By the late 1960s, 64 GALOSH missiles were deployed at four complexes around Moscow.

At the same time, the Soviets were developing systems based on air defense technologies that appeared — and which the Soviets claimed — to have ABM capabilities. The so-called

Leningrad system, based on the GRIFFON high altitude interceptor missile (evidently a forerunner or variant of the SA-5), was under construction by 1960. By the mid-1960s work ceased and the system was dismantled. The Tallinn system, based on the SA-5 missile, soon made its initial appearance in the same area (astride the primary attack route for bombers and missiles originating from the United States) and was subsequently deployed throughout the Soviet Union.

A major debate occurred toward the end of the 1960s concerning the capabilities of these Soviet systems and their intended missions; disagreement about them persists within the intelligence community.[40] A good, if not conclusive, case can be made that the Leningrad and Tallinn systems were designed from the beginning as dual-capable systems for air and antiballistic defense, whatever the deficiencies in their actual capabilities against the rapidly developing U.S. offensive strategic threat throughout the 1960s. It has been argued that the Soviets have consistently employed two distinct approaches to ballistic missile defense, reflected in the differences between the original Moscow and Leningrad systems and their successors — the first, a dedicated BMD system geared to exoatmospheric interception at very long ranges, the second, an upgraded air defense system designed against the full range of threats in the high altitude endoatmospheric regime.[41]

Perhaps the strongest argument on behalf of an ABM capability for the SA-5 system is the fact that the Soviets not only retained but also expanded this system throughout the 1970s, long after cancellation of the only U.S. air-breathing weapons program (the B-70) that posed a high altitude threat.[42] That the Soviets may have wanted a residual deterrent capability against reconnaissance aircraft as well as bombers in high altitude fight profiles is understandable, but it fails to explain why the number of SA-5 launchers doubled during the period 1971–1981. In addition, it has been reported that over a period of some 18 months in 1973–1974, the Soviets conducted some 60 tests of the SA-5 missile system in an "ABM mode" (that is, against ballistic targets).[43] Beginning with his second report to Congress on Soviet arms control violations, the president has formally stated a U.S. government finding that Soviet testing of SAM components concurrently with ABM systems is highly probable, also in violation of their ABM Treaty prohibition on testing nonstrategic systems in an ABM mode.[44]

By the early 1970s, the Soviets had begun development of a somewhat different kind of BMD system. Subsequently known as the ABM-X-3, this system incorporated a new high-performance endoatmospheric missile and a transportable phased array radar (the FLAT TWIN) apparently designed to be rapidly deployable (months rather than years). It has been argued that FLAT TWIN violates the ABM Treaty prohibition against development of ABM systems that are not "fixed types" and, more generally, that it is suggestive of a Soviet intent to lay the groundwork for eventual deployment of a nationwide BMD capability.[45] Also of critical importance in this connection is the construction by the Soviets of a large phased array radar (LPAR) at Krasnoyarsk in southern Siberia that appears identical to the Pechora-class early warning radars constructed during the 1970s on the periphery of the Soviet Union. The Krasnoyarsk radar has been formally determined (and is now almost universally acknowledged) to be a clear violation of the ABM Treaty prohibition against deployment of early warning radars other than on the national periphery and oriented outward. Soviet willingness to openly violate the treaty in this area would appear to suggest that the Krasnoyarsk radar may be intended to fulfill ABM battle management functions in addition to early warning and, hence, may be a critical long lead-time item in the creation of the elements of a comprehensive defense of Soviet national territory. The recent discovery that three additional Pechora-class LPARs are under construction in the western Soviet Union has strongly reinforced this concern.[46]

CURRENT STATUS AND TRENDS IN SOVIET PROGRAMS

The ABM system currently deployed around Moscow has been undergoing a major upgrade since 1980.[47] When completed, the new system will be a two-layer defense consisting of a modified GALOSH missile for long-range interception and a shorter-range high-acceleration interceptor missile (the GAZELLE) designed to operate within the atmosphere. The full 100 missiles permitted under the ABM Treaty are expected to be deployed in silo launchers, which may be reloadable. A new large phased array radar (the PILL BOX) for battle management is being constructed at Pushkino; this will presumably supplement rather than replace the existing DOG HOUSE and CAT HOUSE radars.

Several aspects of the Moscow system are worth stressing. First, the range of the GALOSH missile and the capabilities of its radars have, from the beginning, given the system the potential to defend an area much larger than the city of Moscow. The mission of the system has been officially assessed as defense of the Soviet civil and military command authorities in the Moscow area, rather than defense of the city of Moscow as such.[48] Second, the combination of hardening and reloadability of missile silos suggests that the Soviets intend the system to function in an enduring mode under conditions of protracted conflict. While the large phased array radars supporting the system are clearly very vulnerable to nuclear effects, it should probably be assumed that the Soviets have some confidence in their ability to ensure the survival or reconstitution of relevant radar capabilities. It seems likely that Soviet operational doctrine for the Moscow system calls for retaining some interceptor missiles to deal with follow-up strikes and for employing selective and preferential defense tactics. The large number of hardened relocation sites the Soviets have evidently prepared throughout this area, and other passive measures for protection of leadership cadres, could substantially enhance the effectiveness of the Moscow system in performing the mission indicated.

The ABM-X-3 system, utilizing the FLAT TWIN tracking radar and PAWN SHOP missile guidance radar as well as a high-acceleration interceptor, appears to have been designed as a rapidly deployable system that would provide area defense for critical portions of the USSR. Because it would not be truly mobile and would utilize above-ground launchers, the system appears to have been conceived as providing effective defense only against an initial strike. In view of the limitations of the FLAT TWIN in acquiring targets with low radar cross sections and in tracking many targets simultaneously, the system seems designed to operate with handoff data from the Pechora-class radars now under construction as well as the older early warning and battle management radars and possibly the Pushkino radar. However, the extent to which the system might be able to operate autonomously is, and is likely to remain, uncertain. The recent dismantling of up to five FLAT TWINs at the Soviet test facility at Sary Shagan has been interpreted by some in the U.S. government as a Soviet effort to satisfy U.S. compliance concerns, but it is by no means clear that the system as such has been abandoned.[49]

The Soviets currently have over 9,000 surface-to-air missile (SAM) launchers for strategic defense at over 1,200 sites as well as some 2,250 dedicated interceptor aircraft; in addition, they possess nearly 5,000 launch vehicles for tactical SAMs and some 10,000 air defense radars.[50] Progress in the relevant technologies is inexorably narrowing the gap between SAM and BMD systems, and current generation SAM systems can be expected to be much more capable, at least against certain types of ballistic missiles, than their predecessors.

There is every indication that the Soviets plan to retain large numbers of SA-5s in their inventory and to upgrade the system's general capabilities in the high altitude regime. The other principal modern strategic SAM system is the SA-10, which was first deployed in 1980. Some 80 sites are now operational, nearly half of them near Moscow, suggesting that their primary mission is defense of command and control facilities and other key military and industrial complexes in this area. A mobile variant of the system will provide enhanced survivability. The SA-10 is an all-altitude SAM system that appears to be designed primarily against the low altitude airbreathing threat. Coupled with an anticipated Soviet AWACs system and a new generation of air superiority fighters with look down-shoot down capabilities, the SA-10 should for the first time provide the Soviets with an effective capability against penetrating bombers and cruise missiles in theater and strategic applications. At the same time, it appears that the SA-10 may have the potential to intercept some types of strategic ballistic missiles.[51]

Of equal, if not greater, interest in this connection is the mobile SA-12. This system, which has reportedly been tested against SS-4 medium-range ballistic missiles and is now beginning to be deployed, has apparently been designed as a dual-capable SAM and antitactical ballistic missile (ATBM) system for theater missions.[52] As such, it possesses some inherent capability against strategic ballistic missiles — particularly SLBMs, the RVs of which generally have larger radar cross sections and slower reentry speeds than ICBMs.[53] An even more capable, longer-range, and higher altitude version, the SA-X-12b/GIANT, is currently being flight-tested and is expected to be widely deployed throughout the USSR.[54] There have been reports (so far unconfirmed) that the SA-12 is being deployed with the new mobile SS-25 ICBM, as well as with the SS-18.[55] If this should prove to be the case, it would represent an extremely significant step, suggesting that the Soviets believe the SA-12 can provide defense of ICBMs against airbreathing and perhaps even ballistic missile threats.

Analyses of the effectiveness of all of these SAM systems against ballistic missiles depend decisively on assumptions concerning their ability to accept handoff data from larger battle management or target acquisition radars. If properly supported by such radars, it would appear that both the SA-10 and the SA-12 could add significant point-target coverage to a widespread ABM deployment.[56] Even in the absence of such a deployment, there is reason to suppose that they could act as a valuable adjunct to the existing Moscow system, utilizing data from the Pushkino radar as well as DOG HOUSE, CAT HOUSE, and some or all of the peripheral phased array acquisition radars. The mobility of these systems would give them at least some capability to act as an enduring terminal defense capability in protracted war.

In addition to the conventional BMD and air defense systems just discussed, the Soviets are engaged in intensive research and development of a variety of exotic technologies with applications for strategic defense. The Department of Defense has estimated that the USSR's laser program involves more than 10,000 scientists and engineers and costs the equivalent of $1 billion a year. Prototypes for ground-based lasers for antisatellite and antimissile applications are likely to be available by the late 1980s. An operational laser for air defense is likely to be ready in the early 1990s; a ground-based laser BMD system might be deployable by the late 1990s. Other strong Soviet efforts are underway in the area of particle beam, kinetic energy, and radiofrequency weapons technology. Applications to BMD are not likely before the end of the century. The recent discovery of an elaborate laser facility at Dushanbe in Soviet Central Asia has led to speculation that the Soviets may already be deploying an operational laser ASAT and positioning themselves for more rapid development of a similar BMD system.[57]

TRENDS IN DOCTRINE AND STRATEGY

The cumulative evidence provided by the prominent place of strategic defense in Soviet military doctrine, the history of Soviet strategic defense programs, and current investment in weapons procurement and research and development in this area strongly suggests that strategic defense against ballistic missiles is and will remain a fundamental requirement of Soviet military strategy. Many questions relating to the Soviets' understanding of the effectiveness of their current BMD capabilities, their operational doctrine for BMD, the extent of Soviet concealment and deception relative to BMD and strategic defense generally, and Soviet arms control strategy relative to BMD are difficult or impossible to answer with our current knowledge. Nevertheless, prudence would seem to require that Soviet activities in this area be taken with the utmost seriousness, and that special efforts be made to understand, if only in speculative fashion, the options afforded the Soviets now and in the near term by their existing and prospective strategic defensive capabilities.

Strong circumstantial evidence suggests that the ABM Treaty of 1972, far from dampening Soviet interest in BMD, has provided the Soviets an opportunity to achieve technological parity with the United States in conventional BMD and the potential for technological surprise through research and development in exotic BMD. It has also provided a cover for the gradual upgrading of the BMD capabilities of existing defensive systems, particularly strategic

SAM systems but also relevant communications and data processing capabilities. Whatever their actual intentions, the Soviets appear to have positioned themselves to "break out" (or "creep out") of the ABM Treaty regime should the appropriate circumstances materialize. Whether these circumstances would be determined more by Soviet progress in BMD technology or by the activities of the United States and other political-diplomatic considerations is not easy to say.

A good case can be made that the Soviets have developed two basic options for long-range planning relative to BMD: no arms control and overt territorial defense with dedicated BMD; and arms control, overt defense of the Moscow region, and covert territorial defense with dual-capable SAMs (together with the capability to transition rapidly to a nonarms control environment). The Soviets may well have felt that the advantages forgone by banning dedicated BMD for nationwide defense were more than made up by the constraints placed on U.S. BMD activities across the board. Clearly, the U.S. Strategic Defense Initiative has radically altered Soviet calculations regarding the likely constraining effect of arms control on U.S. actions in the long run. In the short term, however, the Soviets may still feel it is to their advantage to minimize their own demonstrated interest in strategic defense and attempt to maintain the ABM Treaty constraints on the United States. At the same time, for a number of reasons — notably, the continuing inability of the United States or the West generally to respond effectively to Soviet arms control violations or near-violations — they may well be tempted to exercise greater latitude in pursuing their own BMD efforts whether or not these raise treaty-related issues.[58]

This suggests that in the near term the Soviets are likely to engage in "creep out" rather than "break out" from the ABM Treaty and are likely to concentrate their efforts in upgrading the Moscow system and their strategic SAMs rather than in preparing for deployment of the ABM-X-3 system. Such a strategy might also call for rapid development of a gound-based laser system with capabilities against ballistic missiles, perhaps under the cover of an ASAT or air defense system.

That this is the most likely direction of Soviet strategy would seem to be reinforced by recent trends in Soviet doctrine relative to nuclear war. As discussed earlier, increasing emphasis has been given by the Soviets throughout the late 1970s and early 1980s to the requirements of protracted nuclear or general war. Soviet spokesmen have stressed the need to maintain powerful and secure strategic reserve forces and to engage in "strategic maneuver" with these and other forces. These requirements would seem to place a premium on concealment (strategic/operational as well as tactical), dispersal, mobility, and flexibility of operations — qualities associated more readily with the new generation of strategic SAM systems than with dedicated BMD (particularly, as noted earlier, the AMB-X-3 system, which does not seem designed for endurance in conditions of protracted war).

A critical issue relating to Soviet defensive capabilities for protracted war is the survivability of phased array radars for warning, attack assessment, and battle management and of communications between these radars and field-deployed tracking and guidance radars. It may be assumed that the Soviets will place the highest priority on active defense of their large phase array radars — particularly the battle management radars in the Moscow area. On the one hand, it is necessary to wonder whether they have not taken additional steps to ensure the survival or reconstitution of such capabilities, possibly in the form of covert programs of various kinds. On the other hand, it has to be kept in mind that the Soviets probably envision the protracted phases of a general war as requiring defense principally against airbreathing systems rather than against ballistic missiles. In particular, they probably assume that the U.S. ICBM force would not be a significant factor at this stage of a war and may conclude that defense against ragged SLBM attacks as well as the airbreathing threat could be effective even with local radars operating autonomously. This is most likely to be the case in the defense of targets of lesser priority (e.g., OMT and economic assets).

ASSESSING SOVIET CAPABILITIES

There is a long tradition of discounting the effectiveness of Soviet efforts in the BMD area. Historically, the Soviets have had severe difficulties in overcoming some of the key technical obstacles to effective BMD — notably, in developing a high-acceleration interceptor missile, in phased array radar technology, and in computing capacity for battle management. However, it is also clear that the Soviets have made considerable progress in these areas. At least as important, though, is an understanding of the strategic and operational context in which Soviet BMD can be expected to operate, and this element of the analysis is regularly slighted.

Most fundamental is the question of the nature of the basic attack that Soviet strategic defenses are likely to have to sustain. There is a vast difference between an undegraded, coordinated, massive U.S. ICBM strike and a degraded, ragged U.S. retaliatory attack consisting primarily of SLBMs. As discussed earlier, the Soviets have never been certain of their ability to execute a preemptive nuclear strike that would effectively eliminate U.S. offensive strategic forces. They are probably not fully convinced of their ability to inflict an essentially preclusive blow against the U.S. ICBM force, not to speak of the problems they would face in attacking U.S. ballistic missile submarines and strategic bombers; and they no doubt take seriously the possibility that U.S. ICBMs could be launched on tactical warning of a Soviet strike. However, they may be confident enough of their ability to deliver a preclusive or seriously crippling offensive blow to the U.S. ICBM force or its associated command and control elements to model the fundamental structure and doctrine of Soviet strategic defense on this assumption. In other words, the criteria of effectiveness used by the Soviets in evaluating their own BMD may differ radically from the criteria usually employed by Western analysts, who tend to evaluate Soviet systems against an undegraded attack maximized for penetration and/or destruction of Soviet defenses.

When coupled with a damage-limiting Soviet first strike against U.S. strategic forces and C3, then, Soviet strategic defenses look much more formidable than when confronting an undegraded U.S. ICBM strike. ICBMs, both because of their trajectory characteristics and because of the simultaneity of attack that they afford, pose by far the greatest problem for BMD. In addition, of course, ICBMs pose a direct threat to BMD and its supporting infrastructure, particularly because of their ability to execute highly precise sequenced attacks. If the U.S. ICBM force is seriously degraded, it can be safely assumed that most if not all sequenced ICBM attacks could no longer be carried out, that attacks against highest priority hard targets would have a greatly reduced probability of kill, and that synergistic effects from the thorough destruction of certain kinds of target sets (particularly C3) would be largely lost. Failure to effectively suppress Soviet defenses in an initial retaliatory strike, it may be added, could afford the Soviets important leverage in a protracted war, disproportionately reducing the effectiveness of follow-on strikes by withheld U.S. forces and complicating U.S. retargeting and refire efforts. Yet for the United States to place a high priority on assured suppression of Soviet defenses could create exorbitant requirements for prompt ballistic missile warheads.

It is also essential to bear in mind the possibility that Soviet operational and tactical concepts for BMD may differ markedly from those assumed by Western analysts. The Soviets are likely to have fewer inhibitions than U.S. military planners, for example, about detonating nuclear warheads over their own territory. Thus, deficiencies of current Soviet BMD systems in reaction time and accuracy may not seem as disabling to Soviet planners as might otherwise be supposed. For that matter, one cannot entirely dismiss the possibility that the Soviets, under some circumstances, might use their own ICBMs for BMD missions.[59]

NOTES

1. See, for example, Ashton B. Carter, "BMD Applications: Performance and Limitations," in *Ballistic Missile Defense*, ed. Ashton B. Carter and David N. Schwartz (Washington, D.C.: The Brookings Institution, 1984), pp. 98–181.

2. Colin S. Gray, "National Style in Strategy: The American Example," *International Security* 6 (Fall 1981): 21–48; Carnes Lord, "American Strategic Culture," *Comparison Strategy* 5 (Fall 1985): 269–93.

3. See generally Richard Pipes, *Survival Is Not Enough* (New York: Simon and Schuster, 1984), pp. 17–109.

4. See, for example, Colonel I. A. Grudinin, *Dialektika i sovremennoye voyennoye delo* [*Dialectic and Contemporary Military Affairs*] (Moscow: Voyenizdat, 1971), p. 57.

5. Marshal of the Soviet Union V. D. Sokolovskiy, *Soviet Military Strategy*, ed. Harriet Fast Scott (New York: Crane, Russak, 1975), p. 255.

6. General Major Nikolay A. Talenskiy, "Antimissile Systems and the Problem of Disarmament," *International Affairs* 10, October 1964 (reprinted in *Bulletin of the Atomic Scientists*, February 1965, pp. 25–29). For a discussion of Talenskiy and this article, see Raymond L. Garthof, "BMD and East-West Relations," in Carter and Schwartz, *Ballistic Missile Defense*, pp. 292–94.

7. Marshal of the Soviet Union Nikolay V. Ogarkov, *Vsegda v Gotovnosti k Zashcite Otechestva* [*Always Ready to Defend the Motherland*] (Moscow: Voyenizdat, 1982), p. 36.

8. A straightforward explication of the U.S. notion of "damage limitation" was added in the third edition of Sokolovskiy (pp. 62–63) — well after it had ceased to reflect declaratory U.S. policy. This discussion also treats "assured destruction" merely as an aspect of a U.S. warfighting nuclear strategy. For the defensive mission of the SRF see Sokolovskiy, p. 284. See generally Michael J. Deane, *Strategic Defense in Soviet Strategy* (Coral Gables, Florida: Advanced International Studies Institute, University of Miami, 1980).

9. Sokolovskiy, p. 296. The remark that "ballistic missiles employed en masse are still practically invulnerable to existing means of PVO" (p. 431, n. 115) appeared only in the first edition.

10. For an evaluation of recent changes in Soviet declaratory policy relative to nuclear weapons, see Dan L. Strode and Rebecca V. Strode, "Diplomacy and Defense in Soviet National Security Policy," *International Security*, Fall 1983, pp. 92–116.

11. Sokolovskiy, p. 391, n. 31.

12. Defense Minister Dmitri Ustinov's defense of the Brezhnev pledge in *Pravda* (June 12, 1982) is frequently taken as endorsing a LOW posture for Soviet forces; but Ustinov seems to leave the door open for a preemptive option when he remarks that "the imperialist forces will not succeed in ensuring for themselves military superiority either at the state of preparing a nuclear war or at the moment when they try to start that war."

13. General V. I. Zemskov, "Wars of the Contemporary Era," *Voyennaya mysl'* 5 (May 1969): 59.

14. Talenskiy, "Antimissile Systems."

15. Ibid.

16. See, for example, Thomas W. Wolfe, *Soviet Strategy at the Crossroads* (Cambridge, Mass.: Harvard University Press, 1964), pp. 72–78.

17. See the account of Garthoff, "BMD and East-West Relations," pp. 295–96.

18. See particularly Garthoff, "BMD and East-West Relations," pp. 298–314.

19. On this subject see generally Richard S. Soll, "The Soviet Union and Protracted Nuclear War," *Strategic Review* 8 (Fall 1980): 15–28; and Richard B. Foster, "On Prolonged Nuclear War," *International Security Review* 6 (Winter 1981–1982): 497–518.

20. Marshal of the Soviet Union Nikolay V. Ogarkov, "Military Strategy," in *Sovetskaya Voyennaya Entsiklopediya*, Vol. 7 (Moscow: Voyenizdat, 1979), p. 563.

21. Consider particularly then-Minister of Defense Grechko's remark that "war cannot be waged without a reliable and functioning rear" (*Vooruzhenniye Sili Sovetskovo Gosudarstvo* [*The Armed Forces of the Soviet State*] [Moscow: Voyenizdat, 1975], p. 114). A drastic upgrading of the Soviet civil defense program was undertaken beginning in 1973, apparently in response to decisions taken in the late 1960s regarding the potential importance and effectiveness of civil defense measures in overall Soviet strategy. See Leon Gouré, *War Survival in Soviet Strategy: USSR Civil Defense* (Coral Gables, Florida: Center for Advanced International Studies, University of Miami, 1976). For an account of actual measures the Soviets have taken to ensure continued functioning of their economy under conditions of nuclear war, see Department of Defense, *Soviet Military Power* (Washington, D.C.: U.S. Government Printing Office, 1985), p. 52.

22. Colonel General M. A. Gareyev, *M. V. Frunze — Voenniy Teorik* [*M. V. Frunze — Military Theoretician*] (Moscow: Voyenizdat, 1985), pp. 236–46, as translated in *Strategic Review* 13 (Fall 1985): 102–6.

23. Gareyev, *M. V. Frunze*.

24. Ibid.

25. For a discussion of the Gareyev volume in the context of the "third revolution" in Soviet military affairs, see General William E. Odom, "Soviet Force Posture: Dilemmas and Directions," *Problems of Communism* 34 (July-August 1985): 1–14. See also James M. McConnell, "The Irrelevance Today of Sokolovskiy's Book *Military Strategy*," *Defense Analysis* 1 (1985): 243–54.

26. See generally Brian D. Dailey and Patrick J. Parker, eds., *Soviet Strategic Deception* (Lexington, Mass/Toronto: Lexington Books, 1987); as well as Richard H. Shultz and Roy Godson, *Dezinformatsia: Active Measures in Soviet Strategy* (Washington, D.C.: Pergamon-Brassey's, 1984).

27. The only general account is Michael Mihalka, "Soviet Strategic Deception, 1955–1981," *Journal of Strategic Studies* 5 (March 1982): 40–93; reprinted in *Military Deception and Strategic Surprise*, ed. John Gooch and Amos Perlmutter (London: Frank Cass, 1982).

28. A detailed history and analysis of this episode is available in Arnold L. Horelick and Myron Rush, *Strategic Power and Soviet Foreign Policy* (Chicago/London: University of Chicago Press, 1966).

29. Viktor Suvorov, *Inside the Soviet Army* (New York: MacMillan, 1982), pp. 100–7, and "GUSM: The Soviet Service of Strategic Deception," *International Defense Review* 8 (1985): 1235–40. See further Richard J. Heuer, Jr., "Soviet Organization and Doctrine for Strategic Deception," in Dailey and Parker, pp. 42–47.

30. See, for example, Colin S. Gray, "SALT I Aftermath: Have the Soviets Been Cheating?" *Air Force*, November 1975, pp. 28–33.

31. Gouré, *War Survival in Soviet Strategy*, pp. 64–66.

32. General of the Army V. Kulikov, "Anti-air Defense in the System of Defense of the Soviet State," *Vestnik protivovodushnoy oborony* 4 (April 1973): 4. See generally the discussion of Deane, *Strategic Defense in Soviet Strategy*, pp. 77–94.

33. Ibid., pp. 79–80.

34. Marshal of Aviation G. V. Zimin, *Razvitiye Frotivovozdushnoi Oboroni [Development of Anti-air Defense]* (Moscow: Voyenizdat, 1976), pp. 192, 105.

35. "Soviets State Integrated Test of Weapons," *Aviation Week and Space Technology*, June 28, 1982, pp. 20–21.

36. Deane, *Strategic Defense in Soviet Strategy*, pp. 84–94.

37. Ibid., pp. 83–84.

38. According to a recent monograph on Soviet air defense in World War II, its two basic missions were "defense of important administrative-political and industrial-economic centers of the Soviet Union and other very important installations having decisive importance for the state's military-industrial might and defense of field army communications, especially front railroads" (Colonel N. A. Svetlishin, *Voyska PVO strany v Velikoy Otchestvennoy voyne [The National Air Defense Forces in the Great Patriotic War]* [Moscow: Nauka, 1979], p. 290). See Deane, *Strategic Defense in Soviet Strategy*, pp. 23–25.

39. See John Prados, *The Soviet Estimate: U.S. Intelligence Analysis and Russian Military Strength* (New York: The Dial Press, 1982), pp. 151–71; Sayre Stevens, "The Soviet BMD Program," in Carter and Schwartz, pp. 189–209.

40. Prados, *The Soviet Estimate*, pp. 151–71, discusses disagreements between CIA and DIA going back to the early 1960s on the BMD capabilities of the SA-5 and other early Soviet systems.

41. Stevens, "The Soviet BMD Program," pp. 194–95.

42. See especially Prados, *The Soviet Estimate*, pp. 169–71. SA-5 deployments increased at the rate of about 100 launchers a year throughout the 1970s; there were 1,100 SA-5 launchers deployed through the Soviet Union in 1970, 2,000 by 1981. A recent summary of publicly available data on the SA-5 may be found in "Soviets' S-200 SAM System," *Jane's Defense Weekly*, October 12, 1985, pp. 793–94.

43. Gray, "SALT I Aftermath," pp. 28, 30. These tests appear to have involved the SA-5 SQUARE PAIR radar rather than the system's interceptor missile (George Schneiter, "The ABM Treaty Today," in Carter and Schwartz, pp. 239–40).

44. The White House, *Report of the President on Soviet Noncompliance with Arms Control Agreements*, February 1, 1985, pp. 8–9. Extraordinary confirmation of the BMD capability of Soviet strategic SAMs was provided by a Soviet military attache in private conversation with Michael Deane of the University of Miami's Advanced International Studies Institute in Washington in June 1983. Deane's report of the incident appears in U.S. Senate, *Congressional Record*, November 1, 1985, p. S-14591; quoted in Brian D. Dailey, "Deception, Perceptions Management, and Self-Deception in Arms Control: An Examination of the ABM Treaty," in Daily and Parker, p. 246. A useful comparative summary of the findings of the various presidential reports relating to Soviet compliance with the ABM Treaty may be found in William R. Harris, "Soviet *Maskirovka* and Arms Control Verification," in Dailey and Parker, p. 210.

45. Stevens, "The Soviet BMD Program," pp. 211–13; Gray, "SALT I Aftermath," p. 30; *Summary Report of the General Advisory Committee on Arms Control and Disarmament*, October 1984, pp. 9–10.

46. Varying views of the Krasnoyarsk radar issue are discussed in Michael R. Gordon, "CIA Is Skeptical That New Soviet Radar Is Part of an ABM Defense System," *National Journal*, March 9, 1985, pp. 523–26. On the new radars see Rowland Evans and Robert Novak, "Carlucci's First Test," *Washington Post*, December 1, 1986, p. A27; and more generally Department of

Defense, *Soviet Military Power 1987* (Washington, D.C.: U.S. Government Printing Office, 1987), pp. 48–49. The evidence of the new radars has led some officials to press for a formal U.S. government finding that the Soviets are preparing a nationwide ABM system. See Colin Norman, "A Dispute over Soviet ABM Plans," *Science* 235 (January 1987): 524–26.

47. See generally *Soviet Military Power 1987*, pp. 46–47.

48. Department of Defense, *Soviet Military Power 1985*, p. 47.

49. See R. Jeffrey Smith, "Soviet Radars of Concern to U.S. Removed," *Washington Post*, February 25, 1987, p. A20.

50. *Soviet Military Power 1987*, pp. 58–59. For a general discussion, see Gordon MacDonald, Jack Ruina, and Mark Balaschak, "Soviet Strategic Air Defense," in *Cruise Missiles: Technology, Strategy, Politics*, ed. Richard K. Betts (Washington, D.C.: The Brookings Institution, 1981), pp. 53–82.

51. *Soviet Military Power 1987*, pp. 50, 60–61.

52. Schneiter, "The ABM Treaty Today," p. 239. A U.S. official has testified that the SA-12 is being deployed in two configurations, one for air defense and one for BMD (*Defense Daily*, March 9, 1984).

53. Stevens, "The Soviet BMD Program," pp. 215–16.

54. *Soviet Military Power 1987*, p. 61.

55. Tom Diaz, "U.S. Detects New Breach of Arms Treaty by Soviets," *Washington Times*, November 12, 1985, p. 1A; "SA-12 SAMs Deployed to South-Western TVD," *Jane's Defense Weekly*, March 7, 1987, p. 359.

56. *Soviet Military Power 1987*, p. 61.

57. *Soviet Military Power 1987*, pp. 50–52. On the Dushanbe facility see "White House Assesses Reports of Soviet ASAT Laser Facilities," *Aviation Week & Space Technology*, September 15, 1986, p. 21; and William J. Broad, "The Secrets of Soviet Star Wars," *New York Times Magazine*, June 28, 1987, p. 22.

58. On this problem see Representative Henry Hyde, "Trick or Treaty," *Policy Review* (Spring 1987), pp. 26–31; and Carnes Lord, "Verification — Reforming a Theology," *The National Interest* 3 (Spring 1986): 50–60.

59. Consider the claim of "Viktor Suvorov" (*Inside the Soviet Army* [New York: Macmillan, 1982], p. 105) that shortly after the signing of SALT I the Soviets gave the "largest" of their strategic missiles a covert defensive mission or capability.

3

NATO and the Changing Soviet Concept of Control for Theater War

John G. Hines and Phillip A. Petersen

The demands of increasingly complex and possibly prolonged theater warfare have preoccupied Soviet military thinkers since at least the mid-1970s. Operational concepts and capabilities have been reassessed and the structure for control of forces has been modified. Perhaps the most significant command and control change has been the addition of an intermediate level of strategic leadership, called the High Command of Forces (HCOF), between the Soviet Supreme High Command (SHC; in Russian *verkhovnoye glavnokomandovaniye* or VGK) in Moscow and operational forces in the field. HCOFs have been established, in peacetime, opposite NATO's central and southern regions to control forces in what the Soviets call the Western and Southwestern Theaters of Strategic Military Action (TSMA; in Russian *teatr voyennykh deystviy* or TVD: see the Appendix at the end of this chapter).

NATO, the Soviets observe, has maintained a wartime command structure in peacetime for several decades.[1] Allied Command Europe (ACE) comprises three regional commands: AFNORTH (Allied Forces Northern Europe), AFCENT (Allied Forces Central Europe), and AFSOUTH (Allied Forces Southern Europe). In addition, AFCENT has subordinate to it NATO army group commands that also function continuously in peacetime. To date, the Warsaw Pact equivalent to an Army Group, the Front, is formally established only in time of war or for training (even though the front command infrastructure is embedded in

This chapter expands and updates articles published in the March and May 1986 issues of *International Defense Review* as published in the December 1986 and May 1987 issues of *Signal Magazine.*

NATO AND WARSAW PACT APPROACHES TO CONTROL COMPARED

NATO	WARSAW PACT
Effectiveness is served by decentralization of control to the lowest level at which the information and resources required for formation and execution of a sound decision are available. (Resources and information may be pushed downward to support this preference.)	Control is to be maintained at the highest level effective operation will possibly allow. (More information, resources, and experience are available at higher levels.) Methods of enhancing the efficiency and reliability of centralized control are exhausted before decentralization of decision making is considered.
Operational flexibility is largely the product of the responsiveness of discrete subsystems (weapons and operators) and individual units to secondary and unplanned requirements: i.e., the ability to produce an unprogrammed variety of response to a remote or even unanticipated set of contingencies.	Operational flexibility is the product of alternatives and variety structured into the operational plan and combat organization to provide for more contingencies than the opponent is forecast to be able to generate.
Partial system disintegration would be harmful but *not catastrophic* because subsystems are more autonomous in terms of capability and control. Significant system disintegration, however, would greatly degrade system effectiveness. The likelihood of such failure is increased by less NATO attention to maintenance of total system integrity under stress.	Under conditions of significant, or even partial, *system disintegration,* effectiveness of *subsystems* and hence the system *would be greatly degraded* because component subsystems are highly interdependent. Warsaw pact planners try to compensate for this by protecting systems integrity through redundancy, extensive preplanning (structure variety), and by reducing the vulnerability of nodes and links.
NATO forces routinely fail to maximize the synergy made possible through total-system combinations of forces in well-integrated operational strategies.	Warsaw Pact planners forfeit the greater responsiveness and spontaneity that is possible when force is applied through many centers of decision and initiative.

peacetime administrative organs such as Groups of Forces headquarters). One might conclude that NATO has a peacetime command system that, in terms of hierarchical structure, is roughly equivalent to that which the Warsaw Pact considers necessary during wartime.

This chapter looks beyond these apparent similarities in the command structures of the opposing alliances to dissimilarities in how those command systems are likely to work in time of war. To make such a comparison, it is necessary to understand the nature and significance of recent changes in the Soviet theater control system. Part one, therefore, describes and explains these developments from a Soviet perspective and, at the same time, addresses some Western stereotypes of the Soviet command system. For example, the validity of the traditional Western characterization of Soviet control as extremely rigid is examined and found to be simplistic and dangerously misleading. Based on this analysis, the second part compares the NATO command system to that of the Warsaw Pact at the various levels of command from theater down to corps and army. This comparison includes examination of the span of control horizontally over various types of forces (air and ground, forward forces and reserves) and the authority of commanders vertically at various command levels in both alliances, and it discusses how well both systems would be likely to serve wartime operational needs. The chapter concludes with a discussion of the implications of our findings for NATO and suggests solutions for existing inadequacies.

THE SOVIET SYSTEM OF CONTROL FOR THEATER WAR

The Soviets think about control of forces during war in terms of the three types of "strategic military action" that the Soviet Armed Forces must execute: "strikes by strategic nuclear forces" against the enemy in adjacent theaters and on distant continents, strategic operations "to repulse the enemy's aerospace attack" and defend the homeland from strikes by enemy weapons of mass destruction, and offensive and defensive strategic operations in continental or oceanic theaters around the periphery of the Soviet homeland.[2] Everything else — how command systems are structured and specific control measures such as designation of strategic and operational directions — is developed around the kinds of strategic operations various Soviet forces would be expected to have to execute in the event of war.

Soviet thinking about the relative importance of various forms of strategic military action and how they might be executed has been changing since the mid-1960s. In the standard Soviet scenario of the early 1960s, war was expected to be very brief and violent. A future war was expected to begin with a global nuclear exchange and to be followed by theater nuclear strikes and subsequent exploitation and mopping up by ground and air forces.[3] By the late 1960s, however, the Soviets estimated that they had achieved approximate strategic nuclear parity with the United States, and they noted that this shift in the global strategic correlation of forces had led the United States to abandon its strategy of massive retaliation in favor of flexible response.[4] Their assessment of the significance of this and related changes led the Soviets to revise their estimate of the likely "character of future war," especially with respect to the beginning of a major war. Today the dominant Soviet scenario centers on war in continental theaters peripheral to the Soviet Union. In such a war advanced conventional, and possibly some nuclear, weapons would be used, but massive use of central nuclear weapons systems against transoceanic or even theater targets might be postponed indefinitely.[5]

This gradual but deliberate shift in focus to complex, and perhaps, prolonged theater warfare led Soviet military scientists to make a major reexamination of the command system for wartime control of forces. Forces designated to conduct strategic nuclear strikes seem to have moved toward an even greater degree of centralized control at the national level, probably to further ensure that any use of such weapons would reflect pursuit of the objectives of the highest levels of Soviet leadership.[6] At the same time, protection of strategic nuclear weapon systems and control nodes through hardening, redundancy, and mobility seems to have continued to grow in importance given the growing expectation that these systems would be exposed to enemy nonnuclear, and perhaps limited nuclear, attack for an indeterminate length of time while the war was being carried on in theaters around the Soviet periphery.[7]

Predictably, the possibility of prolonged exposure to strategic attack also has led to changes in control of forces that would conduct "strategic operations to repulse the enemy's aerospace attack." There seem to be two trends. The first has been toward expansion of centralized control over the aerospace defense assets of the Air Defense Forces, Air Forces, and Navy. The second trend is toward greater interservice integration of the control systems for these *defense* assets with control of *offensive* strategic nuclear forces. In these two areas no new, special commands seem to have been established. Instead, structural changes appear to be restricted to refinements of the preexisting functional control system under direction of the central leadership. Specifically, the national command authority almost certainly assigns responsibility for control of combined air defense assets to the Air Defense Forces (*Voyska PVO*), and Strategic Nuclear Forces are probably directed by the General Staff on behalf of the national command authority through the established control mechanism of the Strategic Rocket Forces, the Navy, and the Air Forces.

In contrast, new requirements for controlling the main form of strategic military action, strategic operations in peripheral theaters, have led Soviet planners to make what is probably one of the most significant changes in their command and control system in more than two decades. Specifically, Soviet military leaders have added an intermediate level of strategic leadership, called High Commands, between the Supreme High Command (Russian abbreviation VGK) in Moscow and Warsaw Pact Fronts, which are very large combined-arms formations roughly equivalent to NATO Army Groups. These High Commands are being established in peacetime to control forces in the "Theater of Strategic Military Action."

Military Geography

The significance of the peacetime establishment of wartime High Commands of Forces (HCOFs) over several Fronts is often misunderstood in the West, primarily because of confusion about how the recently established HCOFs are related to Soviet concepts of military geography. To help reduce the apparent confusion, we will distinguish Soviet concepts of military geography (*voyennaya geografiya*) and associated control measures from Soviet concepts of strategic leadership (*strategicheskoye rukovodstvo*). It should then be easier to understand how the Soviets relate the two in planning and controlling strategic military operations.

For purposes of planning for war, the Soviets divide the world into a number of hierarchically ordered military-geographical sections. Arranged in a descending order of scale, they are Theater of War, Theater of Strategic Military Action, Strategic Direction, Operational Direction, and Tactical Direction (see Figure 3.1). Starting at the top of the geographical hierarchy, the broadest concept in military geography seems to be that of the Theater of War, abbreviated TW (in Russian *teatr voiny*,

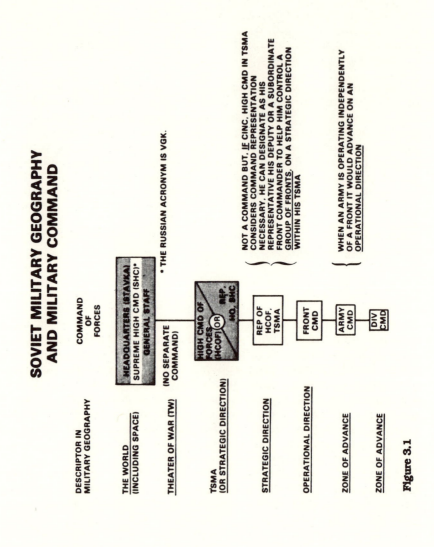

SOVIET MILITARY GEOGRAPHY AND MILITARY COMMAND

DESCRIPTOR IN MILITARY GEOGRAPHY	COMMAND OF FORCES

THE WORLD (INCLUDING SPACE) — HEADQUARTERS (STAVKA) SUPREME HIGH CMD (SHC)* GENERAL STAFF

* THE RUSSIAN ACRONYM IS VGK.

THEATER OF WAR (TW) — (NO SEPARATE COMMAND)

TSMA (OR STRATEGIC DIRECTION) — HIGH CMD OF FORCES (HCOF) (OR) REP. HQ, SHC

STRATEGIC DIRECTION — REP OF HCOF, TSMA

NOT A COMMAND BUT, IF CINC, HIGH CMD IN TSMA CONSIDERS COMMAND REPRESENTATION NECESSARY, HE CAN DESIGNATE AS HIS REPRESENTATIVE HIS DEPUTY OR A SUBORDINATE FRONT COMMANDER TO HELP HIM CONTROL A GROUP OF FRONTS, ON A STRATEGIC DIRECTION WITHIN HIS TSMA

OPERATIONAL DIRECTION — FRONT CMD

ZONE OF ADVANCE — ARMY CMD

WHEN AN ARMY IS OPERATING INDEPENDENTLY OF A FRONT IT WOULD ADVANCE ON AN OPERATIONAL DIRECTION

ZONE OF ADVANCE — DIV CMD

Figure 3.1

abbreviated *TV*). According to an article in the December 1981 Polish *Naval Review*, Theater of War is defined as "the term given to vast areas of land, sea, and air, prepared in a political, economic, and military sense, on which bilateral hostilities are conducted between two states or coalitions." This article also noted, however, that although the boundaries of Theaters of War are defined in a general sense in peacetime, during the course of hostilities "they may stretch to several continents or even over the whole globe — including into space."[8]

The country's military-administrative system, which divides the USSR into 16 Military Districts, is directly connected to the regional structure of the Soviet economy. These Military Districts may be visualized as comprising four regional groups (see Figure 3.2) more or less analogous to the strategic rear of the country and the rears of the potential Theaters of War: regions of the center, Volga area, and Ural in the middle of the European part of the country (the strategic rear of the country); regions of the Northwest, West, and Southwest along the Soviet Union's Western borders (the rear of the Western Theater of War); regions of the South and Southeast along the Southern borders of the country (the rear of the Southern Theater of War); and regions of the East (the rear of the Far Eastern Theater of War).[9]

TSMAs

While finding the concept of Theater of War as a useful way to identify general areas of potential conflict, the Soviets focus their operational planning at the TSMA level. The identities and sizes of TSMAs have changed over time. Europe, for example, was considered to be a single TSMA in the 1960s, but, by the mid-1970s, the Soviets were teaching Voroshilov General Staff Academy students that Europe had been divided into three continental Theaters of Strategic Military Action.[10] During the course of the mid- to late-1970s, the Soviets continued to work out their thoughts on the most appropriate geographical approach to strategic planning. Near Eastern, Middle Eastern, Northeastern, and Northern Theaters of Strategic Military Action appeared and disappeared as strategic planning contingencies. Apparently, the first two were eventually subsumed in the present Southern TSMA, and the latter two, into the present Far Eastern TSMA.

Even the definition of the TSMA has been an issue of bureaucratic contention within the Soviet Armed Forces. By arguing for independent "sea" (*morskoy*) — in addition to Oceanic (*okeanskiy*) — Theaters of Strategic Military Action, the

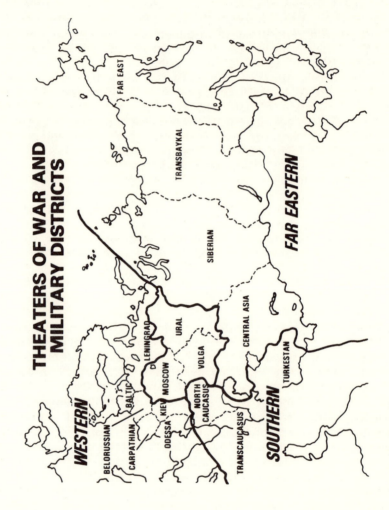

THEATERS OF WAR AND MILITARY DISTRICTS

WESTERN

SOUTHERN

FAR EASTERN

BELORUSSIAN
CARPATHIAN
BALTIC
LENINGRAD
KIEV
MOSCOW
URAL
ODESSA
VOLGA
NORTH CAUCASUS
TRANSCAUCASUS
CENTRAL ASIA
TURKESTAN
SIBERIAN
TRANSBAYKAL
FAR EAST

Figure 3.2

Navy could hope to obtain additional resources and avoid subordinating some of its fleets or flotillas to the operational control of commanders in adjacent continental theaters. The authoritative 1983 *Military Encyclopedic Dictionary*, however, defined the TSMA simply as "that part of the territory of a continent with the coastal waters of the oceans, internal seas and the air space above them (continental TSMA); or the water areas of an ocean, including its islands, the contiguous coastlines of continents and the air space above them (oceanic TSMA), within the boundaries of which are deployed strategic grouping of the Armed Forces and within which military operations are conducted." It appears, therefore, that while the term "sea TSMA" continues to appear in some Soviet military sources, such usage does not imply equality with continental and oceanic TSMAs. In most instances, in fact, an area that could be defined as a sea TSMA is an integral part of a continental TSMA.

By the Soviet's own assessment, "the preparation of a TSMA, is accomplished in advance, in peacetime, and continues in the course of war." In peacetime, construction of land transportation routes, airfields, naval bases, pipelines, fixed systems for detection of submarines, and other kinds of infrastructure construction are planned, budgeted, and conducted under the rubric of the "preparation for war" of the TSMA involved. If hostilities approach, troops and naval forces are to be mobilized and deployed on a TSMA basis. War plans setting out the strategic operations for each TSMA could then be executed with the onset of hostilities.[11]

The Soviets recognize five continental Theaters of Strategic Military Action around the Soviet periphery: the Northwestern, Western, Southwestern, Southern, and the Far Eastern. The Soviets also recognize North America, South America, Australia, Africa, and Antarctica as individual continental TSMAs. The Oceanic TSMAs include the Atlantic, Pacific, Indian, and Arctic Oceans. Figure 3.3 shows approximate Soviet TSMA boundaries.

Lines on a map can be misleading, however, in that "the boundaries of TSMAs can be fixed or variable; they can be adjacent or they can overlap."[12] Figure 3.4 indicates the flexibility of the boundaries of Theaters of Strategic Military Action in Europe. Denmark, for example, lies in the Western TSMA probably because it is assessed by the Soviets to occupy territory critical for the conduct of military operations in Central Europe. At the same time, however, Denmark is a Nordic country and, theoretically, could become involved in a local war in northern Europe. It also would be included, therefore, in the Northwestern TSMA should this TSMA be the focus of military action in Europe. As another illustration of the flexibility of

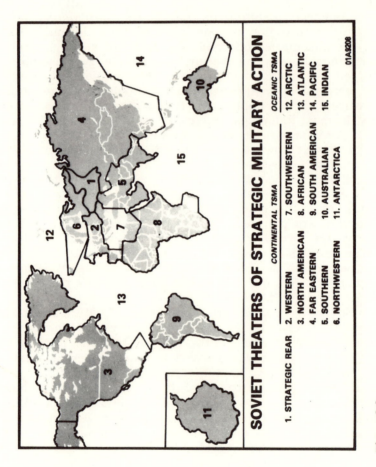

SOVIET THEATERS OF STRATEGIC MILITARY ACTION

CONTINENTAL TSMA

1. STRATEGIC REAR
2. WESTERN
3. NORTH AMERICAN
4. FAR EASTERN
5. SOUTHERN
6. NORTHWESTERN
7. SOUTHWESTERN
8. AFRICAN
9. SOUTH AMERICAN
10. AUSTRALIAN
11. ANTARCTICA

OCEANIC TSMA

12. ARCTIC
13. ATLANTIC
14. PACIFIC
15. INDIAN

01A9208

Figure 3.3

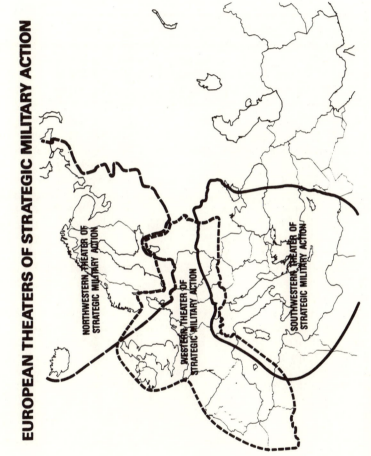

EUROPEAN THEATERS OF STRATEGIC MILITARY ACTION

NORTHWESTERN THEATER OF STRATEGIC MILITARY ACTION

WESTERN THEATER OF STRATEGIC MILITARY ACTION

SOUTHWESTERN THEATER OF STRATEGIC MILITARY ACTION

Figure 3.4

75

TSMA boundaries, forces operating along the common flank between the Western and Southwestern Theaters of Strategic Military Action might find themselves resubordinated from a High Command of Forces in one TSMA to a High Command in another TSMA at some point in an operation to accommodate the anticipated flow of strategic operations in either or both TSMAs. TSMA boundaries either could be shifted or made to overlap to facilitate control coordination.

Voroshilov General Staff Academy lecture materials from the mid-1970s specify precisely what countries and bodies of water are included in each of the peripheral TSMAs. The Northwestern TSMA includes Finland, Sweden, Norway, Iceland, Denmark, the Barents Sea, the Norwegian Sea, the North Sea, and the Baltic Sea. The Western TSMA includes Denmark, the Federal Republic of Germany, the Netherlands, Belgium, Luxemburg, France, Great Britain, Spain, Portugal, Switzerland, Austria, Ireland, northern Morocco, western Algeria, Poland, the German Democratic Republic, Czechoslovakia, the southern part of the Baltic Sea, and the western part of the Mediterranean Sea. The Southwestern TSMA includes Italy, Austria, Switzerland, Yugoslavia, Greece, the western part of Turkey, northern Egypt, Libya, Tunisia, northeastern Algeria, Hungary, Bulgaria, Romania, the western part of the Black Sea, and the eastern part of the Mediterranean Sea. Based on the General Staff Academy and other materials, the Southern TSMA may include the eastern part of Turkey, Iran, Saudi Arabia, Syria, Iraq, Israel, Jordan Lebanon, eastern Egypt, Afghanistan, Pakistan, India, Bangladesh, the eastern part of the Black Sea, and the Caspian Sea. The Far Eastern TSMA includes China, Mongolia, the Republic of Korea, Burma, Indochina (excluding Indonesia), Japan, the Philippines, Alaska, and northern and central Siberia.

The identity and nature of strategic objectives identified around the Soviet periphery constitute the key determinant of the nature and size of the various TSMAs as well as the number and location of "directions" within each TSMA. As explained in a mid-1980s Soviet military lecture, "TSMAs are organized and situated so that each TSMA has strategic and operational objectives." The lecture goes on to explain that because "each TSMA has several strategic objectives, it is necessary to organize and situate each TSMA along several Strategic Directions [the Russian term is *napravleniye*, which may be translated as direction, sector, or axis]," aimed at those objectives. The exact location and scale of these Strategic Directions is determined by the objectives, by "natural features, and the number and placement of existing lines of communication serving these objectives." For example, the Dutch and Belgian North Sea ports (probably grouped with Bonn and the Kiel Canal into a "strategic region") would probably constitute strategic objectives in the northern sector of the Western TSMA. A Strategic Direction would be aimed at this set of objectives, but the location of the terrain over which forces would attack would be determined by the nature of opposing forces, the nature of the terrain (flat, mountainous, or urban), and the location of favorable road and rail networks.

Within each Theater of Strategic Military Action there is one or more of these Strategic Directions. A Strategic Direction consists of a wide strip of land, including contiguous coastal waters and airspace, leading the armed forces of one warring party to the other's most important administrative-political and industrial-economic centers. Strategic Directions involve operational-strategic scale operations, undertaken by combinations of Fronts, fleets, independent armies, and flotillas. Thus a Strategic Direction usually permits operations by many strategic formations of various services.[13] The smallest size force likely to operate on a strategic direction would be a single Front comprising two or more armies. A strategic direction might also accommodate a group of two or more Fronts as was common toward the end of the Great Patriot War.[14]

Each Strategic Direction is, in turn, in the words of the same mid-1980s Soviet military lecture, "organized and situated along several Operational Directions." An Operational Direction is a zone of terrain, to include contiguous coastal waters and its airspace, within which an operational-strategic or operational formation conducts its operation.[15] Within the context of the continental TSMA in which they lie, Operational Directions may be internal or coastal. Normally a Soviet army of two or more divisions would advance on an Operational Direction. Illustrations can help to explain how these various Strategic and Operational Directions might, depending upon the conflict scenario, appear on the ground in the theaters around the Soviet periphery. We caution that these arrows represent military planning tools only and not any Soviet political decision to execute such operations.

Continental TSMAs around the Soviet Periphery

The Western TSMA

The Warsaw Pact considers the "main" TSMA to be the Western in Central Europe.[16] According to lecture materials from the Soviet General Staff Academy, the Western TSMA may be envisioned as comprising two Strategic Directions: north

German and south German. The operational capacity of each of these Strategic Directions is said to be "sufficient for the deployment and military operations of up to two Fronts."

The north German Strategic Direction would be directed against NATO's Northern Army Group (NORTHAG) and those Allied Forces North (AFNORTH) contingents located in Denmark and the Federal German state of Schleswig-Holstein. The northern or coastal Front on the north German Strategic Direction would probably have two initial Operational Directions: one directed against Schleswig-Holstein in AFNORTH and a second directed at the Dutch Corps sector in NORTHAG. The operational axis directed against Schleswig-Holstein would be aimed at seizing the probable immediate Front objective, the Kiel Canal, and subsequent seizure of Jutland. The southern Front on the north German Strategic Direction would probably have at least two initial Operational Directions; one aimed at fixing the I German Corps in its Intra-German Border (IGB) positions and the other at penetrating the British and Dutch Corps sectors. Successful operations on these Operational Directions along the north German Strategic Direction would ensure achieving initial strategic objectives in NORTHAG's rear, specifically the Dutch and Belgian ports and the French border. Destruction of the Dutch and British Corps, and operational-tactical encirclement of the I German Corps would probably be the means by which the Soviets would hope to expedite achieving these objectives.

The south German Strategic Direction would probably be aimed at holding the two German and two American Corps in Central Army Group (CENTAG) in their IGB and FRG-Czech border positions and attempting to encircle them on two major Operational Directions, one through the British and Belgian sectors and the other through Austria. In a protracted conflict, subsequent Operational Directions probably would be grouped along northern and southern Strategic Directions aimed through France at the United Kingdom and the Iberian peninsula (see Figure 3.5). On the southern flank of the Western TSMA, any Warsaw Pact forces moving up the Danube Valley from Hungary would probably initially be subordinated to the HCOF in the Southwestern TSMA, although upon operational success they could become resubordinated to the HCOF in the Western TSMA.

The Southwestern TSMA

According to the same previously mentioned Soviet military academy lecture presented in the mid-1980s, possible Operational Directions (see Figure 3.6) would include the following:

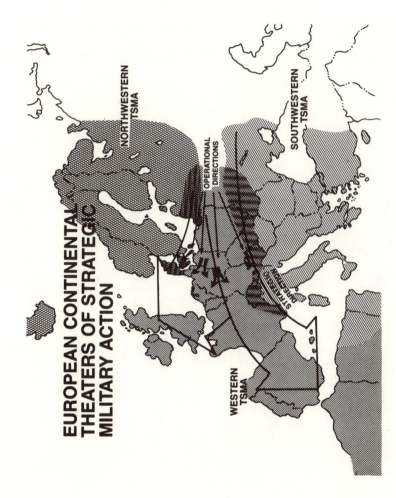

EUROPEAN CONTINENTAL
THEATERS OF STRATEGIC
MILITARY ACTION

NORTHWESTERN
TSMA

OPERATIONAL
DIRECTIONS

SOUTHWESTERN
TSMA

WESTERN
TSMA

Figure 3.5

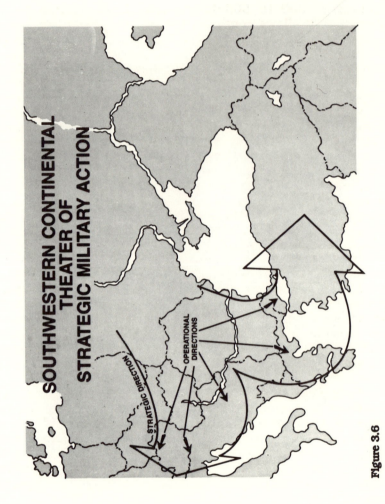

SOUTHWESTERN CONTINENTAL THEATER OF STRATEGIC MILITARY ACTION

STRATEGIC DIRECTION

OPERATIONAL DIRECTIONS

Figure 3.6

A. Alpine Direction: frontage — 180 to 240 kilometers; depth — 550 kilometers; operational density — six to eight divisions.
B. North Italian Direction: frontage — 100 to 200 kilometers; depth — 600 to 750 kilometers; operational density — six to eight divisions.
C. The Adriatic Direction is basically the territory of Yugoslavia: frontage — 300 to 500 kilometers; depth — 500 to 700 kilometers. It allows control of the Adriatic coastline, prevent a major assault landing by NATO, and thus creates favorable conditions for a grouping of forces operating on the north Italian direction. Besides this, by operating on this axis the forces of the Warsaw Pact can cover the primary economic regions and industrial centers of Yugoslavia, Hungary and Romania and control the important lines of communication: Vienna-Belgrade-Athens. The Dinaric Alps stretch from the southern coast to the Adriatic Sea and ports, and constitute a wide mountainous obstacle having operational significance. The most impenetrable sector is the Western sector of the Alps, where no forces exist and there are not sufficient sources of water. The most convenient places for crossing the Dinaric Alps are the valleys of the Bosna and Neretva rivers. The operational density of this axis is 10 to 15 divisions (toward the west from the Sava river it is four to five divisions).
D. Ionian Direction: frontage — 180 to 400 kilometers; depth — 400 to 500 kilometers. This direction provides a grouping of forces an exit from the lower Danube Plain to the coast of the Ionian Sea and the Strait of Otranto. The natural conditions of this direction are very complicated. Therefore, a wide use of combat equipment with high trafficability, airborne assaults, transport aviation and helicopters is advisable. The operational density is only five to six divisions.
E. The Bosporus-Dardanelles Direction provides the creation of conditions for the breakout of a large grouping of Warsaw Pact forces in the straits. The terrain on this direction allows for the use of tank formations as part of combined-arms groupings and for the rapid exploitation of success with the aim of establishing control over the straits. The operational density of this direction is five to six divisions, including two tank divisions.

The Alpine, North Italian and Adriatic Operational Directions would probably be grouped along a single Strategic Direction, and the Ionian and Bosporus-Dardanelles Operational Directions would probably be grouped into another Strategic Direction aimed at establishing control of access to the Black Sea.

The Northwestern TSMA

On the Northern flank, an initial offensive Strategic Direction against the Nordic countries in the Northwestern Theater of Strategic Military Action would undoubtedly center upon the Operational Direction aimed at northern Norway (see Figure 3.7). Assault (amphibious or airborne/heliborne) landing combat actions might be undertaken as a series of tactical assaults in support of this coastal Operational Direction, or such combat actions might be conducted as a sequentially executed assault landing operation conducted on an independent maritime axis directed along the Norwegian coast. Obviously, the operational plan for the Northwestern TSMA takes into consideration contingencies for the conduct of combat actions against Sweden as well. As a result, this northern Operational Direction could also include a tactical axis of advance directed across northern Sweden toward Narvik, Norway. A defensive Operational Direction aimed at southern Finland would probably be used to hold the larger part of Finnish military forces in the South.

It should be pointed out that Iceland could be part of both the continental Northwestern TSMA and the Arctic Oceanic TSMA depending upon the wartime scenario. If a conflict in the Western TSMA did not spread to the Scandinavian Peninsula, combat action in the Northwestern continental TSMA could be limited to Iceland. In this case, the military-political significance of Iceland would be based on its importance to the conduct of strategic action in the Arctic and Atlantic Oceanic TSMAs.

The Far Eastern TSMA

At the opposite end of the Soviet Union in the Far Eastern TSMA (see Figure 3.8), the Soviets apparently envision four Strategic Directions: against the Urumqi Military Region; against the Shenyang and Beijing Military Regions; against Japan, Korea, and the Philippines; and against Alaska. Of these four Strategic Directions in the Far Eastern TSMA, the direction against Northeast China constitutes the keystone of any successful strategic operation involving China and is, by far, the most complex of the possible Strategic Directions. It comprises at least three initial Operational Directions, involving offensive operations by at least three Fronts: the Transbaykal Front against the Beijing Military Region; the Second Far Eastern Front against northern Shenyang Military Region; and the First Far Eastern Front against the eastern Shenyang Military Region.

SOVIET NORTHWESTERN THEATER OF STRATEGIC MILITARY ACTION

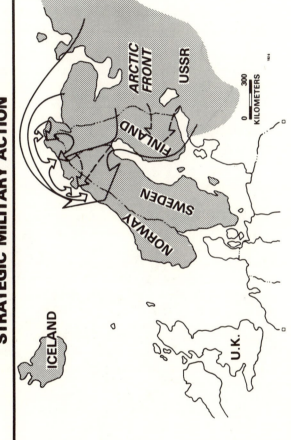

Figure 3.7

SOVIET STRATEGIC/OPERATIONAL DIRECTIONS FAR EASTERN THEATER OF STRATEGIC MILITARY ACTION

3234-5

Figure 3.8

The Southern TSMA

Finally, in the region between central Turkey and China lies the Southern TSMA (see Figure 3.9). The Southern TSMA probably can be divided into two initial Strategic Directions, one directed toward the Middle East, the other toward Iran, Pakistan, and India. Thus, the Turkish border with the Soviet Union is not considered by the Soviets to lie in the same TSMA as the Bosporus and Dardanelles but in the Southern TSMA. This fact apparently reflects at least two Soviet considerations: any Soviet conflict with Pakistan and Iran could involve the United States and Turkey, but not necessarily NATO as an alliance; and in an operational sense, combat actions against the Bosporus and Dardanelles would not involve the coordination of Front boundaries with combat action against eastern Turkey.

The System of Strategic Leadership

The Soviets have developed a comprehensive theory of strategic leadership that corresponds to their highly structured view of military geography. The Soviets explain the intersection of political and military authority at the very top of the command hierarchy as follows:

> The general policy on strengthening national defense and developing the Armed Forces is determined by the Communist Party, its Central Committee, and the Politburo. According to the Constitution, the direction of all the Armed Forces of the USSR is vested in the highest organ of state authority: the Supreme Soviet. The Presidium of the Supreme Soviet organizes the Defense Council.[17]

The Defense Council (*sovet oborony*) unifies the military and civilian leadership so as to ensure centralized political direction of military efforts.

The Defense Council controls the Soviet Armed Forces through the Supreme High Command or SHC (in Russian, *verkhovnogo glavnokommandovaniye* or VGK). The SHC is responsible for "direct leadership of the Armed Forces both *in peacetime* and in war"[18] (emphasis added). Figure 3.10 illustrates the interrelationship of the membership of the Defense Council and the SHC. General Secretary Gorbachev is both the chairman of the Defense Council and the Supreme High Commander.

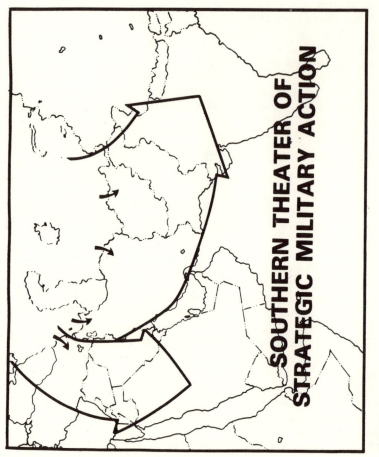

SOUTHERN THEATER OF
STRATEGIC MILITARY ACTION

Figure 3.9

86

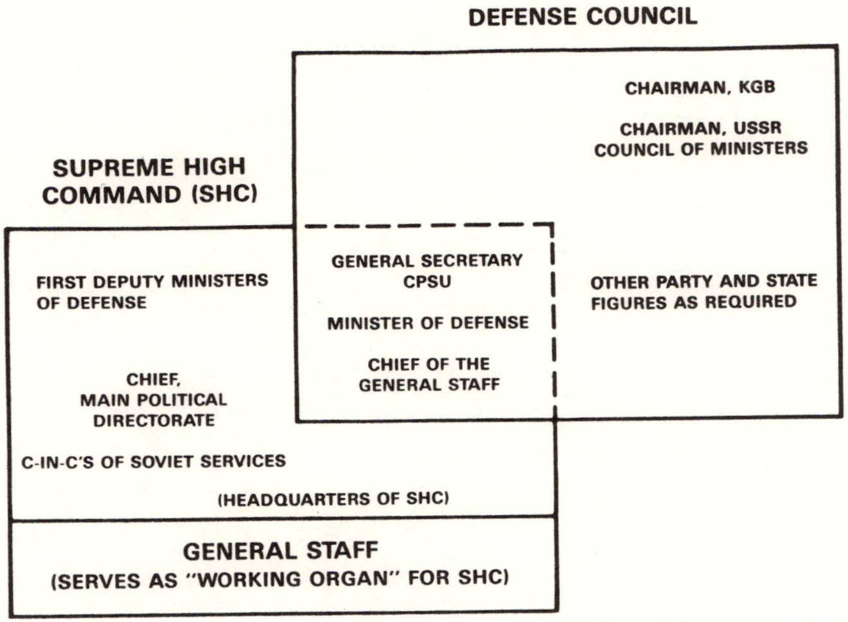

DEFENSE COUNCIL

CHAIRMAN. KGB

CHAIRMAN, USSR
COUNCIL OF MINISTERS

OTHER PARTY AND STATE
FIGURES AS REQUIRED

GENERAL SECRETARY
CPSU

MINISTER OF DEFENSE

CHIEF OF THE
GENERAL STAFF

**SUPREME HIGH
COMMAND (SHC)**

FIRST DEPUTY MINISTERS
OF DEFENSE

CHIEF,
MAIN POLITICAL
DIRECTORATE

C-IN-C'S OF SOVIET SERVICES

(HEADQUARTERS OF SHC)

GENERAL STAFF

(SERVES AS "WORKING ORGAN" FOR SHC)

Figure 3.10

Four Elements of Strategic Command

The SHC is the heart of what the Soviets call their "system of strategic leadership," which comprises the four elements shown in Figure 3.11. The two key components of this system are within the SHC itself. The first and "supreme organ of strategic military leadership" is the Headquarters, SHC (in Russian, *Stavka*, VGK). The "working organ" of the SHC, the General Staff, is the second component. The so-called "intermediate organs of strategic leadership," constituting the third element, consist either of formal High Commands of Forces or representatives of the HQ, SHC and are intended to extend the operational control by the HQ, SHC out to the forces actually engaged in combat. The fourth component is also a system of representatives, in this case an extension of the General Staff. These SHC staff representatives ensure strategic coordination of planning down to the level of division and flotilla.

The "intermediate organs of strategic leadership" bear a closer look because they are the source of so much confusion and controversy in the West today. The major differences between a HCOF and an HQ, SHC representative are the degree of their permanence and the size of their staffs. Existing HCOFs are probably supported by a sizable infrastructure and staff. In fact, each High Command, just like the Supreme High Command, comprises its own headquarters and staff. The HQ, SHC representative, however, is more of a crisis manager. He would be more likely to have only the staff support of a relatively small "operations group" that could move quickly to solve immediate, but more temporary problems. Such a representative could, however, also draw upon the staffs of Fronts and fleets that are temporarily under his control. HQ, SHC representatives could even be dispatched to oversee "wars of national liberation." For example, in the early 1980s then First Deputy Ministers of Defense Petrov and Sokolov served as representatives of the HQ, SHC to "progressive" forces fighting in Ethiopia and Afghanistan.

Both the CINC of the High Command of Forces and the representative of the HQ, SHC would have the full authority of the HQ, SHC and are probably themselves members of the Headquarters. This conclusion is based on the Soviet assessment that a major weakness of World War II HCOFs on Strategic Directions was their lack of authority. They controlled no reserves and had to refer all important decisions to the SHC. The Soviets eventually dissolved the high commands and sent members of the HQ, SHC itself out to the troops to control operations by groups of Fronts. This practice finally evolved into

THE SOVIET SYSTEM OF STRATEGIC LEADERSHIP

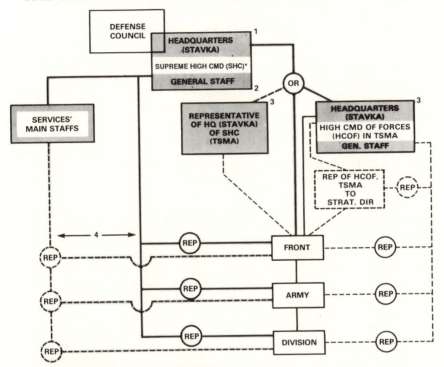

1. SUPREME ORGAN OF STRATEGIC LEADERSHIP

2. WORKING ORGAN

3. INTERMEDIATE ORGANS (GENERAL STAFF AND SPECIAL REPRESENTATIVES ARE ALSO FOUND IN THESE
   CONTROL ELEMENTS)

4. SYSTEM OF SUPREME HIGH CMD. REPRESENTATIVES   *THE RUSSIAN ACRONYM IS "VGK"

Figure 3.11

the reestablishment of an HCOF in the Far East in which the authority of the CINC (Vasilevskiy) was assured by his membership in the HQ, SHC. The entire thrust of Soviet military literature regarding strategic leadership suggests that modern HCOFs are modeled on this World War II command, which incorporated both the authority of an HQ, SHC representative and the organization and permanence of a high command.

The fourth component of Soviet strategic military leadership is the extensive system of SHC staff representatives. Their primary function is to monitor the operational situation to ensure that the overall plans of the Supreme High Command are being respected. They also serve as a direct conduit for communications between lower level units and both the General Staff and the Main Staffs of the five services. This information can form the basis for refining planning and, ultimately, changing support priorities throughout the forces. The staff representatives are either officers of the General Staff with general coordination responsibilities or officers from the Main Staffs of the services who assist, on behalf of the General Staff, in specialized areas such as air, artillery, engineer, and naval support. Although neither the General Staff nor the Main Staffs of the services formally command any forces, this entire staff representative system can be seen to constitute a shadow control system superimposed by the SHC upon the formal organizational structure. Members of the Western military might be inclined to view this as a higher headquarters spy network that would demoralize mid-level commanders. The Soviets, however, have expressed great confidence in the effectiveness of the staff representative system in helping to keep the armed forces focused on the Supreme High Command's strategic objectives rather than on more narrowly defined objectives of the services or of lower-level commanders.

Parallel Operational and Support Structures

The relationship in the Soviet command structure between operational subordination of forces and the military support infrastructure can be seen in Figure 3.12. Fronts (or independent armies) and fleets (or flotillas) constitute the operational components of the system. The Ministry of Defense, Services, and Military Districts constitute the support structure. Note that both the operational and support elements are directly responsive to the HQ, SHC. The HQ, SHC allocates strategic reserves (to include air and nuclear reserves) within the strategic leadership system, depending upon planned requirements and contingencies that arise during the course of

COMMAND RELATIONSHIPS IN THE SOVIET CONTROL SYSTEM

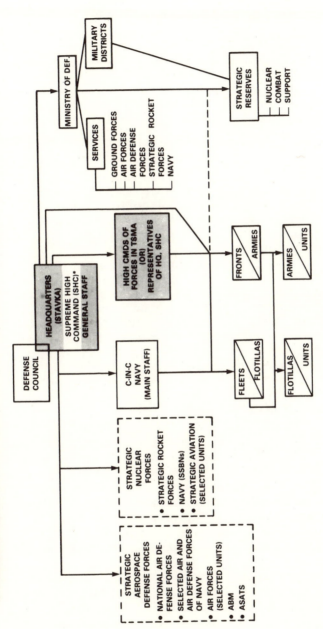

* THE RUSSIAN ACROYNM IS "VGK"

Figure 3.12

conflict. The Soviets do not establish different command structures for conventional and nuclear war; a single system under control of the HQ, SHC exists for conflict of any intensity.

On the support side, the Ministry of Defense does not function as an organ of strategic leadership. It does, however, play a central role in the Soviet control structure through the Services and Military Districts. Peacetime Military Districts do not turn into Fronts and disappear in time of war.[19] The command and staff functions of Fronts that are generated initially are very likely to be already "embedded" in the headquarters of the Military Districts and, in Eastern Europe, in the headquarters of the various Groups of Forces (e.g., Group of Soviet Forces Germany — GSFG). Military Districts continue to exist, however, because they must generate additional forces — perhaps several armies or even another Front. Moreover, the Military Districts are required to support homeland aerospace defense and, in the event of general nuclear war, postnuclear strike reconstruction.

The five Services also continue to function in wartime. Units of the Services are absorbed into the combined-arms command structure of the various Fronts, fleets, and SHC reserves, but the Services themselves continue to exist to help generate new units and sustain those that already exist. Moreover, the Services continue to be indirectly involved in the wartime strategic leadership system. First, the five Service Commanders in Chiefs (CINCs) are members of the Headquarters (*Stavka*) element of the SHC. Second, the Main Staffs of the Services participate in the operational planning process in direct support and response to the General Staff of the SHC.

On the operational side, there is considerable structural flexibility in the Soviet command system. Variants in the subordination of operational commands can be dictated by the HQ, SHC in response to planned or unanticipated wartime requirements. A ground force division or army might be subordinated to a Navy fleet and the fleet itself subordinated, in turn, to an HCOF or a representative of the HQ, SHC in a continental TSMA. Likewise, a ground forces army under command of a Front might control a Navy flotilla in the conduct of an operation (see Figure 3.12).

The Soviets believe that this highly centralized system of strategic leadership, responding to developments of military technology, enables commanders to meet the requirements of modern warfare. They expect that the increasing mobility of forces and the ranges of new and projected weapons are leading to the possibility of warfare on a broader scale than previously experienced. In such a war, success will require progressively greater centralization of control to enable commanders to make effective use of the full capabilities of the modern means of war. Historical and theoretical discussions in Soviet military literature strongly suggest that a highly centralized control structure greatly increases flexibility at the strategic and operational levels where, in the Soviet view, the outcome of conflict would be determined. They recognize that, to avoid the systemic paralysis such centralization might induce, the entire centralized control process must be fully and effectively automated.[20] Thus, the way the Soviets define their own control requirements puts them under considerable pressure to stay abreast of the West in technologies in which they are traditionally weak.

TSMA High Command — The Rationale

Belief that the "beginning period of war" will probably feature large conventional combat actions rather than global strategic nuclear missile strikes places a premium on Soviet readiness to be able to gain and maintain the strategic initiative in a conventional war. The critical feature of such readiness is a command system that would be adequate to effectively control many hundreds of armored, artillery, missile, air, and naval units in the conduct of large-scale offensive operations. There would not be sufficient time to reposture forces of such variety and size from peacetime to wartime organizational structure. Nor would there be time to establish and train special commands capable of directing such forces in wide-ranging, complex operations in large, sometimes continental-size TSMA. Finally, wartime commands established in peacetime could facilitate covert mobilization and integration of reserves into active units during the "prewar" crisis period and the beginning period of war.[21]

Soviet military statements calling for maintenance of a wartime command structure in peacetime have grown stronger since the mid-1970s. A May 1985 statement is most straightforward:

> The course and outcome of the last war revealed the imperative need for the peacetime creation of suitable organs and a scientifically based system of strategic leadership. They need to be maintained in a state that would provide reliable and continuous control of troops and naval forces from the onset of military action *without substantive changes incidental to the transition from a peacetime to a wartime state.*[22]

Since the end of World War II, the Soviets have recognized that, if war began, some form of regional intermediate-level command for control of strategic operations conducted by groups of Fronts would be necessary in some regions.[23] Before the end of the 1960s, had war occurred, the Strategic Direction would have been the most likely level in the scale of military geography at which High Commands would have been established.[24] This would have been consistent with Soviet experience with High Commands of Forces on Strategic Directions and the designation of representatives of HQ, SHC to control groups of Fronts on Strategic Directions in World War II.

By the mid-1970s, however, then Chief of the General Staff Marshal Kulikov indicated that the Soviet military leadership was rethinking the structure of wartime strategic leadership. Kulikov noted that the TSMA rather than the Strategic Direction had been the more effective level for establishment of High Commands of Forces during World War II.[25] Upon Kulikov's appointment as CINC, Warsaw Pact, his successor as chief of the General Staff, Marshal Ogarkov, strongly reaffirmed and refined Kulikov's initiative. The authority of the authors and the forcefulness of their arguments strongly pointed toward establishing HCOFs in TSMAs, not in Theaters of War, and, normally, not in Strategic Directions.

The Evidence That HCOFs Are at the Level of TSMAs

Other indicators have served to reinforce these conclusions. First, the *Soviet Military Encyclopedia* states that a High Command can be established for forces operating "in either a Theater of Strategic Military Action or in a Strategic Direction."[26] In this and similar reference works Theater of War is not included as a candidate for High Commands of Forces.[27] Despite this and the total absence of indications that the Soviets are associating High Commands with Theaters of War, speculation about the existence of such commands continues to appear in Western analytical discussions. This may be attributable, to some extent, to projection of Western thinking about command of geographical regions (e.g., CINC, Europe and CINC, Pacific). A major reason, however, appears to be an inadequate appreciation of the importance the TSMA holds in Soviet thinking about the planning and execution of war. This is often complicated by an even more basic lack of understanding that Theater of War and TSMA are not one and the same. For analysts who do not read Russian, this confusion has been deepened by some well-meaning translators who have taken the liberty of translating *teatr voyennykh deystviy* (TSMA) as "Theater of War" because the latter is a military term familiar to Westerners.

Second, we know from Soviet sources such as the one cited, that it is possible that High Commands could be established either on Strategic Directions or in TSMA. Most evidence indicates, however, that the TSMA has emerged as the level considered by the Soviets to be most appropriate. Arguments in the West that High Commands have been established for Strategic Directions instead of TSMA have been based, in part, on a misunderstanding of the nature of Strategic Directions and how they relate to TSMA. Some have concluded that, unlike the geographical concept TSMA, the Strategic Direction is an independent operational entity of some kind that passes over several TSMA "like a chess piece over chessboard squares."[28] Furthermore it is more likely, the argument goes, that the Soviets would establish High Commands for Strategic Directions representing forces conducting operations than for a geographical region like a TSMA.

In fact, a Strategic Direction, like a TSMA, is a military geographical descriptor that represents terrain where operations may occur. It differs from TSMA in that it designates the general area of the objective as well as the location of potential operations. Furthermore, the Soviet *Military Encyclopedic Dictionary* explains that the Strategic Direction, "is *part* of a TSMA," not an independent entity of forces, nor an equivalent expression for the same terrain. One might conclude that the Strategic Direction does not move (since it is not a formation) and that, as a geographical control measure, it lies within the TSMA of which it is a component. In fact, the *Soviet Military Encyclopedia* explains that (as has been illustrated earlier) "several Strategic Directions might be located within the boundaries of a single TSMA." To use the analogy mentioned above, for any given Strategic Direction, the TSMA is the entire chessboard, not a square.

Ogarkov's Views

Marshal Ogarkov hinted very strongly at the nature and span of control of the reconstituted High Commands in his 1985 update (*History Teaches Vigilance*) of a 1982 book (*Always in Readiness to Defend the Fatherland*). Specifically, in the discussion in which he related "higher military leadership" (*vyshiye voyennoye rukovodstvo*) to the scale of warfare, Ogarkov explained in both versions, that today the "main operation" is "no longer the Front operation" but, instead, the "operation in the TSMA."

In 1985 this sentence was amended to exclude from consideration as the main operation "the operation of a group of Fronts," traditionally carried out on a Strategic Direction. He made this addition almost certainly to make it clear to those within the Soviet military who still did not understand, that the scale of the "modern" operation and the level at which it would be controlled transcended the operation by a group of Fronts on a Strategic Direction.

Also Ogarkov links "higher military leadership," i.e., strategic leadership as discussed earlier, directly to "the main form of military action" the strategic operation in the TSMA, not in the Strategic Direction. In addition, Soviet military literature and reference publications of recent issue refer to strategic military action around the Soviet periphery as the "strategic operation in the TSMA."[29] Strategic Direction is not even offered as a parenthetical alternative. This "strategic operation" is defined by the Soviet *Military Encyclopedic Dictionary* as "the sum total of operations, strikes, and combat actions of large units and formations of the various services of the armed forces, coordinated and interrelated by objective missions, terrain and time and carried out *in accordance with a single concept and plan* for the achievement of strategic objectives." The HQ, SHC has established High Commands around the Soviet periphery to control more effectively forces executing these strategic operations. Unity of command, as the Soviets practice it, would require that all forces executing the strategic operation would come under control of these High Commands. All this strongly suggests that forces executing the strategic operation within a TSMA would be controlled at that level rather than at the level of the Strategic Directions that lie within the TSMA. Figure 3.13 illustrates how the Soviets associate commands of forces in the execution of operations with the various military geographical areas over which those operations would be conducted.

Control on Strategic Directions

Some analysts, including those who acknowledge that the establishment of High Commands of Forces has been at the level of the TSMA, continue to wonder how forces on Strategic Directions within a TSMA would be controlled. Discussions in the Soviet military literature strongly suggest that, when required, the CINC of a High Command of Forces in a given TSMA would designate his own high-level representatives to oversee operations by groups of Fronts on diverging Strategic Directions within the TSMA. One Soviet military writer noted

SOVIET MILITARY GEOGRAPHY AND MILITARY COMMAND

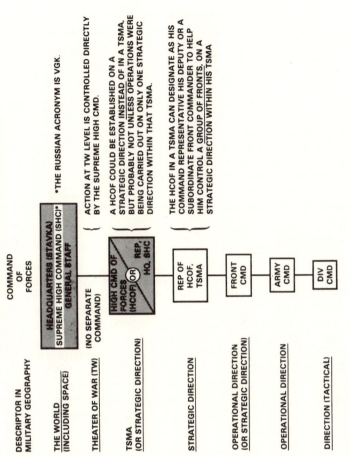

COMMAND OF FORCES

DESCRIPTOR IN MILITARY GEOGRAPHY

THE WORLD (INCLUDING SPACE) — HEADQUARTERS (STAVKA) SUPREME HIGH COMMAND (SHC)* GENERAL STAFF — *THE RUSSIAN ACRONYM IS VGK.

THEATER OF WAR (TW) — (NO SEPARATE COMMAND) — ACTION AT TW LEVEL IS CONTROLLED DIRECTLY BY THE SUPREME HIGH CMD.

TSMA (OR STRATEGIC DIRECTION) — HIGH CMD OF FORCES (HCOF) OR REP, HQ, SHC — A HCOF COULD BE ESTABLISHED ON A STRATEGIC DIRECTION INSTEAD OF IN A TSMA, BUT PROBABLY NOT UNLESS OPERATIONS WERE BEING CARRIED OUT ON ONLY ONE STRATEGIC DIRECTION WITHIN THAT TSMA.

STRATEGIC DIRECTION — REP OF HCOF, TSMA — THE HCOF IN A TSMA CAN DESIGNATE AS HIS COMMAND REPRESENTATIVE HIS DEPUTY OR A SUBORDINATE FRONT COMMANDER TO HELP HIM CONTROL A GROUP OF FRONTS, ON A STRATEGIC DIRECTION WITHIN HIS TSMA.

OPERATIONAL DIRECTION (OR STRATEGIC DIRECTION) — FRONT CMD

OPERATIONAL DIRECTION — ARMY CMD

DIRECTION (TACTICAL) — DIV CMD

Figure 3.13

with approval that these "High Command representatives" could be officers from the CINC's own military council, his chief of staff, chiefs of the major directorates within his staff, or officers of similar responsibility and position. The use of such High Command representatives was standard practice in World War II. Only very rarely were subordinate commanders called to the CINC's headquarters to receive instructions.[30]

Variants of this practice continued when representatives of the HQ, SHC replaced High Commands later in the war. In some instances, an HQ, SHC representative such as Zhukov would leave one of his senior deputies to control one or two Fronts for him while he took responsibility for the overall strategic operation.[31] In other instances he would designate a Front commander to be his deputy and give him control of two or more Fronts in order to free himself to attend to the overall operation.[32] We should expect to see a variant of these methods in a future war, although the most likely approach would be designation by the CINC of a HCOF in a TSMA of his own special deputies for temporary control of forces on Strategic Directions within the TSMA. The nature of the command and command representative relationship probably would be as shown in Figure 3.11.

Existing HCOFs

CINCs of HCOFs have been assigned to command forces in four of the five peripheral continental TSMAs (see Figure 3.14). It appears that no HCOF is being established in the Northwestern TSMA. The apparent absence of a HCOF for the Northwest does not mean that the TSMA does not exist in Soviet military geography but rather that operations in this region are probably not expected to be of sufficient scale to require the peacetime creation of a formal HCOF. In the event of war, therefore, the Arctic Front commander might be the senior combined-arms commander responsible for strategic operations in the Northwestern TSMA. It is possible, however, that given the likely complexity of wartime military requirements in the Northwest region (protection of SSBNs in the adjacent Barents Sea, strategic air defense of European USSR, and the possibility of operations into Scandinavia), a representative of the HQ, SHC might be sent to the region. The absence of an HCOF in the Northwestern TSMA does not mean that the TSMA does not exist. Strategic Leadership and Military Geography are separate concepts. There is probably no Soviet command of any kind for the Australian TSMA, for example, but the Australian TSMA continues to exist in Soviet military geography.

The High Command of the Warsaw Pact is not a wartime operational command. With the exception of Romanian forces,

COMMAND SUBORDINATION IN WARTIME

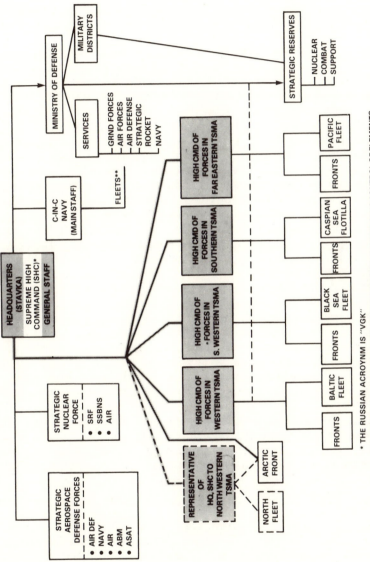

* THE RUSSIAN ACROYNM IS "VGK"

** NORMALLY PLANNING AND COORDINATION REQUIREMENT PLUS CONTROL OF ELEMENTS
OF NORTH SEA FLEET NOT CONTROLLED THROUGH STRATEGIC NUCLEAR FORCES

Figure 3.14

the ground forces, navies, and air forces of the Warsaw Pact allies are integrated directly into the Soviet wartime command structure shown in Figure 3.14.[33] This, of course, raises the question of the wartime role of General of the Army Lushev as CINC of the Warsaw Pact, especially as it might relate to the HCOF in the Western TSMA (WTSMA). It is very likely that Lushev would function in a role not dissimilar to that of a wartime Soviet Military District commander. While the HCOF WTSMA would have operational responsibility for the forces operating in the Western TSMA, Lushev's primary wartime mission would be to ensure that non-Soviet Warsaw Pact forces and associated support are fed quickly and efficiently into the operations conducted in the Western and Southwestern theaters.

The dominance of land warfare in Soviet military thinking is expressed very clearly by the absence of any HCOF in an Oceanic TSMA and by the probable subordination of all but possibly one of the four Soviet fleets to HCOFs in continental TSMAs. The leadership of the Soviet Armed Forces is ground forces dominated, and the fleets are still considered to be primarily maritime support elements to continental operations and a means of extending homeland defense out to sea. The global role of the SSBNs places them in the Strategic Nuclear Forces under control of the Supreme High Command, leaving very few naval forces under operational control of the Navy in time of war. One should bear in mind, however, that the CINC of the Navy, Admiral Chernavin, is a member of HQ, SHC and, in that capacity, can influence how naval forces are used in the various theaters. This influence is reinforced by the role of the Navy Main Staff in preparing the naval sections of strategic plans prepared by the Operations Directorate of the General Staff for the various continental TSMAs.

This discussion might convey the impression that Soviet military thinking is systematic and structured in the extreme and, therefore, very rigid. Although Soviet views of military geography and strategic leadership are more specifically defined than are comparable Western concepts, the manner in which their ideas are applied to "objective conditions" can be quite flexible.

The identities, boundaries, and associated command structures of forces in various TSMAs and Strategic Directions described above reflect how the Soviet military think about organization and control of forces for war around the Soviet periphery. This does not mean that, in the event of war, the Soviets are committed to execute any or all of the operational scenarios implied by the previously identified Strategic and Operational Directions. Even the command structure of forces and the boundaries of TSMA and internal Strategic Directions could be altered radically in response to unanticipated changes that could pose special problems or opportunities. In the early months of World War II, the Soviets made major adjustments in their strategic thinking and command structure as a result of unanticipated developments in initial operations against the Germans. Their concepts of command and operational control continued to change and mature throughout the war. Many of the lessons learned about the need for operational flexibility, coupled with centralized combined-arms control, underlie the changes the Soviets have been implementing over the past decade.

COMPARING WARSAW PACT AND NATO COMMAND SYSTEMS

The Soviets have concluded that the TSMA (equivalent to the area of a NATO regional command) rather than the Front (equivalent to a NATO Army Group) is now the level at which military forces must be controlled. NATO, however, continues to focus the command and control function at the corps level. The NATO corps, roughly equivalent to a Soviet army, is already one level in the hierarchy below the Front/Army Group level which Ogarkov considered to be too limited for effectively waging war at the theater level[34] (see Figures 3.15 and 3.16).

The low level at which NATO focuses command and control largely reflects the international and democratic nature of our alliance. The corps is the highest level at which NATO military organizations maintain national integrity. Predictably, national military organizations develop and refine operational concepts (including associated approaches to command and control) within the scope of forces commanders can train and employ at the national level. Hence, methods for effectively employing and directing large operational and operational-strategic forces on a scale that transcends corps simply do not receive much serious attention. The vagueness and the single-service (army) nature of the U.S. military's attempt to develop a doctrine for "echelons above corps" (EAC) is indicative of the difficulty we in NATO have in solving institutional and, hence, conceptual elements of the problem.

In contrast, the Soviets are routinely discussing, and practicing, how to control and employ forces on an operational and theater-strategic scale. This is hardly surprising because the Soviets can field entire Fronts (NATO Army Group) com-prised exclusively of Soviet forces. Moreover, because of the autocratic nature of the Warsaw Pact "coalition," the Soviets

CONCEPT AND FOCUS OF CONTROL FOR COMBAT OPERATIONS

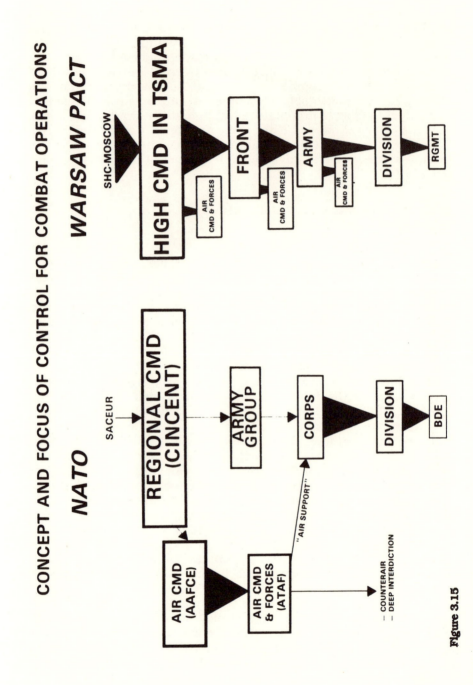

Figure 3.15

STRUCTURAL AND PERCEPTUAL DIFFERENCES
IN COMMAND OF COMBAT OPERATIONS

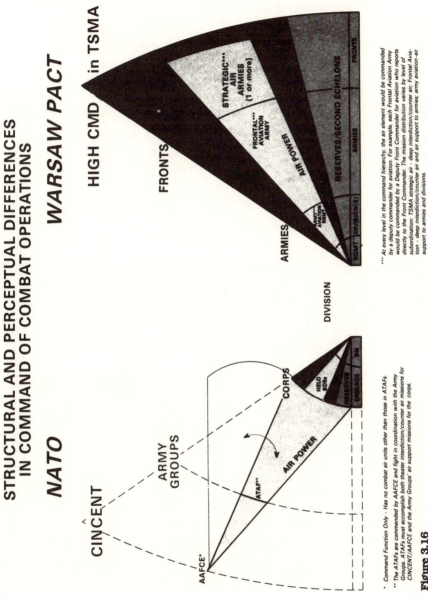

NATO

CINCENT

ARMY GROUPS

CORPS

DIVISION

AAFCE*

ATAF**

AIR POWER

HELO BDEs

RESERVES

BRIGADE

BN

*   Command Function Only - Has no combat air units other than those in ATAFs.
** The ATAFs are commanded by AAFCE and fight in coordination with the Army Groups. ATAFs must accomplish both theater interdiction/counter air missions for CINCENT/AAFCE and the Army Groups' air support missions for the corps.

WARSAW PACT

HIGH CMD in TSMA

FRONTS

ARMIES

STRATEGIC*** AIR ARMIES (1 or more)

FRONTAL*** AVIATION ARMY

AIR POWER

ARMY*** AVIATION RGMT

RESERVES/SECOND ECHELONS

ARMY* | DIVISION(S) | ARMIES | FRONTS

*** At every level in the command hierarchy, the air element would be commanded by a deputy commander for aviation. For example, each Frontal Aviation Army would be commanded by a Deputy Front Commander for aviation who reports directly to the Front Commander. The mission distribution varies by level of subordination: TSMA strategic air - deep interdiction/counter air; Frontal Aviation - deep interdiction/counter air and air support to armies; army aviation-air support to armies and divisions.

Figure 3.16

103

dominate the command structure of non-Soviet Pact Fronts as well as the HCOFs in the Western and Southeastern TSMA. A recent authoritative study concluded that the initiation of combat operations by the Pact "will not be the result of collective deliberation made by . . . the member states, but rather a direct reflection of a decision made solely in Moscow." Even "mobilization and force generation . . . would occur . . . *en masse* as [in] a single multinational army."[35] Of course, the Soviets also control the vast expanses of territory needed for conducting wide-ranging maneuver of combined air and ground forces. As a consequence, Soviet military scientists and commanders have a much broader organizational, political, and geographical context within which to think about employing and directing very large groupings of forces of different nationalities and services.

The discussion that follows will compare the NATO and Warsaw Pact command structure giving particular attention to the command hierarchy at "echelons above corps."

NATO's Army Group

Turning first to NATO, one sees that military leaders, especially army officers, tend to think of theater war in terms of the "corps battle." This perspective so thoroughly pervades operational thinking that, in an important sense, the corps commander is at the top of NATO's battle management hierarchy. Commanders above the corps commander are not there to direct him in the execution of a larger plan as much as they are there to coordinate support for him as he executes his own plan to defend a piece of terrain rarely more than 100 kilometers wide and 50 kilometers deep.

The level of command immediately above corps, the NATO Army Group, is equivalent to the Warsaw Pact Front. However, the extent of the Army Group commander's operational control and the reserve forces and firepower he can use to influence the course of any operation are somewhat more limited than are those at the disposal of a Pact Front Commander. Essentially, the NATO Army Group must coordinate the actions of already committed subordinate corps as they battle attacking Pact forces according to their various national tactical doctrines. Should the Army Group commander detect the development of a major operational-scale threat (or opportunity) in one particular sector along the Army Group's frontage, he might have to redistribute the committed forces of one national corps from one sector to reinforce the sector of another national corps. Failure to redistribute forces rapidly could result in enemy success on an operational-strategic scale that would threaten the survival of the entire Army Group, if not the forces of the entire region.

The Army Group commander may be able to apply additional firepower against the developing threat using Allied Tactical Air Forces' (ATAF) air sorties made available to him by CINCENT (CINC Allied Forces Central Europe, which would be the equivalent to a Pact HCOF in a TSMA). Nevertheless, in most respects, the Army Group commander would depend upon subordinate corps for the combat resources he would need to influence the course of conflict at his level.

The Warsaw Pact Front and the HCOF

The Pact Front commander, in contrast, would dictate priorities and missions to subordinate armies (equivalent to NATO corps). He would normally control sizable reserve forces and firepower (his second echelon army plus combined-arms and special reserves consisting of several divisions, an air assault brigade, an artillery division, and his own army of Frontal Aviation), which he could readily use to shift the weight of his main attack almost anywhere within his strategic direction without drawing upon forces from armies already committed. Moreover, should he choose to accept tactical stalemate in one or more army sectors to ensure operational-strategic success for the Front through weighting other sectors, he clearly would have the resources, authority, and span of control to do so. This rather impressive operational-strategic Front command system is not new in the structure of the Warsaw Pact troop control. But Ogarkov assessed it to be inadequate for the effective prosecution of theater-strategic war.

The HCOF at TSMA level is designed to meet this need for a theater-level perspective over the conduct of the strategic operation. The C-in-C of an HCOF would bring to bear additional forces (second echelon Fronts and airborne and amphibious forces) and fire support (additional aircraft, missiles, and artillery) and, as necessary, reallocate the resources of Fronts already engaged to add weight to those operational directions expected to offer most promise for strategic success. As a Front commander would with armies, the HCOF C-in-C would choose to have some Fronts (comprising perhaps two to three armies — eight to sixteen divisions) fight their own major battles (*srazheniya*) without significant external reinforcement while he would marshal operational and strategic reserves on selected directions for rapid execution of the TSMA strategic operation directed toward winning the war.

NATO's Regional Commands and Air Resources

The NATO regional commands, such as AFCENT, are equivalent in the hierarchy to the Warsaw Pact HCOF in a TSMA.[36] But one must question the degree to which CINCENT could influence the actions of the Army Groups and their subordinate corps. In terms of ground maneuver forces, CINCENT is simply one more level removed from the primary focus of control and combat resources — the national corps. The primary resource with which the CINCENT could influence the course of the war is air power (Allied Air Forces Central Europe — AAFCE). It could, of course, be argued that concentrating combat aircraft control at the regional level reflects a truly strategic approach to the problem by ensuring the most efficient use of air power in theater-strategic war.

The fact that air power is subordinated only at the regional level is more likely, however, to reflect the relative independence of the air force command function from that of "ground" armies in Western military thinking. For, while the much greater range of their weapons systems causes NATO air force commanders to think about theater warfare on a somewhat larger geographical scale than do their army counterparts, they tend to focus on the air threat and sometimes view support to the ground war as a competing, less time sensitive and, perhaps, less important mission. Although predictable and understandable, given the institutional independence of Western air forces since World War II, these peacetime bureaucratic biases, unfortunately, have a strong influence on operational thinking and would affect the conduct of wartime operations.

As illustrated on Figures 3.15 and 3.16, functional independence has invested considerable operational independence in the air force command element at every level. As a result, control of air combat power is, in many respects, external to and superimposed upon the primary command and operational decision centers such as Army Group and CINCENT. In the command hierarchy AAFCE is subordinated to CINCENT. In practice, however, AAFCE would more likely work with AFCENT as a more-or-less equal partner in allocating air sorties between theater air missions and support of the Army Groups.

The two allied tactical air forces each working with an Army Group — the 2nd and 4th ATAFs with NORTHAG (Northern Army Group) and CENTAG (Central Army Group) respectively — would then coordinate allocation of the air support sorties received from AAFCE/AFCENT down to the various national corps. To help manage the process, AAFCE has established a somewhat elaborate tactical air control and coordination system, designed to expedite coordination throughout the hierarchy. From the perspective of the ground commanders, however, this entire coordination process could be time consuming, inconsistent, and fragile because it would assume tremendous cooperation among the various national air forces and between allied air and ground commands under the great stress of competing wartime operational demands. The continued absence of a common NATO positive identification system (IFF) among the various national air forces could further reduce the flexibility of the allied air commands in meeting those demands.

Soviet HCOFs and Combined Arms

Within the Warsaw Pact, in contrast, air command and resources are fully integrated, from top to bottom, into a single combined-arms command structure. This command at TSMA level would even include naval forces supporting a strategic operation from contiguous seas (the Soviet Baltic Fleet and the naval forces of the GDR and Poland in the Western TSMA) and air units allotted to him from the strategic reserve by the Supreme High Command in Moscow. The deputy commanders for air, air defense, and naval forces would assist in carrying out the combined-arms strategic operation. (The Front commander has a similar command relationship with his deputy commanders for air forces and air defense.) The chief combined-arms commanders in the TSMA and in each of the Fronts typically would be very senior ground forces officers with considerable exercise experience in commanding large forces of different services in the conduct of operational-strategic and strategic operations. Their NATO counterparts, on the other hand, may be limited to providing an international coordination and information exchange function in a somewhat loose confederation of national corps and air forces striving to defeat a common enemy (see Figure 3.15).

IMPLICATIONS FOR NATO

It might appear at first that NATO could benefit from the shift in the Soviet focus of control from Front up to the HCOF in the TSMA. Warsaw Pact wartime control, already established in peacetime, would be more centralized than before and, hence, more vulnerable to disruption or destruction. Pact leaders would, however, attempt to reduce, if not eliminate, their vulnerability by thorough contingency planning and by increasing the hardening, redundancy, and mobility of command centers and supporting communications systems.

An increase in the rigidity of the Pact command structure resulting from a reduction of the responsiveness of the system to lower-level commanders may be another illusory benefit. Pact army (equivalent to NATO corps) commanders already have more maneuver units, air assault assets, and much more air, artillery, and logistics support under their direct control than do most NATO corps commanders, and, hence, they may not be seriously affected by a less responsive chain of command. In fact, a major objective of the reorganization of the Soviet and Warsaw Pact armed forces over the past decade has been to provide lower levels of command with a more truly combined-arms mix with which to conduct operations at each level. Even the tank regiment commander now commands his own artillery battalion and his own motorized rifle (BMP) battalion.

The Soviets, citing their own historical experience, argue that this top-down autocratic system, in practice, would allow considerable flexibility and responsiveness to operational and strategic opportunities on a theater scale. At the heart of their argument is the conviction that the key to operational flexibility and success is the ability of commanders at TSMA level to make optimum use of large reserves. They would have greater freedom to change plans, even during an operation, having uncommitted forces for major alternative contingencies. The authority to maneuver large reserves rapidly also improves the chances to effect surprise against an opponent who lacks similar flexibility.[37]

Conversely, a command without control of significant reserves cannot directly affect the course of battle and is, therefore, no command at all, simply a switchboard or possibly a bottleneck in the information flow between commands at higher and lower levels. Restriction of tactical commanders to a relatively narrow range of battle drills is acceptable, and even desirable, in the context of operational-strategic planning in which the predictability of implementation of the tactical plan is essential. Tactical failure is to be offset by operational-strategic adjustments in the course of the operation or campaign.

NATO's Tactical Mindset

The Warsaw Pact has increasingly more mobile assault forces and a continuously evolving offensive doctrine that calls for deployment of major elements of these forces more than 200 kilometers into NATO territory within less than a week from the time hostilities have begun.[38] NATO also has combat aircraft that can do great damage over distances of hundreds of kilometers in a matter of minutes. Its maneuver forces have sufficient mobility to move great distances and selected elements can redeploy laterally or in depth in a matter of hours or, in the case of aircraft, minutes.

The difference is that the Warsaw Pact not only has forces designed to achieve operational-strategic objectives, it is designing and exercising a command structure on a scale adequate to control those forces. NATO despite having weapons and forces capable of carrying on warfare on an operational-strategic scale, is severely limited by its tactical mindset. The Soviet changes represent both a lesson and a warning to NATO.

The Lesson

The central importance of what are essentially operational-tactical corps commands in NATO's overall control system is reflected also in national military doctrines, which rarely transcend solutions to problems of tactical dimensions. NATO has failed to expand its concept of control to encompass the extensive scale of intercoalition warfare that is determined by the instruments of war now possessed by both sides.

The Warning

The Soviets have recognized the need to adopt a broader concept of control to accommodate new "objective conditions." In creating an HCOF at the TSMA level, the Soviets have folded an already well-developed tactical (division) and operational/operational-strategic (army/Front) command system into a still more comprehensive strategic structure designed to control larger-scale theater-strategic operations.

NATO Approaches to Operational Thinking

Meanwhile, some NATO members are striving to expand from tactical and operational-tactical (division and corps) concepts to a broader level of military doctrine called operational art, which would govern the conduct of warfare by "echelons above corps." The West still tends, however, to approach operational art from below. Tactical concepts become the basic building blocks for operational art and operational success and, by extension, strategic success. Operational success tends to be regarded as the unplanned, but hoped-for, results of many sequential successes at the tactical level. In fact, some Western defense analysts have even defined operational art as "grand tactics."[39] The Western military planning environment, defined as it is by its nature as a coalition of more or less political equals, tends to make it very difficult for NATO planners to rise beyond the corps and division trenches of national-level organizational concerns to achieve a coalition-wide theater-strategic perspective.

In contrast, in Soviet military doctrine, tactical success is defined from above. The commander at the operational level establishes the objectives for lower tactical units, which, when achieved, create the conditions necessary for operational success at his level. Operational success, in turn, is the achievement of operational objectives previously established by the commander at the strategic level (see Figure 3.16).

Why NATO Needs Operational Control

Ogarkov's assessment that the impressive operational-strategic command system at Front level is inadequate for control of theater war suggests that NATO already has been conceptually outflanked. The Soviets are now pressing their advantage on a broad organizational and operational level that falls so far outside NATO's experience that the latter has difficulty understanding why the changes are important. For example, some would argue that NATO does not need more centralized control. They would contend that the focus of NATO's command structure, decentralized as it is down to corps level and below, is perfectly appropriate for the defense. Only a high-speed offensive such as that described in Warsaw Pact doctrinal writings requires a high degree of command centralization to ensure optimum coordination of fire and maneuver and proper timing of commitment of forces throughout the theater. NATO corps need only intercept the advancing Pact armies and defeat them as they arrive.

The argument itself is indicative of a tactical approach to theater-strategic war. The corps defends to a depth the Soviets define as the "tactical zone of defense," the first 30 kilometers to 50 kilometers west of the FEBA, which they would plan to penetrate in selected, relatively narrow, sectors within hours from the time they have begun the offensive by means of concentrating overwhelming firepower (air, missile, and artillery) in conjunction with maneuvering by airborne, air assault, and armored forces. They would strive to extend the penetration to a depth of more than 100 kilometers and seek to execute preplanned large-scale encirclements of entire NATO corps.

Because NATO is committed to a defensive posture, it would be irresponsible not to plan for the possibility of Warsaw Pact success in some sectors and, indeed, even in one or more major directions (see Figure 3.17). Such Pact successes would confront our defending corps with operational scale penetrations requiring an operational sale response and a command authority with a commensurate span of control.

Corps would have neither the information, the mobility, nor the forces to deal with successful penetration of such depth and magnitude. In fact, because of their proximity to unfolding events, corps level officers might report distorted impressions. A corps commander astride a major Warsaw Pact penetration corridor might not have the means even to assess the significance of the unfolding situation and certainly not the means to deal with the weight of fires and forces confronting him. Commanders of corps experiencing tactical penetrations of 15 kilometers to 25 kilometers in Pact secondary attacks, given their significance at corps level, might tend to exaggerate the operational significance of the enemy's successes. They probably would generate increasingly more strident requests to Army Group for scarce air sorties and logistics support in competition with Army Group and CINCENT requirements to limit the impact of major operational penetrations in other sectors.

Perhaps the most disturbing figures in such a scenario would be corps commanders who are holding or even advancing somewhat in those sectors where the Pact Front or HCOFs chose not to weight the attack. They would be accurately reporting victory — winning the corps battle — while Army Group and CINCENT could be trying desperately to fend off operational or strategic encirclement. Such corps might be analogous to a courageous squad fighting valiantly and successfully in a darkened building throughout the night only to discover at first light that the entire block has been in enemy hands for hours.

The major point is that, even in defense, the alliance would need a truly operational and strategic command system with a timely and accurate intelligence acquisition function and necessary combat resources to effect operational-strategic defeat of the opponent at the moment of his operational-tactical scale success.

The Soviet View of NATO's Command System

The asymmetries in NATO and Warsaw Pact command systems could even affect the quality of deterrence itself. Deterrence is a function of the enemy perceptions, and indications show the Soviets somewhat less impressed than is NATO with a command system focused on the corps level.

The Corps Level Is Not Impressive

In Soviet terminology, a corps may be classified as an *ob"edineniye* or a *soyedineniye*. The first is a major operational-scale formation comprising large elements of several different arms and, in some cases, different services capable of

WARTIME COMMAND SYSTEMS OF OPPOSING FORCES IN CENTRAL EUROPE

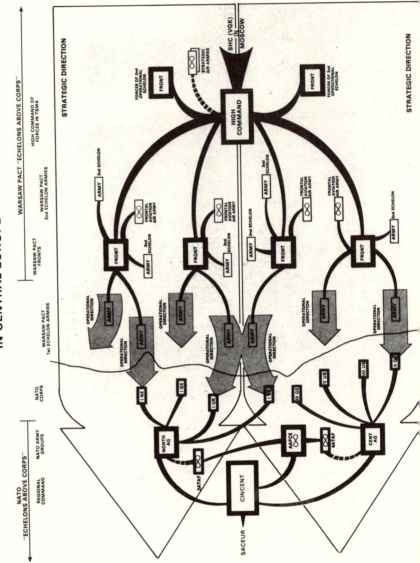

FIGURE 3.17

A stylized portrayal of the opposing forces that could be deployed within one to two weeks of mobilization in the central region. It attempts to capture, in a general way, the composition and possible disposition of forces and the relative depth of territory initially available to each side. The number of Warsaw Pact Fronts forward and the areas where each would concentrate its main attack could vary depending upon mobilization and attack scenarios. Additional forces from the United States and France are assumed to be not yet available. The lines of command on the NATO side are inverted to indicate the dependency of higher headquarters on subordinate, committed units for the resources needed to influence battle outcomes. NATO corps and air commands are emphasized to indicate the de facto locus of principal command authority in the alliance.

Source (for Strategic Directions and density of Fronts): Lecture materials from the Voroshilov General Staff Academy.

113

operational missions 50 kilometers to 500 kilometers deep into enemy defenses. For example, Soviet armies are *ob'edineniya*. In contrast, a *soyedineniye* is essentially a special, sometimes oversized, division, that is to say, an operational-tactical or greater tactical formation with a tactical span of control. Although such a corps may be expected to be able to accomplish missions in the enemy's operational depth, it would normally do so under control of a larger organization with a truly operational span of control, such as an army or Front.

Soviet and NATO divisions are called *soyedineniya*, or tactical formations.[40] But a 1983 textbook on NATO armies uses the term "*soyedineniya*" for NATO corps as well. Although certain French, German, and British corps are called "greater tactical" and some U.S. corps even "operational-tactical," because of their missions, all are designated *soyedineniya* with a tactical focus and span of control.[41] Hence the national corps, the mainstay of NATO's command organization, is regarded as little more than a super division.

History's Lessons about Western Coalitions

The Soviets tend to have a fairly low regard for the military effectiveness of Western military coalitions in which issues of control are not clearly defined. Soviet military writers have noted considerable dysfunctional rigidity at the higher end of the command hierarchy in Western alliances and illustrate this historically with the example of the U.S.-British forces in Europe during World War II: "Most decisions were made at the strategic level after long and difficult negotiations," even "to determine objectives, missions, and initiation times of combat action for American and English army groups." Repeated breakdowns in coordination between allied forces at the operational level were, in the Soviet view, "one of the main reasons why the allied armies were held up at the Siegfried line." The ultimate demonstration of the ineffectiveness of the Western system of strategic leadership was the inability of the U.S.-British coalition "to effect a single operation of encirclement and destruction of major groupings of enemy forces."[42]

In the spring of 1984 the chief of staff of the Warsaw Pact forces made some specific observations about the relevance of historical experience to NATO's current command and control problems: "It is not accidental that NATO's problems with interaction between very large formations (army groups) and national commands (corps and their national controlling ministries) are causing considerable concern which has led to a great deal of work to correct the problem. The main efforts are directed at timely determination of the sequence and times of turning forces over to control of the NATO command, and the division of spheres of responsibility between the large formations (army groups) and national control organs."[43]

None of these observations are meant to suggest that the Soviets think that NATO could be defeated easily. They do help to illustrate, however, that the Soviets are very sensitive to the role of the system of command and control in making their assessment of the overall combat effectiveness of a coalition.

NOTES

1. Major General R. Simoyan, "Teatry voyennykh deystviy v. plannakh NATO" ["Theaters of Strategic Military Action in NATO Plans"], series published in *Krasnaya zvezda* [Red Star], July 27, August 8 and 10, 1979.

2. M. M. Kir'yan, *Problemy Voyennoy teorii v sovetskikh nauchno-spravochnykh isdaniyakh'* [*Problems of Military Theory in Soviet Scientific Reference Publications*] (Moscow: Nauka, 1985), p. 61; and M. I. Cherenichenko, "Strategicheskaya Operatsiya" ["Strategic Operation"], *Sovetskaya voyennaya entsiklopedia* [*Soviet Military Encyclopedia*, hereafter *S.V.E.*], Vol. 7, pp. 551, 552.

3. V. D. Sokolovskiy, ed., *Voyennaya strategiya* [*Military Strategy*], 3rd edition (Moscow: Voyenizdat, 1968), pp. 226, 234, 235, 255-92, 331.

4. B. V. Panov, et al., *Istoriya voyennogo iskusstva* [*History of Military Art*] (Moscow: Voyenizdat, 1984), pp. 498-99.

5. The source that most directly and explicitly revises Sokolovskiy's single-scenario view of war was written by Deputy to the Chief of the General Staff Colonel-General M. A. Gareyev in his book, *M. V. Frunze — Voyennyy teoretik: vzglyady M. V. Frunze i sovremennaya voyennaya teoriya* [*M. V. Frunze — Military Theoretician: The Views of M. V. Frunze and Modern Military Theory*] (Moscow: Voyenizdat, 1985), pp. 239-41, 380, 381.

6. See, for example, Marshal of the Soviet Union I. Bagramyan and Colonel, Docent, I. Vyrodov, "Rol' predstaviteley stavki vgk v gody voyny: organizatsiya i metody ikh raboty" ["The Role of Representatives of the Headquarters, VGK in the War Years: Organization and Methods of Their Work"], *Voyenno-istoricheskiy zhurnal* [*Military Historical Journal* hereafter *Vizh.*] 8 (August 1980): 33.

7. Global war with highly capable conventional weapons is envisioned in an increasing number of Soviet military sources. See, for example, N. V. Ogarkov, "The Defense of Socialism: The Experience of History and the Present," *Krasnaya zvezda*, May 9, 1984, p. 3; and L. I. Ol'shtynskiy, *Vzaimodeystviye armii i flota* [*Interaction of the Army and Navy*] (Moscow: Voyenizdat, 1983), p. 132. The most responsible discussion of Soviet thinking about limited nuclear use can be found in Notra Trulock III, "Soviet Perspectives on Limited Nuclear War," in *Swords and Shields: NATO, the USSR, and New Choices for Long-Range Offense and Defense*, ed. Fred S. Hoffman, Albert Wohlstetter, and David S. Yost (Lexington, Mass.: Lexington Books, 1987). Trulock's research includes open sources and lecture materials from the Voroshilov General Staff Academy. Also see John G. Hines, Phillip A. Petersen, and Notra Trulock III, "Soviet Military Theory from 1945-2000: Implications for NATO," *The Washington Quarterly*, Fall 1986, pp. 117-37.

8. Lieutenant Commander (Diploma) Zygmunt Binieda, "Ogolne pojecie teatru dzialan wojennych" ["The General Concept of a Theater of Strategic

Military Action"], *Przeglad morski* [*Polish Naval Review*] 12 (1981): 3.

9. *Politicheskaya i voennaya geografiya* [*Political and Military Geography*] (Moscow: Voyenizdat, 1980), pp. 92–93, 116–17.

10. Warsaw Pact defectors trained in the 1960s were so instructed. See, for example, Viktor Suvorov, "Strategic Command and Control: The Soviet Approach," *International Defense Review* 17 (1984): 1815.

11. "Podgotovka TVD" ["Preparation of the TSMA"], *S.V.E.*, Vol. 6 (Moscow: Voyenizdat, 1978), p. 384.

12. Binieda, p. 4.

13. "Strategicheskoye napravleniye" ["Strategic Direction"], *S.V.E.*, Vol. 7 (1979), p. 555; and *Voyennyy entsiklopedisheskiy slovar'* [*Military Encyclopedic Dictionary*, hereafter *V.E.S.*] (Moscow: Voyenizdat, 1983), p. 711.

14. "Front," *V.E.S.* (Moscow: Voyenizdat), p. 787

15. "Operatsionnoye napravleniye" ["Operational Direction"], *V.E.S.*, p. 516; and *S.V.E.*, Vol. 6, p. 64.

16. Colonel (Diploma) Pilot Aleksander Musial, "Kharacter i znaczenie operacji powietrznych we wspolczesnych dzialanizch wojennych" ["The Character and Importance of Air Operations in Modern Warfare"], *Przeglad wojsk lotniczych i wojsk obrony powietrznej kraju* [*Polish Air Forces and Air Defense Review*] 3 (1982): 13.

17. S. A. Tyushkevish, *The Soviet Armed Forces: A History of Their Organizational Development* (Moscow: 1978), trans. U.S. Air Force Soviet Military Thought Series, No. 19 (Washington, D.C.: U.S. Government Printing Office, undated), p. 459.

18. Colonel M. P. Skirdo, *Narod, Armiya, Polkovodets* [*The People, the Army, the Commander*] (Moscow, 1970), trans. U.S. Air Force Soviet Military Thought Series, No. 14 (Washington, D.C.: U.S. Government Printing Office, undated), p. 109.

19. John Erickson, Lynn Hansen, Amnon Sella, et al., "College Station Paper 2 — Organizing for War: The Soviet Military Establishment View through the Prism of the Military District," College Station Papers Series (College Station, Texas, 1983), pp. xxxi, xxvii.

20. General of the Army P. Lashchenko, "Sovershenstvovaniye sposobev okruzheniya i unichtozheniya krupnykh gruppirovoka protivnika po opytu volikoy otechestvennoy voyny" ["Perfection of Methods of Encircling and Destroying Large-Scale Enemy Groupings Based on the Experience of the Great Patriotic War"], *Vizh.* 2 (February 1985): 31.

21. These themes are repeated and refined in a great volume of Soviet military literature on strategic leadership. For a discussion of the need to be able to quickly mobilize reserves while avoiding provocation of an enemy response, see Gareyev, op. cit., pp. 241, 242. (Editor's note: Marshal N. V. Ogarkov noted in 1982 that "it is inexpedient to maintain Armed Forces in peacetime which are fully deployed in the strength required in case of war. No nation is economically capable of doing this, nor is there any particular need to do so." He goes on to note that a certain portion of the armed forces is in a continuous state of readiness (at full strength in personnel and equipment) while another portion is prepared for rapid mobilization and deployment. See Ogarkov, *Vsegda v gotovnosti k zashchite otechestva* [*Always in Readiness to Defend the Homeland*] (Moscow: Voyenizdat, 1982), p. 58.

22. General of the Army A. M. Mayorov, First Deputy Commander of the Ground Forces, "Strategicheskoye rukovodstvo v velikoy otechestvennoy voyne" ["Strategic Leadership in the Great Patriotic War"], *Vizh.* 5 (May 1985): 39.

23. Skirdo, op. cit., pp. 117–18.

24. Warsaw Pact defectors trained in the 1960s were so instructed. See, for example, Viktor Suvorov, "Strategic Command and Control: The Soviet Approach," *International Defense Review* 17 (1984): 1813–20.

25. V. Kulikov, "Strategicheskoe rukovodstvo vooruzhennymi silami" ["Strategic Leadership of the Armed Forces"], *Vizh.* 6 (June 1975): 15–16.

26. See "Glavnoe komandovaniye," *S.V.E.*, Vol. 2 (Moscow: Voyenizdat, 1976), p. 562.

27. Brigadier John Hemsley, "The Influence of Technology upon Soviet Operational Doctrine." A lecture given at the Royal United Services Institute February 13, 1986. Hemsley incorrectly speculates that the three TSMAs in the West (the Northwestern, Western, and Southwestern) have now been grouped together "to one large TVD" under the command of Ogarkov and that there are additional High Commands that have been established on the Northwestern, Western, and Southwestern strategic directions. He wrongly asserted that Marshal Kulikov held the High Command of Forces of the Western "strategic direction."

28. This and numerous other factual and analytical errors can be found in Jack Sullivan and Tom Symonds, "Soviet Troop Control: Challenging Myths," U.S. Air Force Intelligence Research Division Special Research Item, April 1985.

29. "Strategiya, voyennaya" ["Strategy, Military"], *S.V.E.*, Vol. 7, p. 564; *V.E.S.*, p. 712; and "Strategicheskaya operatsiya" ["Strategic Operation"], *V.E.S.*, p. 710.

30. Colonel I. Vyrodov, "O rukovodstve voyennymi deystviyami strategicheskikh gruppirovok voysk vo vtoroy mirovoy voyne" ["On the Direction of Military Action of Strategic Groupings of Forces in the Second World War"], *Vizh.* 4 (April 1979): 19.

31. Bagramyan and Vyrodov, op. cit., p. 30.

32. Ibid., p. 29.

33. The most authoritative discussion of the current state of Warsaw Pact command structure can be found in John J. Yurechko, "Command and Control for Coalitional Warfare: The Soviet Approach," *Signal,* December 1985, pp. 34–39; reprinted in Stephen J. Cimbala, ed., *Soviet C3* (Washington, D.C.: AFCEA International Press, 1987), pp. 17–34. Yurechko's analysis is explicitly confirmed by the revelation of a highly placed Polish officer who worked on the Polish General Staff until his defection in November 1981. The officer attested that in 1979 and 1980 all Warsaw Pact members except Romania signed a "Statute of the Combined (Warsaw Pact) Armed Forces and Wartime Control Organs" that surrendered control of the armed forces of the East European states directly to the Soviet Supreme High Command in the event of war. Even the Polish fleet would be directly integrated into the Soviet Baltic Fleet. Ryszard Jerzy Kuklinski, "Wojna z narodem widziana od srodka" ["The War Against the Nation Seen from Within"], *Kultura,* No. 4/475, Paris, pp. 53–54.

34. Marshal of the Soviet Union Nikolay V. Ogarkov, *Istoria uchit bditel'nosti* [*History Teaches Vigilance*] (Moscow: Voyenizdat, 1985), pp. 36–37.

35. Yurechko, op. cit., for an abbreviated version of this study.

36. In the Central Region, AFCENT would be opposed by the HCOF in the Western TSMA whose responsibility would also include part of AFNORTH — specifically Denmark and the Danish straits.

37. Soviet military experts have made these points in numerous evaluations of "lessons learned" from history. Two instructive examples are Army General A. M. Mayorov, "Strategicheskoye rukovodstvo v velikoy ostechestvennoy voyne" ["Strategic Leadership in the Great Patriotic War"], *Vizh.* 5 (May 1985): 37–39; and Marshal of the Soviet Union I. Bagramyan and Colonel I. Vyrodov, "Rol' predstaviteley stavki vgk v gody voyny: organizatziya i

metody ikh raboty" ["The Role of Representatives of the Headquarters, Supreme High Command in the War Years: The Organization and Methods of Their Work"], *Vizh.* 8 (August 1980): 31.

38.   See John G. Hines, "Soviet Front Operations in Europe — Planning for Encirclement," *A Report from a Conference at Sundvollen, April 25-27, 1985* (Oslo: Forsvarets Hogskolefurenig [Alumni Association of the Norwegian Defense College], 1986).

39.   Attributed to Basil Liddell-Hart in Edward N. Luttwak, "The Operational Level of Warfare," *International Security,* Winter 1980-1981, p. 61.

40.   "Divisiya" ["Division"] *V.E.S.* (Moscow: Voyenizdat, 1983), p. 233.

41.   N. K. Glazunov and N. S. Nikitin, *Operatsiya i boy [The Operation and Battle],* (Moscow: Voyenizdat, 1983), pp. 70, 169, 258, 266.

42.   Colonel General P. K. Altukhov, "Osobennosti upravleniya ob'edineniyami i soyedineniyami koalitsionnogo sostava po opytu voyny (1939-1945)" ["The Peculiarities of Control of Very Large and Large Coalition Units Based on the Experience of the War (1939-1945)], *Vizh.* 3 (March 1982): 51.

43.   Army General Gribkov, "Opyt upravleniya koakitsionnymi gruppirovkami voysk" ["The Experience of Controlling Coalition Force Groupings"], *Vizh.* 3 (March 1984): 34.

APPENDIX: TRANSLATING A CONCEPT

Many Western specialists on the Soviet military have chosen to abandon use of the Russian acronym "TVD" as arcane and unhelpful in communicating to nonspecialists what the Soviet concept stands for. To the understandable confusion of nonspecialists, at least three different translations have been used in the past six years. Theater of Military Operations (TMO) is the most widely used, and the authors have used the expression "Theater of Military Action." The GRU defector, Victor Suvorov, acknowledged that TVD means "theater of actions on a strategic scale" but he also argued for continued use of the term "TVD" to discourage Western analysts from distorting the concept to fit their own preconceptions.

We agree with Suvorov's translation but disagree with his advice not to use it. Because "TVD" doesn't mean anything to Western readers, they are very likely to make their own assumptions about what the concept represents. We feel that an accurate translation of "TVD" will narrow the range of possible creative Western interpretations. Specifically, we believe the most accurate and useful translation of the Soviet military term, *teatr voyennykh deystviy* is, as Suvorov suggested, Theater of Strategic Military Action (TSMA). (Russian uses the plural *deystviya*, which literally means "actions," for describing more than one act. In English the word "action" in the singular already expresses the idea of a number or series of acts, especially in its military usage.)

In the 1983 Soviet *Military Encyclopedic Dictionary* and in a 1985 Soviet book devoted to clarifying military terminology (Kiryan), the term *voyennye deystviya* in the expression *teatr voyennykh deystviy* is defined as referring exclusively to military action on a strategic scale. The same sources note that for smaller scale action at the operational and tactical levels the Soviets use a different expression, *boyeviye deystviya,* literally "combat action." The phrase, "military operations," in the widely used translation, "Theater of Military Operations," therefore is a mistranslation of the term *voyenniya deystviya.* Moreover, TMO fails to communicate to the nonspecialist what Soviet military planners grasp immediately when they hear the expression TVD — a region identified for military action on a strategic scale. The English term, "Theater of Military Action," accurately translates the individual Russian words, but still fails to translate the specialized Soviet military meaning of the entire expression, "Theater of Strategic Military Action."

The Soviets do not use the expression *teatr strategicheskikh deystviy* (theater of strategic action) most probably because *voyennye deystviya* (military action) is a broader concept than strategic action. Strategic action tends to exclude smaller scale operations and tactics whereas military action encompasses all levels of warfare, up to and including strategic, and is, therefore, more appropriate for describing the full range of military activity associated with theater conflict.

II

The Management of Geostrategic Conflict: Escalation, Control, and War Termination

4

Strategic Priorities and U.S. Options: Escalation and Extended War

Colin S. Gray

THE STRATEGIC CONTEXT

The national military strategy adopted and pursued by the United States should be congruent with support of the policy goals that ought to be its justification. In practice, policy can be so vague or so influenced by a desire to stimulate particular domestic and foreign perceptions of will, that, in effect, it yields no guidance of real utility to defense planners. If the global containment of Soviet power is the central guiding purpose for U.S. national security policy, with the proximate goal of denying Moscow a substantially unchallenged hegemony over Eurasia, then the framework for U.S. strategy design is not difficult to identify — although room remains for important debate over means and methods.

The geostrategic reality of the West's interrupted, on-shore containing line in Eurasia is considerably stronger than superficial study of a map could lead one to believe. In principle, the Soviet Union, utilizing the value of the initiative, could select vulnerable targets of opportunity that would not lend themselves easily to local defense. But, in practice, a flagrant act of Soviet aggression that was geostrategically very limited in its immediate goals would forfeit the potentially (large) war-winning value of surprise, in aid of securing only a modest gain. Successful local Soviet offensive action — against Norway or Turkey, for example — might trigger the unravelling of NATO, if NATO-Europe decided that the action in question demonstrated that the alliance could neither protect nor, plausibly, promise to liberate. Nonetheless, more probable results of Soviet aggression on so limited a scale would be general Western mobilization and, if time permitted, rearmament, and the conduct of a geographically unconstrained scale of military response at times and places of U.S. or NATO choosing. In short, one important function of relatively weak forward defenses is to compel the enemy to fight, albeit perhaps only on a modest scale, and thereby declare the intensity of his intentions.

Horizontal escalation has not been debated competently in recent years. Execution of such escalation, it should be emphasized, would reflect the facts that attractive steps in vertical escalation would not be available and that the premier general-purpose force instrument of the maritime alliance, superior naval power, inherently is suitable for such missions (by way of contrast to heavy, mechanized Army formations). Critics of horizontal escalation point, correctly, both to the improbability of finding strategic compensation through gains on the Soviet flanks for the short-war loss of NATO territory in Central-Western Europe, and to the dangers of vertical escalation that would accompany horizontal escalation. The critics, by and large, have created a "straw target."[1] In the context of a stalemated NATO-Warsaw Pact ground war in Central Europe, horizontal escalation would be nothing more than common sense; whereas should NATO lose a ground war in Europe, a United States determined to continue the war would be compelled to pursue a peripheral strategy.

Far more troubling than any prospect of horizontal escalation on the part of the West is the possibility of its exercise by a Soviet Union that chose to exploit the "wrong footing" of the United States in a region logistically far removed from Central Europe. Writing about U.S. improvements in strategic mobility, Secretary of Defense Weinberger advised, "Once these programs are complete, we will be able to deploy seven divisions in Southwest Asia."[2] How would NATO-Europe be reinforced if U.S. strategic air and sealift were fully employed sustaining a major expeditionary force in Southwest Asia? It may be sensible for the United States to be able to deploy a multidivision force to Southwest Asia — but not in the context of continuing NATO dependence upon U.S. rapid reinforcement. One should recall the anxieties of 1950–1951 as to whether Korea was "the wrong war, at the wrong place, at the wrong time, and with the wrong enemy [presumably this last point, at least, would not apply]" in General Bradley's words.[3]

The "two ocean" problem that the USSR's strategic geography poses for the U.S. Navy may be a dilemma for U.S. uniformed planners and operators, but it is a net asset of enormous significance for the West. The Soviet Union has no choice other than to contemplate the prospect of a two(plus)-front war.[4] But even that definition is optimistic for Moscow, given that the Asian front encompasses, potentially, the entirety of the frontier with China and, more plausibly still, confrontation with a U.S. military power anchored in South Korea and on an island chain reaching from Luzon, in the Philippines, through Hokkaido, in Japan, and the Aleutians and then to Alaska — and expressed in the form of a manifestly superior maritime power projection capability. The importance in Soviet calculation of the second front in Asia (a certain second front with U.S. maritime power and a possible second/third front vis-à-vis China) must depend upon how optimistically they would view the prospects for a rapid favorable decision in the West.

If Soviet leaders believe that their forces could inflict a definitive defeat upon NATO in Europe in the course of two-to-four weeks and that Soviet nuclear capabilities would function very reliably as a counterdeterrent, then even substantial military setbacks in the Far East, or along the Chinese frontier, could be endured, *pro tem.* Indeed, in that context, Soviet anticipation of suffering considerable disadvantage in Asia should not serve very usefully to enhance deterrence. But, if Soviet leaders were far from confident that a definitive theater victory in Europe would in practice be secured in days or a few weeks, or if they feared that an undefeated (save in Europe) United States, undamaged at home, would choose and be able to continue to prosecute global war, or if they expected to suffer very great nuclear damage at home in the course of winning a campaign or war in Europe — then, the prospect of loss in the Far East would have to assume a status of very considerable importance and should enhance deterrence usefully.

Common sense as well as contemporary defense reformers remind us that strategy is an exercise in making choices. In practice, many important choices are, and should be recognized as, foreordained by geopolitics. Moreover, as William Kaufmann insists, U.S. freedom of action in choice of strategic objectives is somewhat constrained by the fact that the overall strategic posture, and certainly the political purpose of the Western Alliance, is defensive in character. To the substantial degree to which the U.S./NATO choice of strategic objectives must flow from the scale, kind, locations, and assessed intentions of a Soviet attack, Western strategy is generically reactive in nature. The flexibility with which superior naval power can be applied is important in principle, as the United States and NATO seek to shape an overall strategy that leans on relative Western strengths and exploits relative Soviet weaknesses. But, the strategic value of superior naval power is to a degree offset by the very substantial inaccessibility of the core areas of power in the Soviet

Union to the direct application of pressure from the sea, and the geostrategic vulnerability of peninsular Europe to the long suit of Soviet power, mechanized ground forces.[5]

The principal restriction upon choice of strategy for NATO and for the United States is geopolitical in nature. Whatever the U.S./NATO choice among military instruments and the operational methods chosen for their employment, the primary immediate objective of the alliance has to be to defeat a Soviet invasion of West Germany (in the first instance). Insofar as NATO is concerned (although not necessarily the United States as a separate national security community) Western Europe from the Baltic to the Adriatic does comprise prospectively the main theater of operations. Arguments over the implications of this inalienable fact comprise the heart of the recent debate over U.S. national military strategy. Much of this debate — between self-described continentalists/coalitionists and maritime advocates[6] — has reflected considerable mutual misunderstanding (some, no doubt, willful in origin), the attacking of imaginary debating positions, and an absence of history-based prudence.[7] Maritime-oriented analysis of the geostrategic situation of the West yields a number of propositions.

First, U.S. (and allied) maritime advantage is critically important — not just desirable, but literally essential — for the deterrence of war, in that the credible promise of the U.S. exercise of sea control is a necessary precondition for the conduct of protracted armed conflict in and about Eurasia-Africa. Needless to add, perhaps, Western ability to enforce a long war on the Soviet Union could be defeated if U.S. strategic nuclear forces were insufficient to impose escalation discipline or if the United States was denied a sufficient quality of working control of the key sea lines of communication.

Second, if NATO's ground and tactical air forces go down in defeat in a matter of days, U.S. and allied naval forces cannot provide immediate strategic compensation through the achievement of success of comparable strategic value elsewhere. Furthermore, there is no way in which NATO's maritime assets could be employed in the course of a European campaign of, say, two-weeks' duration, such as to have a truly major impact on the battle of the Central Front. There is nothing very surprising about this. British naval power could not intervene directly, respectively, to thwart the execution of the Schlieffen Plan in August-September 1914, or the Ludendorff Offensive of March 1918, or the unfolding of the Manstein Plan in May 1940.

Third, if NATO's ground and tactical air forces can remain in the field somewhere in Western Europe, U.S. and allied naval power would play an essential role in NATO's military recovery —

through provision of working control of the SLOCs and, increasingly, through flexibility in sea-based power projection (nautical maneuver) against a Soviet imperium that is vulnerable to attack on many geographical axes. Some proponents and critics of the maritime strategy have tended to debate the strategy out of its appropriate operational context. U.S. and allied naval power is not going to save NATO-Europe in the event of a catastrophe, May 1940-style, on the Central Front. But, sensible proponents of the case for the importance of Western maritime preponderance do not claim otherwise.

Fourth, U.S. working control of the relevant lines of maritime communications will be essential whether or not a Soviet ground-forces' offensive can be held in Central Europe. In U.S. perspective, war in Europe might be only a campaign, it need not comprise the war, and it is very important for deterrence that Soviet leaders understand this point. Always assuming the functioning of strategic nuclear counterdeterrence, in the event of U.S. military expulsion from continental Europe the U.S. Navy again would assume its historic role of being the first line of the nation's defense.

Fifth, the recent U.S. debate over the maritime strategy allegedly versus a continental strategy misses the point that the debate should not be over the relative merits of landpower or seapower in U.S. national military strategy. The United States cannot be a landpower beyond North America unless she is a seapower, and seapower has strategic meaning only insofar as it has influence on events on land.

Altogether there is today in the United States an imprudent obsession with one, admittedly exceedingly important, problem: the difficulty of holding and repelling a Soviet ground assault in Central Europe. This author yields to no one in his recognition of the strategic importance to the United States of keeping the Soviet Union essentially landlocked and healthily distracted from the full-fledged exercise of (maritime) *Weltpolitik* by continental security problems (NATO in the West, China in the East, unstable clients in Eastern Europe, and fanatical Moslems to the south). However that recognition, and acknowledgment that the cutting edge of Soviet military power lies in its ground forces, should not translate into an argument for a stronger U.S. Army and tactical air force at the expense of the U.S. Navy. These points are particularly important:

The prospect of protracted armed conflict should prove particularly deterring to the Soviet Union.[8] The entry price the United States must pay in order to threaten plausibly to impose such a conflict comprises a very convincing strategic nuclear counterdeterrent and preponderance at sea (although not, of course, preponderance everywhere at sea).[9]

It would be vastly preferable for the Soviet Union to confront the prospect of a protracted conflict with a U.S. bridgehead intact in continental NATO-Europe. But, the case for a U.S. Navy able to ensure U.S. use of maritime communications for transportation and for power projection is equally strong, whether or not the protracted conflict includes an active continental NATO-European dimension.

The argument that the U.S. Navy could sink the Soviet Navy in its surface (and attack [and some strategic-nuclear] submarine) entirety and yet still contribute not at all to the defense of NATO's Central Front is a popular trivialization of strategy discussion.[10] (The same point could have been made with reference to Admiral Jellicoe's Grand Fleet of 1914, with equal lack of cogency.) Lest the point is still obscure — only ready, deployed, and rapidly transportable ground and tactical air forces can preclude a Soviet *Blitzkrieg* victory in a one-to-two-week war in Central-Western Europe. U.S. and allied maritime power is not obviously relevant to the mission (the arguments to the contrary are not very persuasive). The case for very strong U.S. naval forces is: to ensure that U.S. reinforcements arrive rapidly so as to avoid a short war defeat for NATO; to keep NATO "in the field" in a war that lasts more than a few weeks; to exploit Soviet weaknesses on its flanks in a protracted war; to apply pressure on the Soviet Union for war termination through the sinking of more and more of its SSBN force; if needs be, to enable the United States to wage a protracted war in Asia and Africa should Europe fall; and truly *in extremis*, to contest a siege of the Americas if the Soviet Union should achieve hegemony over Eurasia and set about the translation of her superior continental landpower into a challenge for (selectively local) maritime superiority.

As happens not infrequently in defense debates, the orientation toward particular disagreements over naval force posture, operational deployment, and missions (e.g., over large carriers versus small carriers, power projection versus sea control) has had the effect of distorting the debate over national military strategy. From the public literature of the 1980s, one could derive the impression that the case for and against a 600-ship U.S. Navy with 15 carrier task forces hangs critically upon the answers to such questions as these: should the Navy promptly assault the home bastions of Soviet naval power in the event of war? And, could successive campaigns against "the flanks" contribute vitally to the defense of NATO's Central Front? This is a classic example of the wrong questions generating, necessarily, irrelevant answers.

NATO and the United States cannot, or cannot sensibly, choose between strength at sea and strength for the holding of Western Europe on land, because NATO cannot hold on land if it cannot control its trans-Atlantic SLOC. A maritime strategy is mandated for the United States by reason of the geography of its competition with the Soviet Union. Some critics of U.S. naval augmentation and modernization are committing the abominable error of reducing the hypothetical future war almost strictly to a brief campaign for an initial (and possibly definitive) decision in Central Europe (victory — that is to say stalemate *après* 1914 — or defeat — that is to say *après* May 1940) and neglecting to enquire what might happen next. To be fair, or perhaps to spread the blame, proponents of the maritime strategy who choose to place emphasis upon the (very) short-war contribution of the U.S. Navy, feed and invite continuation of this error.

Given the strong plausibility of the propositions that the ability to sustain a protracted global conflict may be critically important for the deterrence of war and that nuclear counter-deterrence renders protracted U.S.-Soviet armed conflict very probable indeed — *whether or not NATO holds in Western Europe* — several caveats must be noted concerning the development and operational uses of naval power.

First, the Western Alliance as a whole obviously should not construct a maritime-overbalanced reply to what is, in the first instance, essentially a landpower threat. However, it does not follow from this elementary point that the United States should not have a maritime-heavy orientation in its general purpose force.[11]

Second, U.S. and NATO maritime power should not be used in such a way as to enhance the prospect of a precipitate rate of vertical escalation.[12] For enhancement of prewar deterrence it is important that Soviet leaders should anticipate their Western foes being willing to adopt any and all means necessary to defeat Soviet strategy. Those means include endeavors to exploit differences of interest and commitment within the Soviet empire, denial of any absolute sanctuary status to Soviet home territory, and willingness to use nuclear weapons. However, in operational practice the United States and Great Britain, preeminently though not necessarily exclusively within NATO, may choose to accord Soviet territory sanctuary status in order to minimize the risks to U.S. and British territory.

Lest there be any misunderstanding, the second caveat reflects no more than a concern for due consideration in planning and force execution. Certainly it does not assume that assaults against the Soviet coasts must be unwise under all circumstances or that freedom of choice, the initiative, necessarily will rest with the United States. Moreover, it does not assume that U.S. maritime strategy is committed to any immediate offensive against the coastal bastions of Soviet seapower, regardless of strategic conditions or tactical circumstances. As Admiral Watkins has written:

> Early forward movement of carrier battle forces provides prudent positioning of our forces in order to support the requirements of the unified commanders and to roll back Soviet forces, should war come. It does not imply some immediate "Charge of the Light Brigade" attack on the Kola Peninsula or any other specific target.[13]

Even if the essence of strategy, or perhaps of the quality required of a strategist, is the moral courage to make difficult choices, the real scope for strategic choice in U.S. national military strategy is rather less than frequently is asserted to be the case. If the United States continues down the path of global containment, employing a mix of multilateral and bilateral alliance ties as the political framework, geostrategic and political considerations serve vastly to narrow the scope for U.S. innovation in strategy. In principle, the United States could choose to emphasize in her national military strategy strategic forces (offensive and defensive), landpower, and seapower.

A STRATEGIC FORCES' ORIENTATION

In practice, the requisite superiority, or military advantage for escalation dominance, literally may not be achievable through strategic forces. Moreover, for good or ill, since the latter part of the 1960s the United States explicitly has eschewed strategic superiority — the basis in the 1950s for extended nuclear deterrence — as a strategic policy objective. The SDI might serve to restore some genuine U.S. strategic-force advantage if weaponized in multilayer form and married to strategic offensive forces modernized to defeat emerging Soviet active defenses. But it would be prudent for U.S. planners and commentators to recognize the plain aversion in Western political culture to such a bid for the restoration of superiority, as well as the improbability of its technical accomplishment under current, peacetime circumstances.

As long as the United States lacks the ability to limit the level of damage that it might suffer at home as a consequence of nuclear operations that escalated out of a theater conflict, U.S. strategic forces must be relegated to the status of shield, and not sword, of the republic. The shield role is already critical and entirely indispensable. In effect, U.S. strategic forces, whatever the balance as between offense and defense in the posture, can function usefully in war fairly strictly as a counterdeterrent. That is to say those forces should be capable of denying Soviet leaders any attractive options for escalating out of a stalemated or losing theater, or more likely multitheater, campaign(s) in search of victory through the functional equivalent of a Napoleonic "decisive battle" in the homeland-to-homeland mode.

This is not to suggest that a strategic-nuclear standoff does not cast a shadow over local and theater conflict, inclining combatants to caution lest Clausewitz's "grammar of war"[14] and "friction"[15] produce a combat slide to a scale of violence that was not desired. But it is to suggest that the "generous margin" of strength that the U.S. geopolitical theorist Nicholas Spykman claimed to be necessary for a "positive foreign policy," is unlikely to be secured through improvements in the strategic forces' posture.[16] Spykman, writing in 1942, spoke of the value of "a margin of force which can be freely used." In terms of an objective analysis of the strategic forces' balance, although not in terms of contemporary U.S. political perception, the aircraft of SAC and of the U.S. Navy provided such a margin in the 1950s. The prospects for restoration of U.S. freedom of action vis-à-vis its strategic forces must be judged to be dim.

A LANDPOWER FOCUS

Next, there is a cluster of strategic luminaries who claim that there is a stand off, at best, in the strategic forces' balance; Western maritime power is, and will remain, greatly superior to Soviet maritime power, but that the Soviet empire, unlike the Japanese empire, is not at all vulnerable to pressure at, or from the, sea (the USSR does not have important SLOCs, vulnerable and valuable insular possessions, and coasts easy of access to seaborne assault that are close to the centers of national power); and that, therefore, in the words of Edward Luttwak, "the ground-forces divisions are the basic currency of East-West strategy."[17]

Not for the first time, indeed really for the third time (previous ventures were in 1951–1952 and 1961–1965) some U.S. strategists, official and unofficial, are repeating what Sir Douglas Haig told Lloyd George in 1916–1918 and what George Marshall told Churchill in 1942–1944: there is no effective alternative to meeting the continental superpower enemy on his own terms (with landpower in the principal theater of operations, that is to say on the ground in Europe). Four generic difficulties beset the advocates of a heavy continental-landpower orientation to U.S. national military strategy.

First, in preparing so substantially nearly for the worst-case event (the absolutely worst-case event would be a Soviet preventive nuclear assault on the continental United States) of a Soviet attack in Europe, the United States would risk being severely deficient in flexible, prudently usable military power relevant to most other insecurity scenarios around Rimland Eurasia (the Gulf, for the most obvious example). U.S. policy makers would be doing the reverse of capitalizing upon U.S. geostrategic strengths were they to lock up more military power in, and committed to, a European garrison.

Second, proponents of a continentalist-landpower focus should not be permitted, in the excitement of debate, to neglect the point that the continent most in question is an ocean away. If the war is decided in Europe in five to ten days, with minimum — or, more likely, less — notice for countermobilization, then SLOC protection and support of NATO's flanks may well be close to irrelevant. But, what if the war is not over in five to ten days? More to the point perhaps, what if NATO fares poorly in the field but the U.S. President wishes to continue the war where he effectively can, that is to say in regions apart from peninsular Europe? This second point must be extended beyond the reminder that U.S. landpower overseas must rest upon working control of the seas, to include the caveat that a Soviet enemy, either thwarted on land or so successful on land that he fears U.S./NATO nuclear initiatives in desperation, will need to be discouraged from launching preventive/preemptive nuclear attacks.

Third, it is commonplace to argue that conventional deterrence cannot be regarded as entirely reliable.[18] One must add, somewhat hastily, that no form of deterrence can be thoroughly reliable. Notwithstanding the apparent fact that conventional deterrence is strengthened very usefully by the awesome nuclear dangers that loom over it, one cannot ignore the point that robust conventional capabilities may, on balance, have the undesired effect of reducing deterrence. Substantial ramparts of nonnuclear stopping power necessarily must flag a NATO intention to attempt a nonnuclear defense. There is much to recommend such a course, but proponents of a thoroughly nonnuclear defense have to face the possible problems that they may be offering the Soviet Union, or encouraging Soviet belief that it has, a nonnuclear option for theater war and, thereby, may be reducing seriously the risks that Soviet leaders anticipate as they consider military adventure. A very successful nonnuclear defense could well motivate the Soviet Union to escalate in a quest for victory by other means and in other climes.

History is replete with cases of the failure of conventional deterrence. Such deterrence undoubtedly is different, to a degree, between nuclear-armed, as contrasted with nonnuclear-armed, coalitions. But, nonetheless, it would be prudent to be alert to the dangerous possibility that the benefit to NATO of a military condition wherein very early resort to nuclear weapons would not be essential may have to be paid for in the coin of some diminution in overall deterrent effect.

Fourth, it is very far from certain that a U.S. continental-landpower reorientation is practicable. In theory there is no difficulty translating the economic assets of NATO into designs for conventional forces, strategy, operational art, and tactics, but practice could be very different. One is not in the realm of purely speculative theory with regard to the probability of NATO actually fielding a truly robust conventional defense. There is to hand, after all, the continuous coalition experience of four decades. That experience has to suggest to an unprejudiced observer that the prospects of NATO purchasing and then sustaining a quantity and quality of military power suitable to offset the Soviet ground forces on their own terms, are not overly good. At the very least, given the fate of the "Lisbon goals" of 1952, of the Kennedy version of flexible response in the 1960s, and of the Carter administration/NATO 1978 Long-Term Defense Program (LTDP), it is not unreasonable to say that the burden of proof rests upon those who argue that NATO can field a very robust conventional deterrent.

This fourth point has two distinct dimensions, the general military and the political. The latter dimension refers to the severe limits that the U.S. Army could achieve for the defense of Central Europe, virtually no matter how well favored it was to be in terms of relative funding preference in the defense budget. Forward defense on the Central Front is a coalition enterprise. While the U.S. Seventh Army can improve its ability to defend its two corps areas, there are very practical limits to the extent to which improvements in the fighting power of U.S. ground forces can substitute for major deficiencies on the part of allies. The U.S. Congress, one may be certain, would not permit an augmentation of the U.S. ground defense role in Europe.

Major questions pertain to the feasibility of NATO fielding a truly reliable conventional war-fighting deterrent in Central Europe. U.S. "military reformers," and others, busily have been rediscovering the wheel of recent years (e.g., the very ambiguous and much abused concept of maneuver)[19] and have been seeking inspiration in somewhat romanticized interpretations of the performance of the German Army on the Eastern Front, in Normandy, and on the frontiers of the Reich on the Siegfried Line.[20] The purpose of this discussion is not to distinguish the more from the less plausible ways in which NATO's landpower might be developed and employed effectively. Instead, the purpose here is to suggest that the chorus of criticism to which variants of U.S. maritime strategy currently have been subjected does not rest self-evidently upon a fully persuasive landpower story.

The ranks of continental-landpower strategists contain advocates of *field fortification* (*après* the Siegfried, not the Maginot, Line) — undampened by the political rejection of this option by the Federal Republic of Germany; of new "*emerging technologies*" (ET) — although the critical distinction between weapon and force survivability continues to elude many; of ET-related (dependent) ideas of *deep-strike and follow-on forces attack* (FOFA) — which probably would be an exceedingly expensive way of attempting that which military history suggests to be incapable of having decisive effect; and of *maneuver* — an idea as old as war itself which has come to assume near-mystical significance in the reformers' credo, notwithstanding the politically mandated maldeployment of NATO's more mobile, "maneuver" ground assets, the absence of "maneuver forces" in deep theater reserve, and the inconvenient fact of a lack of depth of geography in the theater, among other factors. Much can be said in favor of all of these elements — fortification, new technology, interdiction, and maneuver (to cite but a few of the favorites) — but, severally or in combination, they do not yield anything even close to a guarantee of successful defense.[21] Utilizing deception for surprise and then attempting disruption of the NATO front through deep armored/mechanized penetration and widespread *Spetsnaz* and airborne force employment, Warsaw Pact forces might achieve an unravelling of NATO's defenses so devastating at the outset of war that recovery would be improbable. This is not a prediction, but it is asserted here as a distinct possibility that requires frank recognition of those who argue in a landpower versus seapower mode, in favor of the former, are to be answered suitably.

On both political and military grounds, the case for the United States' continuing to make a continental landpower commitment to Europe is a strong one. Nonetheless, advocates of a greater U.S. landpower contribution to NATO in Europe, albeit for the best of motives, are encouraging U.S. policy to move in the wrong direction. The task of defending NATO-European territory on the ground should be a mission primarily, and increasingly, entrusted to Europeans. NATO-European countries, now long-recovered from the ravages of World War II, should not be treated as wards of Washington, but rather as allies. These European allies need to believe that, to the degree feasible, their destiny is in their own hands. Moreover, if Americans are to remain tolerably content with their entangling alliance connection with Europe, it is most important that the terms of implementation of that connection be judged to be just. In short, Europeans should be seen to do as much as they are able toward their own defense — not merely as little as they deem consistent with U.S. Congressional tolerance. Americans should not assess U.S. society to be needlessly at very early nuclear risk for reason of allied unwillingness to provide the locally affordable means of sustaining a nonnuclear defense.[22]

Consideration in detail of the purposes and character of the necessary U.S. continental commitment to NATO-Europe, appraised in the context both of the prospects for success in the land battle and of the political evolution of the alliance, transcends the mandate directing the course of this analysis.

A MARITIME EMPHASIS

In this section, as in the discussion of a landpower focus, the subject is the focus or emphasis for the United States, not for the Western Alliance as a whole. It should go without saying that the most serious strategic problem facing NATO-Europe is the possibility of invasion by Warsaw Pact ground forces and that the problem has to be met on its own ground-forces' terms. But, given the very great economic strength of the United States' Eurasian allies, it does not go without saying that continental campaigning à la Eisenhower should be the principal emphasis in, or contemplated end-product of, U.S. general-purpose force planning.

A war in Europe could be lost, not only in Europe but also indirectly, as a consequence of an interrupted trans-Atlantic SLOC and through Soviet ability to swing forces from the Chinese frontier to the European theater (as Stalin did with many of his divisions from Siberia and Central Asia in November-December 1941). Furthermore, in circumstances short of war in Europe, the U.S.-organized and led alliance structure in Europe and Asia would be placed under potentially fatal strain were the Soviet Union able to deny the West (and Japan) access to Gulf oil. Oil from that region is by no means of critical significance for the United States, but it is vital for the economies of many of its major allies.

If the territorial security of Western Europe could be defended only by a much augmented and modernized U.S. Army and by U.S. tactical air power, then there would be a strong case for reorienting U.S. military investment. However, plainly that is not, and will not be, the situation. Indeed, it is no exaggeration to say that the very strong emphasis placed upon the forward NATO commitment by the Carter administration reflected not so much a careful appraisal of U.S. national military strategy as a political belief that, in the aftermath of Vietnam, the NATO track was relatively noncontroversial in the U.S. Congress.

War against a great continental power cannot be won, although it can be lost, at sea. The U.S. armed forces should be balanced both with reference to capabilities provided by the alliance as a whole and with regard to prospective commitment in pursuit of the specific objectives into which U.S. vital interests translate. Those forces should not be balanced as by some astrategic algorithm of "fair shares" for the separate services or without reference to the existence of front-line allies who, one must presume, are even more interested in deterring or repelling geographically contiguous landpower than is the United States.

Endorsement of a maritime emphasis in U.S. national military strategy — with its proper expression in force structure — does not mean: that one is blind to the landpower character of the Soviet threat to the territorial integrity of NATO-Europe; that one fails to recognize the relative inaccessibility of much of the Soviet imperium to pressure from the sea; or that one is determined to hazard U.S. carrier task forces in very severely contested areas on the Soviet maritime frontier at the very outset of a war. The case for a maritime emphasis in U.S. national military strategy rests upon the following considerations:

Recognition that it is politically essential and militarily efficient for NATO-Europe to provide the overwhelming majority of the ready and rapidly mobilizable ground forces for local defense.

Recognition of the fact that working control of key SLOCs would be absolutely essential if NATO were to be able to sustain a conflict in Europe and/or if the United States were to prosecute a more protracted war — regardless of how the campaign in Europe had developed.

Recognition of the likely global character, or certain global potential, of a protracted conflict and of the importance of providing such strategically useful distraction on the very far-flung flanks of Soviet power as could be achieved at tolerable cost. If NATO can hold, if with great difficulty, in the center, it will begin to be very important indeed that Soviet leaders should feel pressed in the Far North, in southern Europe, and — above all — generally feel overextended in the European theater of operations as a consequence both of U.S. operations in the North-East Pacific and of the (probably latent) Chinese threat that flanks their entire position in the East.

Appreciation of the fact that, although the benchmark for adequacy in military preparation would be provided by the test of battle in the event of a Soviet invasion,[23] the United States and her allies are operating day by day in a condition of war in peace. There are few security problems in peacetime to which U.S. naval power is not more or less relevant. Always assuming an adequate framework for the deterrence of major war in Europe, the real action in East-West security relations will involve regional problems and, both for political and military reasons, U.S. naval forces will comprise the lion's share of, as well as the *sine qua non* for, Washington's response.

NOTES

1. This discussion is adapted from Chapter 4 of my *Maritime Strategy, Geopolitics, and the Defense of the West* (New York: Ramapo Press [for the National Strategy Information Center], 1986). The subjects introduced here are treated at length in my forthcoming books: *The Geopolitics of Super Power* (Lexington, Ky.: University Press of Kentucky, 1988); and *The Wartime Influence of Sea Power on Land Power* (provisional title). For example, see Joshua M. Epstein, "Horizontal Escalation: Sour Notes of a Recurrent Theme," *International Security* 8 (Winter 1983–1984): 19–31.

2. *Annual Report to the Congress, Fiscal Year 1987*, (Washington, D.C.: U.S. Government Printing Office, February 5, 1986), p. 52.

3. U.S. Congress, Senate Committees on Armed Services and Foreign Relations, *Military Situation in the Far East, Hearings*, 82nd Cong., 1st sess. (Washington, D.C.: U.S. Government Printing Office, 1951), pp. 731–32.

4. See General P. X. Kelly, "The Amphibious Warfare Strategy," in *The Maritime Strategy*, Admiral James D. Watkins et al., U.S. Naval Institute *Proceedings, Supplement* (January 1986).

5. Sir Halford Mackinder defined what first he termed "The Geographical Pivot of History," and later the "Heartland" of the "World Island" of Eurasia, in terms of its inaccessibility to seapower. See Halford J. Mackinder, *Democratic Ideas and Reality* (New York: W. W. Norton, 1962; first pub. 1942), pp. 241–64.

6. The leading continentalist tract remains Robert W. Komer, *Maritime Strategy or Coalition Defense?* (Cambridge, Mass.: Abt Books, 1984).

7. Robert Komer, for example, has sought to clarify his opposition to current U.S. maritime strategy by explaining: "My argument is that overinvestment in a carrier heavy Navy at the expense of other capabilities could be tantamount to making it impossible to defend Europe, or the Persian Gulf, for that matter." "Comment and Discussion: 'Northern Flank Maritime

Offensive'," *Proceedings* 112/1/995 (January 1986): 19. It is a matter of indisputable fact (for once) that the Reagan administration has not funded the U.S. Navy "at the expense" of other capabilities. At the close of the Carter administration the Navy had 38 percent of the defense budget (to the Army's 28 percent), while for FY 1986 the Navy percentage is 35 percent (to the Army's 27.5 percent). Komer (ibid.) also misunderstands the rationale for horizontal escalation. He states: "The core of my argument is that winning consolation prizes like Cuba, Nicaragua, Angola, Ethiopia, or South Yemen would be utterly inadequate compensation for the loss of far more vital areas to Soviet landpower." Aside from the tautology in his argument, one can only say, first, "Amen," and second, ask, "Who is making claims to the contrary?" Noteworthy contributions to the ongoing debate include John J. Mearsheimer, "A Strategic Misstep: The Maritime Strategy and Deterrence in Europe," *International Security* 2 (Fall 1986): 3–57; Linton F. Brooks, "Naval Power and National Security: The Case for the Maritime Strategy," *International Security* 2 (Fall 1986): 58–88; and Jack Beatty, "In Harm's Way," *The Atlantic,* May 1987, pp. 37–46, 48–49, 52–53.

    8.   See Colin S. Gray, "Global Protracted War: Conduct and Termination," in *Strategic War Termination,* ed. Stephen J. Cimbala (New York: Praeger, 1986), pp. 75–96; and Linton F. Brooks, "Conflict Termination through Maritime Leverage," in *Conflict Termination and Military Strategy: Coercion, Persuasion, and War,* ed. Stephen J. Cimbala and Keith A. Dunn (Boulder, Colo.: Westview Press, 1987), pp. 161–72.

    9.   For an argument of timeless value on the meaning of command of the sea and what it permits, see Julian S. Corbett, *Some Principles of Maritime Strategy* (Annapolis, Md.: Naval Institute Press, 1972; first pub. 1911), Part II, Chapter 1.

    10.   Guilty parties include Komer, *Maritime Strategy or Coalition Defense,* Chapter 7 (particularly pp. 67–68); and Edward N. Luttwak, *The Pentagon and the Art of War: The Question of Military Reform* (New York: Simon and Schuster, 1984), pp. 111 and 261–64. Some of the roots of Komer's misunderstanding of the character and value of maritime power are revealed in his brief and inaccurate treatment of the contribution of the British Royal Navy to victory in 1914–1918 (pp. 43–44). Komer, and others of his persuasion, would benefit from Richard Hough, *The Great War at Sea, 1914–1918* (Oxford: Oxford University Press, 1983).

    11.   This argument is advanced ably in Jeffrey Record, *Revising U.S. Military Strategy: Tailoring Means to Ends* (Washington, D.C.: Pergamon-Brassey's, 1984).

    12.   Pertinent discussion is provided in Linton F. Brooks, "Escalation and Naval Strategy," *Proceedings* 110 (August 1984): 33–37. The dangers of nuclear escalation at sea are well advertised, and indeed overemphasized, in: Barry R. Posen, "Inadvertent Nuclear War? Escalation and NATO's Northern Flank," *International Security* 7 (Fall 1982): 28–54; and Desmond Ball, "Nuclear War at Sea," *International Security* 10 (Winter 1985–1986): 3–31.

    13.   Watkins, "The Maritime Strategy," in *The Maritime Strategy,* Watkins et al. p. 10.

    14.   Carl von Clausewitz, *On War,* ed. and trans. Michael Howard and Peter Paret (Princeton, N.J.: Princeton University Press, 1976; first pub. 1832), p. 605.

    15.   Ibid., pp. 119–21.

    16.   Nicholas J. Spykman, *America's Strategy in World Politics: The United States and the Balance of Power* (Hamden, Conn.: Archon Books, 1970; first pub. 1942), p. 21.

    17.   Luttwak, *The Pentagon and the Art of War,* p. 120 (also see p. 64).

18.   Richard K. Betts, "Conventional Deterrence: Predictive Uncertainty and Policy Confidence," *World Politics* 37 (January 1985): 153–79; and "Compound Deterrence vs. No-First-Use: What's Wrong Is What's Right," *Orbis* 28 (Winter 1985): 697–718.

19.   See William S. Lind, *Maneuver Warfare Handbook* (Boulder, Colo.: Westview Press, 1985). A thought-provoking critique of the military reformers is Richard K. Betts, "Conventional Strategy: New Critics, Old Choices," *International Security* 7 (Spring 1983): 140–62.

20.   See Dennis E. Showalter, "A Dubious Heritage: The Military Legacy of the Russo-German War," *Air University Review* 36 (March-April 1985): 4–23.

21.   The difficulty of judging how well NATO might fare "on the night" is well illustrated in Barry R. Posen, "Measuring the European Conventional Balance: Coping with Complexity in Threat Assessment," *International Security* 9 (Winter 1984/85): 47–88.

22.   See Earl C. Ravenal, "Counterforce and Alliance: The Ultimate Connection," *International Security* 6 (Spring 1982): 26–43.

23.   "The decisions by arms is for all major and minor operations in war what cash payment is in commerce. Regardless how complex the relationship between the two parties, regardless how rarely settlements actually occur, they can never be entirely absent." Clausewitz, *On War*, p. 97.

5

Soviet C3: Present and Future Questions for U.S. Policy

Stephen J. Cimbala

This chapter looks at the Soviet view of command and control and some of its implications for U.S. defense policies. The Soviet concept of control differs considerably from the Western one. The Soviets speak of control or "troop control" to include all those things that must be done to enable forces to accomplish their missions in wartime.[1] Generically this includes not only the technical apparatus for monitoring subordinates and for communicating orders to them. It also includes an understanding of the qualitative factors that influence leadership, the intangibles attendant to the motivation of combat forces, and the "friction" attendant to unfolding any war plans under battlefield conditions.[2] Thus the Western notion of control is a kind of systemic auditing or a systems analysis whereas the Soviet concept includes cultural and psychological components that are deeply rooted in their history and experiences. Above all else, their memories, personal and professional, of Soviet experience in the Great Patriotic War are ever-present testimony to their commitment that war shall never again push the regime near to the breaking point nor the society near to disintegration. Of secondary importance to World War II, but nonetheless memorable to students of Soviet history, the Czarist regime crumbled during World War I after its war effort faltered and its armed forces rebelled.

Therefore, the issue of control in the Soviet Union begins with the control by the Communist Party of the Soviet Union

Portions of this chapter appeared in Stephen J. Cimbala, ed., *Soviet C3* (Washington, D.C.: AFCEA International Press, 1987). Used with permission.

over its armed forces in peacetime and in war. According to the *Officer's Handbook*:

> The undivided leadership of the Armed Forces by the Party and its Central Committee is the objective law of their life and combat activities. This law is determined by the role which our Party plays in the life of Soviet society, as its leading and guiding force.[3]

The connection between the Party and its armed forces affirms the theoretical connection between war and politics, which is explained with the following emphasis: "War is inseparably linked with the political system out of which it grows. Politics engenders war. War is politics throughout, its continuation and implementation by violent means."[4] Wars are evaluated by their political content, i.e., in terms of the "class" interest on whose behalf they are being waged. Wars "in defense of the socialist Fatherland" are the most important and call for "a combination of the political, economic, military, moral, scientific and technical and other factors which determine the defense capacity and security of own state and other socialist countries."[5]

Soviet military doctrine "determines the means, ways, and methods of ensuring the reliable defense of the Soviet Socialist State from imperialist aggression" by incorporating the nature of future warfare, methods of waging armed combat, and the preparedness of the armed forces and Soviet people to defeat any aggressor. Military doctrine has two aspects: political, concerned with the political evaluation of the military tasks of the state, and technical, which "determines the military-technical tasks of the armed forces, and the means, methods and forms of armed combat."[6]

These relationships between war and politics, on one hand, and between the military-technical and sociopolitical aspects of Soviet military doctrine, on the other, are not coincidental. They are formative even in the case of nuclear war. According to the authors of *Marxism-Leninism on War and Army*:

> Marxist-Leninist methodology make it possible to solve the question of the interrelation between politics and armed force in the possible nuclear war in a consistently scientific way. As regards its essence, such a war would also be a continuation of the politics of classes and states by violent means.[7]

Thus, apolitical wars are inconceivable, in the sense that all wars, and especially nuclear war, would have a political cause.

This does not mean that any particular war would be politically sensible, i.e., that it would advance Soviet aims as the leadership defined them. The Soviet leadership is very much aware that a U.S. or NATO nuclear attack on their homeland would create unprecedented societal destruction and jeopardize the stability of the regime. Thus Marxist-Leninist writers can at one and the same time aver that nuclear war is "the heaviest crime that could be committed against humanity" and task their armed forces to win such a war if it is imposed upon them.[8] The military-technical impact of nuclear weapons on combat operations and their control is acknowledged as revolutionary, even as the political character of imperialist wars is defined as immutable. According to General-Lieutenant I. G. Zav'yalov, writing in the Soviet military publication *Red Star* (*Krasnaya zvezda*):

> As a result of the influence of nuclear weapons, whole subdivisions, units and even formations can lose their combat capacity within a few minutes. Large territories will become useless for immediate continuation of the operation. Combat actions along many axes will become isolated and local in nature, *troop control will be interrupted*, and because of the break in the originally outlined plans for combat actions, *new decisions* will have to be made within *restricted time limits*.[9] (Italics supplied.)

Thus the devastation that nuclear weapons may do is not the primary concern of the Soviet commander, although collateral damage injurious to his own mission is unwelcome. More dissuading to him is the possible loss of control and the need to improvise decisions under stress, decisions that higher commanders might not approve and that the lower commander might not have practiced making. In addition, nuclear weapons also have the potential to disrupt the entire linkage among the components of military art as perceived by the Soviets: strategy, operational art, and tactics. They provide for the simultaneous accomplishment of strategic, operational, and tactical tasks.[10]

These military-technical implications, of the risks for Soviet forces engaged in nuclear combat, are not acknowledged at the cost of creating artificial barriers between conventional and nuclear weapons when properly employed. Many important principles of military art, in the Soviet view, apply to both conventional and nuclear war, including those principles of troop control. Admitting that new conventional and nuclear weapons make high demands on troop control, an authoritative Soviet writer explains as follows:

> To control troops flexibly and effectively means to stay constantly informed about a sharply and rapidly changing situation, to foresee opportunities for switching from one mode of operation to another, to constantly maintain in readiness and bring into action at the proper moment those forces and equipment which can appropriately influence the course of events, and at the proper moment to make the necessary changes in established plans and relay these to the troops.[11]

Soviet commanders at the Front (army group) and army levels may have the flexibility to improvise within the theater-strategic plan of the General Staff. But it is unlikely that this improvisation will be encouraged much lower on the ladder. Division commanders will have very specific orders about when and how they are to accomplish their missions. Deviation from the prescribed game plan poses a threat to a professional career, unless the deviation proves to have been successful after the fact. This may be a risk that Soviet unit and subunit commanders are willing to run in wartime, but they are almost certain not to take risks with their careers in military exercises.

There is also the problem for the USSR that its operational strategy for war in Europe is supposedly dependent upon marshaling numerous divisions from the western military districts of the Soviet Union. These are to be joined to the battle near the Forward Line of Troops, which has meanwhile, according to Soviet expectations, been pushed somewhere into the midsection of the Federal Republic. However, those divisions from the Carpathian and Byelorussian military districts of the USSR will be moving into aggressive air interdiction and other onslaughts targeted against Pact forces and command, control, and communications (C3) targets (or C3I for the additional component of intelligence). Unless the Soviet control system works very well and proves to be superior even to the German system that launched the *blitzkrieg* against France in 1940, it will have its work cut out to push its first echelon forces into NATO's rear while giving sanctuary to its reinforcing divisions held farther back. In order to do this, the USSR must have a system that is reconnaissance-pulled for its forward divisions and one that is command-pushed for its rearward ones. The Soviet system will be more command-pushed than reconnaissance-pulled across the board, unlike the German panzers (although not all German divisions in World War II). A command-pushed system may have difficulty sustaining the flow of reserve divisions into the meeting engagements, which will take on the character of a helter-skelter battle throughout Germany. Of course, this problem of a rapidly changing template will also affect NATO C3, which has the added encumbrance of adjustment to a multinational corps structure with less than complete interoperability.

Much depends upon how much effective warning NATO gets and what NATO chooses to do with it. Effective warning means that NATO must respond within the decision cycle of the Pact if the Pact is weighing actual aggression in the balance. The most difficult case for the USSR would be one in which Soviet officials concluded (by whatever process) that there was a strong chance of NATO attack, although not a certainty of it. Soviet planners would be weighing the risk of preemption against the potential cost of not doing so. NATO would be deciding whether its intelligence and warning indicators had yet crossed the threshold of response and, if so, what kind of response would deter the Pact from any premeditated aggression. Both sides would weigh into the balance the implications of protecting their C3, including commanders and communications. From the Soviet perspective, a faster and more decisive attack might allow them to maintain troop control whereas a protracted conflict could dissolve it. Loss of control at the unit and subunit levels could then trickle upward into the truncation of the chain of political and military command theater-wide. The effects could range, in the Soviet view, from the simple loss of effectiveness to the worst-case scenario, in which troop control breaks into a mobocracy of teeming revolt.

THRESHOLDS, ESCALATION CONTROL, AND SOVIET C3

U.S. commentators misattribute to the Soviet Union perspectives that may not be transferable from our strategic culture to theirs.[12] Soviet awareness of Western theories of escalation control is not the same as endorsement of them. Hopeful proponents of controlled warfighting, conventional or nuclear, in Europe can draw upon a variety of Soviet, and U.S., liturgical statements to support their views. Prominent Soviet writers can be cited as optimistic, or pessimistic, about the possibility of observing limitations on escalation once war has begun.

Despite their dissimilarities, NATO and Soviet concepts of escalation can be compared in order to derive insights about the expectations each might hold once war began. NATO strategy calls for direct defense with conventional forces (deliberate escalation to the use of theater nuclear weapons of conventional defenses cannot hold) and, ultimately, employment of U.S. strategic forces. Implicit in this strategy, adopted in 1967 as MC-14/3, is the assumption that NATO will field conventional forces adequate to avoid "early first use" of nuclear weapons. In fact, NATO has fallen short of this requirement. NATO's former Supreme Allied Commander, General Bernard Rogers, urged that NATO improve its conventional forces by having members increase their expenditures by an average of 4 percent in real terms (discounting for inflation) over the next decade.[13] This objective is also unlikely to be met.

NATO's deficiencies in conventional forces create an expectation of early first use of nuclear weapons by the West. Concern that this expectation is self-defeating for NATO has been expressed by prominent former policy makers and strategists, including former U.S. Secretary of Defense Robert McNamara.[14] In his recent book *Blundering into Disaster,* McNamara endorses the recommendations of prestigious European Security Study to improve NATO conventional defenses for four principal missions: blunting the initial Soviet/Warsaw Pact attack, eroding the attackers' airpower, interdicting the follow-on forces and other reinforcements the Pact would need to sustain an attack in Europe, and disrupting Soviet/Pact command, control, and communications.[15] These deficiencies in NATO conventional forces relative to their plausible missions are all the more regrettable, according to U.S. analysts, because the USSR is now showing more apparent interest in a conventional option, or an extended conventional phase during war in Europe, than formerly.[16]

Also implicit in NATO "flexible response" strategy is the assumption that U.S. strategic nuclear forces must be capable of dissuading the Soviet Union from initiating theater or strategic nuclear conflict if its conventional war plan is negated. This is not commonly understood, or acknowledged, by some writers whose understandable fears of strategic nuclear war have led to a diminution of the roles of strategic forces compared to other forces. The coupling of U.S. strategic nuclear forces to NATO theater nuclear and conventional forces is an intentional, and not coincidental, attribute of NATO strategy. It is not an unfortunate necessity that can be circumvented by improved conventional or theater nuclear forces. Quite the contrary, U.S. strategic nuclear forces must be highly competent relative to Soviet strategic forces whatever the balance of forces in the European theater. Some advocates of the "572" deployments by NATO of Pershing II and GLCM missiles talked as if some balance of

NATO and Soviet "Eurostrategic" forces, once attained, could substitute for any uncertainties about the employment of U.S. strategic forces. There is no self-sufficient balance of theater forces that can be evaluated apart from the credibility of U.S. strategic nuclear forces. What will deter the Soviet Union from escalation to the use of operational-tactical (Front level) or operational-strategic (theater of operations, TVD or TSMA) is not only their expectation that they will be on the losing end of a regional firepower exchange but also their expectation that the exchange will escalate to the use of U.S. strategic forces against targets in Europe and the Soviet homeland. Thus theater nuclear forces, however much they may be improved, are like conventional forces not a substitute for more credible U.S. strategic forces if Soviet first use, and subsequent nuclear escalation, is to be deterred.

The above argument has important implications from the Soviet perspective. There is some evidence in Soviet writing and exercises that they might be willing to distinguish among tactical, operational-tactical, and operational-strategic nuclear employment.[17] The Soviets might recognize a threshold between operational-tactical and operational-strategic uses of nuclear weapons. In the former case, delivery means including SS-22 and SS-23 surface-to-surface missiles, and frontal aviation could deliver nuclear strikes against NATO SSMs, nuclear storage sites, and nuclear-capable aircraft, in addition to NATO air defenses, corps C3I, and operational reserves. Operational-strategic employment of nuclear weapons would use intermediate-range and strategic ballistic missiles and long-range aviation against a variety of military and command targets, including NATO theater C3I headquarters.

Soviet ability or willingness to distinguish between theater-strategic nuclear war and intercontinental or global war, however, would be very doubtful. So-called limited nuclear attacks by the Soviets, for example, against 34 U.S. bases, which contained most U.S. combat tactical air and the military airlift to transport U.S. ground force divisions to Europe, might be incorporated into their Eurostrategic war plan. The attacks, although directed against targets in the continental United States, could be accomplished with ten kiloton airbursts at each base, which minimized prompt fatalities. If the USSR also included 12 additional bases with U.S. ground force divisions, they would have targeted all U.S. general purpose ground and tactical air forces that could affect the war in Europe for at least one month while keeping collateral damage well below the threshold of massive societal destruction.[18] It might seem obvious by peacetime standards that this was a strategic attack in the sense that it was comparable to a homeland-to-homeland exchange with ICBMs and SLBMs, but, in the event, policy makers could decide otherwise, especially if they were Western policy makers with strategic nuclear forces at best equivalent to those of the USSR. Another illustration of the difficulty, in preserving any distinction between European theater strategic nuclear warfare and global war is provided by U.S. maritime strategy as promulgated by former Secretary of the Navy John Lehman and uniformed naval officers.[19] U.S. naval general purpose forces would seek to establish primacy in the Norwegian Sea and to place at risk the survivability of Soviet ballistic missile submarines (SSBNs) in their protected bastions near the Kola Peninsula soon after conventional war in Europe has broken out. The Navy argues that progressive attrition of Soviet SSBNs during forward operations into Soviet controlled waters will raise the perceived costs of escalation for the USSR and induce them to consider war termination on terms more favorable to NATO. According to Admiral James D. Watkins, then Chief of Naval Operations:

> The Soviets place great weight on the nuclear correlation of forces, even during the time before nuclear weapons have been used. Maritime forces can influence that correlation, both by destroying Soviet ballistic missile submarines and by improving our own nuclear posture, through deployment of carriers and Tomahawk platforms around the periphery of the Soviet Union.[20]

The advisability of this strategy from an operational standpoint is not at issue here, although others have judged it negatively.[21] These operations, if successfully carried out, would create fewer incentives for a Soviet distinction, if NATO is counting on one, between operational-strategic (theater-strategic) and intercontinental warfare, nuclear or otherwise.

The example of U.S. maritime strategy does raise another point, and that has to do with the kinds of escalation advocates of improved conventional forces might substitute for the vertical escalation inherent in nuclear weapons. The first alternative is horizontal escalation, the extension of war in Europe to other theaters of operation outside Europe. The second is temporal escalation, the effort to prolong the war until one side's resources have exhausted or stalemated the other. The third is what we might call "surprise escalation," in which unexpected operational and tactical maneuvers are converted into strategic and politically decisive results. An example is the Nazi attack against France in 1940.

The first alternative, horizontal escalation to theaters of operation outside of Europe, is a strategy not totally under the control of NATO for its successful execution. Entry by the People's Republic of China into a NATO-Warsaw Pact conflict would open a "second front" which might dissuade the USSR from continuing the war in Europe, but, short of that, it is difficult to construct a war-widening sequence that is unilaterally favorable to the West (unless irrelevant to the outcome in Europe, for example, bashing Soviet client states in the Third World). The U.S. maritime strategy offers a variant of horizontal escalation only if NATO can protect its sea lanes of communication between Europe and North America long enough for strikes on the Soviet periphery to pay dividends, provided that NATO ground and tactical air forces on the Central Front are not summarily defeated.[22]

The second alternative, temporal escalation, is to turn a conventional war in Europe into a protracted war of attrition in order to stalemate Soviet advances and then to terminate the conflict before NATO is required to use nuclear weapons.[23] There are several problems with this alternative, which appears superficially attractive when static indices comparing the economic performances of the United States and its OECD allies, including Japan, are compared with the Soviet Union and its allies. First, a protracted conventional war under contemporary conditions, without the introduction by either side of nuclear weapons, is not likely to repeat the experience of World War II by continuing for four years. Given reasonable projections about rates of personnel loss, rates of ammunition consumption, and other expenditure rates in modern high-intensity combat, a period of three to four months would be a "long" war in Europe. Under those conditions, it is not at all obvious that the Soviet Union would be faced with sustainable inferiority.[24] Several years is, of course, a different matter, but a continuation of coalition warfare between the two alliances, under present conditions, for several years seems highly improbable, although protracted conventional war of uncertain duration is not excluded in Soviet discussions of wartime possibilities.[25] A second problem with the protracted war scenario, from the Western standpoint, is that it allows time for allied political consensus to disintegrate as the fear of nuclear escalation hangs over the battlefield and over efforts to negotiate an acceptable peace. A third difficulty is that an extended conventional war, if it successfully threatened the cohesion of the Soviet glacis in Eastern Europe, would almost certainly prompt their use of theater nuclear weapons to break the stalemate in Western Europe.

A third option for either side, which would in theory avoid vertical escalation, is the option of surprise, regarding the kind of attack launched or the timing and character of the attack. The Soviet Union, for example, might attack from a standing start with its divisions in the Group of Soviet Forces Germany (GSFG) in a slash-and-grab thrust into NATO's operational depth, preparing the way for encirclement of NATO forward defenses.[26] As counterpoint, an unexpected and potentially decisive NATO use of conventional forces, according to Samuel Huntington, might be a conventional retaliatory offensive into Eastern Europe simultaneous with a Soviet conventional attack against Western Europe.[27] Each of these options, while appealing conceptually to expert analysts, has practical problems of implementation. In each instance, the Soviet *blitzkrieg* or the NATO conventional retaliation would be operating at a very thin margin of force structure relative to its probable success.[28] Intelligence misestimates or tactical contretemps could leave forward moving forces isolated and then destroyed. Moreover, each of these operationally daring approaches requires that "real time" command, control, and communications operate with maximum effectiveness while that of the opponent is seriously disrupted.

It seems fair to suppose, in view of the preceding discussion, that the problem of nuclear escalation cannot be avoided by NATO, and it is not obvious that it should be. NATO cannot go too far in the direction of making conventional warfare credible, without lowering the threshold between "no war" and "any war," which is far more meaningful than the thresholds separating kinds of war in Europe.[29] If the problem of nuclear escalation cannot be avoided by conventional deterrence and defense exclusive of probable nuclear use, then the other option is not nuclear avoidance, but nuclear transcendence.

Strategic Defense

If nuclear avoidance is not possible, nuclear transcendence is thought by some to be another plausible path to stable deterrence. A U.S. Strategic Defense Initiative or Soviet research and development efforts might lead to nonnuclear defenses that could limit the damage from nuclear offenses, and ultimately, make those offenses irrelevant. This vision was presented by President Reagan in his March 23, 1983, speech and is now institutionalized in the Strategic Defense Initiative Office in the Pentagon. We will not go into all the pros and cons of SDI here; a large literature has already accumulated. The present discussion will simply note some of the C3 issues attendant to moving from a world dominated by strategic offensive forces to one in which defenses are preeminent, if such an evolution can be brought about.

The first issue is that the problem of C3 for strategic defenses, theirs and ours, cannot be disaggregated from the C3 requirements for strategic forces as a whole. In the near future, even if defensive technologies prove to be viable, they will be deployed alongside offenses, not in place of them. A mixed force of offenses and defenses will require subtle C3 arrangements for connecting National Command Authorities, force commanders, and command posts with the retaliatory forces themselves.[30] Thus the problem of C3 software as discussed by software experts may make the task seem overly difficult technically yet insufficiently complicated from the perspective of group decision making. Providing the appropriate users with the information that they need, at the time they need it, and in a form in which it is useful to them, will be more taxing to designers than writing millions of lines of software.

Second, the technologies that make possible credible U.S. or Soviet ballistic missile defenses may also be tasked to put those defenses at risk. The deployment of space-based kinetic kill vehicles (SBKKV) as boost phase defenses could work to the advantage of the attacker, instead of the defender, if the attacker used the same technology to suppress the defenses. And the prospect of defense suppression will be even more appealing if directed energy weapons such as lasers or particle beams can be deployed in space and made invulnerable to attack from the ground. One can imagine two sides with space-based defenses, which are also very competent antisatellite (ASAT) weapons, each capable of suppressing the other's defenses against ballistic missiles. Of course, Soviet doctrine, which has always held that offenses and defenses work together, will be less surprised than U.S. proponents of defenses, who find that defensive technologies have now contributed to the possible success of an offensive strategy. This expectation by the USSR is evident in the statements of Soviet leaders in opposition to SDI as an alleged component of a U.S. credible first strike capability.

Therefore, the primary importance of active and passive defenses, whatever they contribute to damage limitation, is what they contribute to deterrence. One issue pertinent to C3I in this regard, which requires more extended discussion, is whether U.S. SDI or NATO theater ballistic missile defenses (ATBMs) could help to protect command centers and other potentially vulnerable targets and thus reduce the temptation for early countercommand attacks at the theater or strategic (intercontinental) level. One of the unfortunate incentives for Soviet nuclear escalation in Europe is the possibility that theater-based

C3 relevant to strategic deterrence would be destroyed much more easily by nuclear weapons than by conventional weapons, although both NATO and the Soviet Union are considering deep attack weapons of greater range and lethality.[31]

Third, U.S. strategic defenses could be contributory to stability under some conditions by making retaliatory forces and supporting command systems less vulnerable to Soviet preemption. There is little doubt that U.S. ICBMs based in fixed silos will have to be launched "under attack" (if in fact they can be) in order to survive preemptive attack.[32] In addition, the perceived U.S. necessity for this operational capability, however far back it is thought to be on the policy-preferred menu, raises the Soviet expectation that it will have to do likewise with its most capable and modern land-based missiles. Apparently the USSR is already prepared for preemption, launch under attack, or retaliation as modes of operation for its ICBM forces, which constitute about two-thirds of its force loadings but approximately 90 percent of its ready inventory.[33] The Soviet Union is already deploying mobile land-based strategic missiles, and the United States may follow suit with Midgetman small ICBM in the 1990s or with 50 MX deployed in a rail mobile (rail garrison) configuration even sooner. Mobile land-based missiles would presumably add to ICBM survivability compared to fixed ICBMs, although there might be offsetting strategic and economic costs. The U.S. Midgetman was approved for full-scale development in December 1986 on the assumption that it will be a single warhead missile with hard target accuracy although Congress allowed its weight to reach 37,000 pounds in order to accommodate penetration aids against future Soviet defenses, if needed.[34] Single warhead missiles are not as attractive as targets com-pared to MIRV missiles, so the arithmetic of preemption looks less favorable to the prospective attacker and better to the defender. Soviet attackers would have to use megatonnage adequate to barrage likely Midgetman deployment areas, which could be quite substantial with even tactical warning; strategic warning would create an almost impossible problem of dispersal for prospective targeters. It is also not inconceivable that the small ICBMs could be defended with mobile or fixed terminal or terminal/ midcourse defenses.[35] Midgetman will present new command and control problems, however, which will grow with enlargement of its dispersal area to include U.S. roads outside military reservations.

Postattack Command and Control

In the worst case, outbreak of a U.S.-Soviet strategic nuclear war, the survival of commanders and the fidelity of the command structure will be as important, or more important, than the survivability of forces themselves. "Fidelity" means that the command system must do more than survive physical attack on itself, incidental or deliberate. It must, subsequent to attack, perform with sufficient flexibility and continuity so that the United States is not forced to choose between gross retaliatory options or none. This point has been misunderstood by both "hawks" and "doves" in the strategic debate, so it merits expansion.

The first issue is crisis stability. If either side anticipates that its central political command will be destroyed early in war, then it has a strong incentive to preempt, and to preempt against the central political command of the opponent. However, that central command is not a fixed physical entity only. It is a complex organism that may survive dedicated attack with unpredictable and pathological behavior. U.S. experts disagree whether the Soviet Union would deliberately attempt to suppress the U.S. National Command Authorities and highest military leadership if it felt war was unavoidable. It seems safe to assume that the U.S. leadership will not be spared deliberately from the collateral damage attendant to Soviet attacks against military and war-related economic targets. Soviet as well as U.S. planners could reason that U.S. leadership left intact with much of its country destroyed would have a significant incentive to settle for peace, compared to an uncertain or presumptuous leadership.[36] However, the issue may not be drawn as neatly as this. The fear of command suppression will begin to be more realistic, on either side, after conventional war has begun and C3 based in the theater is attenuated. If the sharp operational end of theater C3 is gradually being disrupted deliberately or coincidentally, the expectation of more disruption to follow creates a serious pressure for escalation. For the Soviet Union attempting to estimate the rate at which deterioration of C3 will become a strategic, as opposed to a tactical, problem, the concept of critical time for a mission related to control time for execution of authorized commands becomes very important. The USSR might, for example, have reacted to survivability-enhancing deployments of Pershing II and GLCM by nuclear preemption, especially if short-range nuclear forces had already been used and the "fog of war" made estimates very brittle.[37]

The second problem is delegation of authority. During a nuclear crisis, the United States wants to be certain that an authoritative Soviet leadership, in full control of its military forces and command system, interprets correctly U.S. signals and messages. If conventional war erupted in Europe, or elsewhere involving direct conflict between U.S. and Soviet forces, the authenticity and cohesion of Soviet leadership would be an asset to NATO, not a liability. A succession crisis within the Politburo during a superpower confrontation might contribute to uncertain decision making in the USSR, which the United States, under duress, could interpret as stonewalling while preparing to attack. Nikita Khrushchev's two very different messages to President Kennedy during the Cuban missile crisis offer indirect evidence that the Politburo was not of a consensual mind about how to handle the crisis once U.S. resolve to have the missiles removed became apparent. Although the U.S. president did present consistent positions in his communications to the USSR, the crisis management in the White House did not take into account important U.S. naval standard operating procedures, including those relevant to establishing the blockade line and to trailing Soviet submarines in Caribbean, Atlantic, and Pacific waters.[38] The U.S. situation illustrates something important about any large military command system, including the Soviet one. Delegation of authority is a misleading focus for understanding how the system may actually operate. Authority is a legal concept, implying written delegation of plenary power downward from the top to the lower echelons of a hierarchy.

In command systems, as in other technologically complex and "tightly coupled" organizations, delegation of authority is less the issue than effective assumption of the initiative by subordinates when the alternative is to suffer de facto loss of mission competency.[39] Command systems and commanders will not just drop dead, literally or figuratively. They will adapt to existing conditions to the best of their ability. Thus a proper understanding of the U.S. command system, and seemingly the Soviet system as well, is that delegation of competency will take place regardless of the arrangements having been made for delegation of authority. Of course, one could argue, on the basis of Soviet World War II experience and the initial successes of the Nazi invasion in June 1941, that the Soviet Union might have more difficulty delegating authority and competency than would the United States or its NATO allies. However, the Soviet approaches cannot necessarily be projected from Soviet World War II experiences because none of Stalin's successors has had a grip on the system of comparable tenacity. The vulnerability of the USSR in June of 1941 may attest to the weakness rather than the strength of centralized control, but despite his misestimates of Hitler's intentions, Stalin rapidly recovered his bearings, and the command system adapted remarkably well over the long haul. Nuclear weapons might not give the Soviet command system the same latitude for mistakes in the future, however, which argues for U.S. sensitivity to the possibility of Soviet preemption in a crisis that appears to be escaping control. In the worst case for either superpower, theater commanders-in-chief who might be isolated from their national command authorities will be striking back with an improvised and disaggregated war plan. Such a retaliation, however discombobulated it is, under present conditions would at least guarantee widespread societal destruction.

A third issue is the role of intelligence relative to the ascertaining of opponents' intentions and capabilities, before and during war. The United States, for its part, may now be correcting an unfortunate tendency of the past, to rely on the presumed infallibility of technical collection at the expense of intelligence derived from human sources.[40] According to Ernest R. May, the major powers before World War I made generally accurate estimates of one another's intentions ("proclivities") but failed to assess accurately their capabilities. Between World War I and II, the situation was reversed, with capabilities being more or less successfully estimated, but intentions not.[41] Of course, major intelligence services, given their scope and tasking, are bound to make both kinds of errors in the course of doing their jobs, and we are likely to know more about errors than successes on the basis of published literature.[42] Estimating is not a science but an art form, incorporating scientific inference and plain hunches, not to mention an element of luck.

On the edge of superpower confrontation, important information about the intentions of either side will be important to the other in the short term. Capabilities do not change rapidly relative to the gross size and flexibility of U.S. and Soviet arsenals. Therefore, erroneous estimates will be errors in predicting intent, not capacity. There is a subtle danger here of inferring intentions from capabilities. Although conventional wisdom might suggest that U.S. war plans and force acquisition ought to be based on worst-case estimates, in the middle of an actual crisis a U.S. president would not want to exclude other than worst-case assumptions. Kennedy's management of the Cuban missile crisis shows how this willingness to include hopeful alternatives in the decision maker's calculus can work to the benefit of war avoidance while still accomplishing policy objectives. Beginning with the blockade and leaving open the option of escalation, Kennedy allowed Khrushchev the option of not forcing the confrontation onto a more dangerous and crisis unstable path. Moreover, the U.S. president also sought to provide the Soviet premier a face-saving exit, which would preclude the personal humiliation of Khrushchev as well as the national humiliation of the USSR.[43] This slow squeeze on the

USSR while holding onto U.S. political demands allowed for Soviet misestimates of U.S. intentions that might have provoked war had the United States, in its initial response to the discovery of the missiles, launched an invasion of Cuba or an air strike against the island.

Related to this concern, of course, is the problem of strategic deception or *maskirovka*, as the Soviets are inclined to discuss it. Soviet *maskirovka* is a multidimensional concept that includes both active deception and passive measures, including camouflage and concealment.[44] The United States can expect that Soviet peacetime and wartime intelligence activities will include measures to deceive opponents about their intentions and capabilities, which are not as transparent as Western fetishists of technical collection might assume. Some very important things about the Soviet force structure, in terms of the ways in which it would operate following a Soviet decision that war was likely, are not known with high confidence by Western assessors. The USSR has apparently never placed its strategic nuclear forces on highest alert.[45] The Soviet approach to deception is judged as very different from the U.S. perspective as the Soviet approach borrows from Pavlovian psychology, cybernetics, and Marxist philosophy. According to Roger Beaumont, "In any case, the Soviets have examined many aspects of command and control on much deeper and broader levels than has been the case in the West."[46] According to Donald C. Daniel and Katherine L. Herbig, the German effort to deceive the Soviet Union about the plans for Operation Barbarossa before the invasion of June 1941 illustrates the "M-type" deception, deceptions that focus the attention of the target on one wrong alternative. This is in distinction to the "A-type" deception, in which ambiguity is created to induce confusion into the decision-making process of the target in order to preclude its focusing on the correct answer.[47]

Soviet military operations in World War II partook of both types of deception noted by Daniel and Herbig. Operational planning for Soviet counterattacks at Stalingrad and the planning of their Belorussian campaign included considerable attention to *maskirovka*. Operation Uranus for the defense of Stalingrad was planned by Marshals Zhukov and Vasilevskiy from September through November of 1942. This operation had to be prepared very carefully, in order to mask the counterattack that would follow successful defense of the inner city. Security was so tight that Soviet Army Group commanders Rokossovskiy and Yeremenko were not informed of plans until the middle of October, when army groups were ordered to go over to the defensive to deceive German intelligence. While visible efforts were directed toward the construction of defenses, the Soviets amassed huge reserves 200 miles from Stalingrad and moved reinforcements only at night under strict radio silence.[48] Another Soviet operational deception, Mars, was scheduled in case the Germans might remove forces from their Army Group Center to support the attack on Stalingrad.[49]

These successful Soviet operational deceptions also hold less obvious lessons. They were made possible by a larger context in which the "victim" made self-defeating strategic and political errors of omission and commission. The Germans, for example, did not have to get several armies committed to the Stalingrad pocket in the first place; the capture of Stalingrad came to have more symbolic than operational or strategic significance. The inner city house-to-house (if not cellar-to-cellar) fighting was an art form in which the Russians excelled, and the costs paid by the Nazis were considerable. This is not the first occasion, nor undoubtedly the last, in which the capture of salient points on a map becomes an end in itself for commanders whose operational objectives are confounded by strategic confusion. The larger issue in this regard, of course, was Hitler's willingness even to engage in a two-front war with the USSR and its Western allies simultaneously, a high policy misjudgment, which resulted in part from German underestimation of Soviet sustainability for protracted conflict. The essential German misjudgment in this regard was not, as is commonly supposed, an underestimation of Soviet reserve divisions and capabilities for industrial reconstitution, although that certainly occurred. The most important German misestimate was the assumption that Soviet strategic command and control would be unable to react successfully following early and spectacular operational victories by the Germans in the western USSR. This assumption was not so unreasonable given the Nazis' experience with the French in 1940. The French were not militarily defeated so much as they were militarily disoriented and then politically discouraged. Nazi *blitzkrieg* operations fell not only upon defenders who were poorly prepared operationally but also upon French politicians whose repertoire included no alternative to conciliation. German operations created the potential for strategic political victory against the French, but French governmental fatalism and defeatism provided the *coup de grâce*.

The collapse of the French command system in 1940, in contrast to the revival and eventual triumph of the Soviet one in 1945, carries significance beyond the illustrations of operational deception and Soviet interest in *maskirovka*. The greatest deceptions are self-deceptions. Deception is a component of surprise. Surprise includes deception and other measures to do the unexpected in implausible ways. The paradox of surprise is that the more improbable it is, the higher the payoff if it occurs.[50] Thus it may turn out that, under some conditions of desperation or anticipation, a strategic nuclear surprise might take place despite the commonly held notion that nuclear war is irrational and self-defeating. Paradoxically, the very expectation that nuclear war is self-defeating may lead to vulnerability to strategic nuclear surprise. Strategic nuclear surprise would be most surprising if it were to remove key elements of the adversary's command system in the earliest stages of war. Undoubtedly, Soviet planners of strategic nuclear surprise would reckon against the obstacles to success, which are indeed formidable.[51] If we assume, however, that nuclear surprise might occur out of the "grey" instead of the "blue" after an alerted U.S. force was stood down, then it becomes somewhat less inconceivable although not any less risky. Most analysts would agree that the risks under normal peacetime condition are so awesome that only foolish leaders would risk nuclear suicide. During superpower crises, however, foolishness will appear to be wise to policy makers who fear preemption of loss or control.[52]

STRATEGY, POLITICS, AND THE OFFENSIVE

The discussion of surprise leads naturally to the concern in the West about Soviet emphasis upon the offensive in operational and strategic writing. However, two different genres of Soviet discussion must be kept distinct. As Condoleeza Rice explains in a recent essay:

> The tension between political activity and the military offensive has remained largely unresolved since Frunze. Modern-day Soviet strategy attempts to make a distinction between military-political doctrine, which is supreme and essentially defensive, and military-technical doctrine (similar to strategy), which upholds the primacy of the offensive and the need for surprise and initiative. This is a distinction that fails to remove the confusion, and the Soviets themselves elaborate no further.[53]

The distinction between military-political and military-technical doctrine might in Western terminology be better described as the difference between sociopolitical and operational modes of analysis because both are so manifest in the work of Clausewitz and other noted Western strategists.[54] Western readers exposed to heavy doses of the "sociology of knowledge" literature will have some (limited) appreciation of the *Weltanschauung* from which Marxism derives its categorical imperatives. The state must, as an essential matter, be prepared for war by anticipating the kinds of enemies it will have to fight and the character of the class nature of war causation. This last point is obscure to many Western readers who assume that either the distinction between bourgeoisie and proletariat is obsolete in the modern-day welfare state and/or that the Soviets no longer really believe in it. However, Soviet sociopolitical doctrine (military-political as above) is based upon the notion that wars are caused by the international class struggle. This class struggle has ontological significance in Marxist thought. Its long term implication is that no single conflict can eradicate the threat that imperialism and capitalism represent to the survival of Soviet socialism, in their perspective. This has serious implications for the Soviet distinction between military-political and military-technical thought as that distinction applies to nuclear war between the capitalist and socialist blocs. As Raymond L. Garthoff has noted, with regard to the development of Soviet military doctrine in the 1970s:

> In its political, or war versus peace, policy dimension, military doctrine was thus moving *away* from question of waging war to place greater stress on preventing war, although its military-technical or war-fighting component continued to emphasize preparedness to wage war decisively, and with a particular accent on offensive operations and on being prepared to wage all-out warfare if nuclear war should come.[55]

As reluctant cobelligerents in World War II, the Soviets are well aware of the costs of major war, especially if they are forced to engage in it with underprepared command systems. Stalin's incapacity in the early days of Barbarossa is now legendary, but more important for Soviet field armies were the early and catastrophic operational losses sustained by USSR forces, which were poorly deployed and trained for the expected conflict. Soviet lack of preparation for the events of June 22, 1941, reflected in part the dramatic purges of the High Command in 1937–1938 for reasons that are still not altogether clear.[56] If the "down" side of the Great Patriotic War for the USSR was its early defeats, the "up" side can be found in its adaptation under stress to the requirements for protracted war, sustainability and endurance. The major achievement of the USSR in World War II came not in the finesse demonstrated in military operations, although important and successful improvisation did take place, but in the Soviet capacity to mobilize the entire society and economy for war.[57]

For obvious reasons based upon that same experience, Soviet military leaders have decided that, if they are charged with the responsibility to go to war by their political leadership, then surprise, boldness, and an offensive operational cast pay large dividends. This tenor in Soviet military scholarship has been apparent since the publication of the important work by A. A. Sidorenko.[58] Recently Western analysts make fewer references to Sidorenko because of his emphasis on the role of nuclear weapons in Soviet offensive theater operations. Contemporary U.S. analysis suggests that Soviet operational art now emphasizes a preferred model of theater-strategic conventional warfare with the escalation to nuclear use avoided if possible.[59] Part of the difficulty in estimating Soviet "operational" approaches from a Blue-views-Red perspective is that Blue is apt to define "operational" in at least three different senses. First, operational is a perspective on the conduct of actual campaigns, as opposed to the logistical or societal perspective.[60] Second, the term operational refers, in Western writing about "operational art," to campaigns from theater level down to division.[61] Third, operational represents a way of thinking about the conduct of theater-level campaigns, and, in particular, about the command systems and its role in the success or failure of military operations.[62]

This third usage of the concept of the operational can be applied to the development of Soviet military thought by Triandifilov and Tukhachevsky, among others, about deep operations, based on their understandings of World War I experience and on their contacts with Germans during the postwar period.[63] It seems apparent that Soviet geography with vast steppes, long borders, and the potential for encirclement by military opponents also suggested an interest in operations of high speed and great depth. Indeed, once they recovered their bearings and began to take the offensive in World War II, the Soviets demonstrated, very much against doctrinal expectations between 1938 and 1940, that they were capable of conducting operations with unprecedented mass and mobility. Study of the Russian Civil War had suggested to some Soviet analysts a forecast of things to come. As Lt. Col. David M. Glantz has indicated:

The concept of mobile operations on a broad front in great depth, the rapid redeployment of forces over wide expanses of territory, the use of shock groups for creating penetrations and the widespread use of cavalry forces as "mobile groups" exploiting offensive success were all legacies of the civil war.[64]

Improvisation was made necessary by the requirement for the Workers' and Peasants' Red Army (RKKA), created by decree in January 1918, to adapt to the requirements of civil war and the expectation of continuing external intervention in the revolution. Soviet military historians note the conduct of bold and daring cavalry operations deep in the rear of the opponent, the decisiveness of the offensive, and the development of expertise in the conduct of fast moving "meeting engagements."[65] Compulsory military service was introduced in 1918 in contrast to the earlier expectation that the armed forces could be staffed by voluntary enlistments. Commanders who were the "revolutionary strata of the proletariat and the soldier masses," however politically qualified, lacked "sufficient knowledge and experience and were not able to organize combat action and direct troops as they should."[66] Former Czarist military officers who were willing to serve the new regime were called upon in order to provide professional leadership.

Superimposed upon this Soviet understanding of their unique historical experience has been the age of military automation and its attendant high technology cast implied for contemporary military operations. For the Soviet Union, this influences expectations about troop control in several ways. Future conventional military operations, which the Red Army may be required to execute, will occur at unprecedented speed and over wide distances. Therefore, the Soviet emphasis on top-down command systems for the efficient carrying out of a superior commander's operational-strategic concept must be combined with allowance for tactical flexibility in maneuver battalions and divisions. The United States has a difficult enough time doing this, and the requirement for the Soviet Union to combine fixity and flexibility into one game plan will be even more stressful.[67]

CONCLUSION

Previously success in military strategy depended upon brute force or fast movement. Successful military suasion or war fighting in the future will depend upon closing the decision loop faster than the opponent. The Soviet military literature indicates that their leaders recognize this. Soviet planners cannot foresee the precise paths to war any more than NATO planners can. The best plans have the "if . . . then" character, and will undoubtedly require modification under the pressure of nuclear crisis management or conventional combat.

Superpower arms control proposals have for the most part been devoted to the reduction of inventories of weapons. The decision matrices of the U.S. and Soviet political leaderships and of their globally dispersed force commanders matter more. So, too, do the organizational repertoires and institutional memories which would be activated during crisis and war. Crisis presents special challenges to U.S. and Soviet leaders. During peacetime and in war the relationship between political and military leaders, and therefore between force and policy, is relatively settled, compared to the crisis time situation. Crisis brings about unexpected strains on a system which does not yet know whether it will revert to "normal" peacetime standards or spill over into actual fighting.

For the Soviet political and military decision making system, the implications of *perestroika* are as profound as they are for the modernization of the Soviet economy. Nothing very limited or partial will guarantee the necessary degree of innovation. On the other hand, any reforms more radical than partial ones threaten vested interests. The Soviet High Command has established planning parameters based on its World War II experience with surprise, multifront offensives, and decisive political victory. A new political context for superpower postwar relations has now been proposed by Soviet General Secretary Gorbachev. The military implications of this new context are profound: conventional forces sufficient for defense but not for attack, and a gradually reduced dependency upon nuclear weapons, prefatory toward their ultimate elimination from global arsenals.[68]

Whether this vision of defensive sufficiency and nuclear disarmament will be fully realized is not known. Regardless, the period of transition from the present to a future, defensively oriented Soviet military establishment is fraught with difficulty for the Soviet leadership. Defensive sufficiency at the operational level requires aggressive technology innovation and the willingness to experiment with new forms of command and control. Only if the Soviet armed forces are more qualitatively secure can they afford to be quantitatively less impressive.

NOTES

1. Soviet concepts of command and control are explained in John Hemsley, *Soviet Troop Control* (Oxford: Brassey's, 1982), Chapter 1.

2. According to Clausewitz: "Everything in war is very simple, but the simplest thing is difficult. The difficulties accumulate and end by producing a kind of friction that is inconceivable unless one has experienced war." Carl von Clausewitz, *On War*, ed. and trans. Michael Howard and Peter Paret (Princeton: Princeton University Press, 1976), p. 119.

3. General-Major S. N. Kozlov, *The Officer's Handbook* (Moscow, 1971), p. 13. Published under the auspices of the U.S. Air Force and translated by the DGIS Multilingual Section, Translation Bureau, Secretary of State Department, Ottawa, Canada.

4. Ibid., p. 41.

5. Ibid., p. 43.

6. Ibid., p. 62.

7. Colonel B. Byely, et al., *Marxism-Leninism on War and Army* (Moscow: Progress Publishers, 1973), p. 28.

8. Ibid., p. 30.

9. General-Lieutenant I. G. Zav'yalov, "The New Weapon and Military Art," *Krasnaya zvezda,* October 30, 1970, in *Selected Soviet Military Writings 1970–1975* (Washington, D.C.: U.S. Government Printing Office, undated), p. 209.

10. Ibid.

11. Ibid., p. 210. On Soviet military doctrine, see John J. Dziak, *Soviet Perceptions of Military Power: The Interaction of Theory and Practice* (New York: National Strategy Information Center/Crane, Russak, 1981), Chapter 3.

12. Colin S. Gray, *Nuclear Strategy and National Style* (Lanham, Md.: Hamilton Press, 1986), Chapter 3, pp. 65–96.

13. Stanley R. Sloan, *NATO's Future: Toward a New Transatlantic Bargain* (Washington, D.C.: National Defense University Press, 1985), p. 141.

14. McGeorge Bundy, George F. Kennan, Robert S. McNamara, and Gerard Smith, "Nuclear Weapons and the Atlantic Alliance," *Foreign Affairs,* Spring 1982, pp. 753–68. See also Robert S. McNamara, *Blundering into Disaster* (New York: Pantheon Books, 1986).

15. McNamara, *Blundering into Disaster,* p. 120. See also *Strengthening Conventional Defenses in Europe: Proposals for the 1980s,* Report of the European Security Study (New York: St. Martin's Press, 1983).

16. John G. Hines, Phillip A. Petersen, and Notra Trulock III, "Soviet Military Theory from 1945–2000: Implications for NATO," *Washington Quarterly* 9 (Fall 1986): 117–37. Counterarguments to the argument that the Soviets are more interested in preserving conventional-nuclear thresholds are noted in Joseph D. Douglass, Jr., and Amoretta M. Hoeber, *Conventional War and Escalation: The Soviet View* (New York: National Strategy Information Center/Crane, Russak, 1981).

17. Paul K. Davis and Peter J. E. Stan, *Concepts and Models of Escalation* (Santa Monica, Calif.: Rand Corporation, May 1984), pp. 26–27.

18. Albert Wohlstetter and Richard Brody, "Continuing Control as a Requirement for Deterring," Chapter 5, in Carter, Steinbruner, and Zraket, eds., *Managing Nuclear Operations,* p. 162.

19. John F. Lehman, Jr., "The 600 Ship Navy," and Admiral James D. Watkins, USN, "The Maritime Strategy," pp. 30–40 and 2–17 in *Proceedings of the U.S. Naval Institute,* January 1986.

20. Watkins, "The Maritime Strategy," p. 14.

21. On inadvertent war, see Barry R. Posen, "Inadvertent Nuclear War? Escalation and NATO's Northern Flank," pp. 85–112 in *Strategy and Nuclear Deterrence,* ed. Steven E. Miller (Princeton: Princeton University Press, 1984); and Paul Bracken, "Accidental Nuclear War," in *Hawks, Doves and Owls,* ed. Allison, Carnesale, and Nye, Chapter 2.

22. John J. Mearsheimer, "A Strategic Misstep: The Maritime Strategy and Deterrence in Europe," *International Security* 2 (Fall 1986): 3–57.

23. John J. Mearsheimer, *Conventional Deterrence* (Ithaca, N.Y.: Cornell University Press, 1983), pp. 165–88.

24. On the sustainability of NATO and the Warsaw Pact under standard mobilization scenarios, see William P. Mako, *U.S. Ground Forces and the Defense of Central Europe* (Washington, D.C.: The Brookings Institution, 1983).

25. See James M. McConnell, *The Soviet Shift in Emphasis from Nuclear to Conventional*, Center for Naval Analyses, CRC 490–Vol. II, June 1983.

26. Peter H. Vigor, *Soviet Blitzkrieg Theory* (New York: St. Martin's Press, 1983), pp. 183–205.

27. Samuel P. Huntington, "The Renewal of Strategy," in *The Strategic Imperative*, ed. Huntington (Cambridge, Mass.: Ballinger, 1982), pp. 1–52.

28. Keith A. Dunn and William O. Staudenmaier, "A NATO Conventional Retaliatory Strategy: Its Strategic and Force Structure Implications," in *Military Strategy in Transition: Defense and Deterrence in the 1980s*, eds. Dunn and Staudenmaier (Boulder, Colo.: Westview Press, 1984), pp. 187–212.

29. Benjamin S. Lambeth, "On Thresholds in Soviet Military Thought," in *Strategic Responses to Conflict in the 1980s*, ed. William J. Taylor, Jr., Steven A. Maaranen, and Gerrit W. Gong (Washington, D.C.: Center for Strategic and International Studies/Lexington Books, 1984), pp. 173–82.

30. On C3 issues attendant to SDI, see Theodore Jarvis, "Nuclear Operations and Strategic Defense," in *Managing Nuclear Operations*, ed. Carter, Steinbruner, and Zraket, pp. 661–78; and Stephen J. Cimbala, "Artificial Intelligence and SDI: Corollaries or Compatriots?" in *Artificial Intelligence and National Security*, ed. Cimbala (Lexington, Mass.: Lexington Books, 1987), pp. 203–14.

31. Wohlstetter and Brody, "Continuing Control as a Requirement for Deterring," p. 181.

32. Difficulties inherent in launching ICBMs under attack are discussed in Ashton B. Carter, "Assessing Command System Vulnerability," in *Managing Nuclear Operations*, ed. Carter, Steinbruner, and Zraket, p. 578–82, esp. p. 580. See also Office of Technology Assessment, *MX Missile Basing* (Washington, D.C.: U.S. Government Printing Office, September 1981), Chapter 4; and John Steinbruner, "Launch under Attack," *Scientific American* 250 (January 1984): 37–47.

33. Stephen M. Meyer, "Soviet Nuclear Operations," *Signal*, December 1986, pp. 41–60.

34. See Blair Stewart, "Technology Impacts on ICBM Modernization: Hard Mobile Launchers and Deep Basing," in *Missiles for the Nineties*, ed. Barry Schneider, Colin S. Gray, and Keith B. Payne (Boulder, Colo.: Westview Press, 1984), pp. 29–41.

35. Near-term BMD options are discussed in William A. Davis, Jr., *Asymmetries in U.S. and Soviet Strategic Defense Programs: Implications for Near-Term American Deployment Options* (Cambridge, Mass.: Institute for Foreign Policy Analysis, Special Report, 1986).

36. On the problem of ambiguous command, see Bracken, *The Command and Control of Nuclear Forces*, pp. 224–32.

37. Soviet writers have proposed three generic measures for assessment of control efficiency: critical time, control time, and performance time. Critical time is the time within which the mission must be completed to be successful. Control time is the time required by the decision cycle from intelligence gathering to the transmission of authenticated orders. Performance time is the time required to complete tasks once orders have been received. For an application to Soviet TNF, see Stephen M. Meyer, *Soviet Theater Nuclear Forces, part II: Capabilities and Implications*, Adelphi Papers 188 (Winter 1983–1984), pp. 37–38.

38. Graham T. Allison, *Essence of Decision* (Boston: Little, Brown, 1971), p. 138.

39. On the concept of coupling in organizations, see Charles Perrow, *Normal Accidents* (New York: Basic Books, 1984), esp. Chapter 3.

40. For illustrative evidence, see Admiral Stansfield Turner, *Secrecy and Democracy: The CIA in Transition* (Boston: Houghton Mifflin, 1985).

41. Ernest R. May, "Conclusions; Capabilities and Proclivities," in *Knowing One's Enemies*, ed. May (Princeton: Princeton University Press, 1984), pp. 503–42.

42. Christopher Andrew, *Her Majesty's Secret Service: The Making of the British Intelligence Community* (New York: Viking Books, 1986).

43. The importance of giving Khrushchev a way out in Cuba is stressed in Allison, *Essence of Decision*, pp. 223–28. The ExCom or special presidential crisis management team had already decided that the U.S. response to a shooting down of a single U-2 intelligence aircraft by Soviet surface-to-air missiles (SAMs) based in Cuba would be to destroy the SAM site. If a second U-2 were downed, the United States would destroy all the sites; the air force had prepared plans for these contingencies. In the event, President Kennedy demurred to allow more time for negotiations to succeed.

44. The *Dictionary of Basic Military Terms* defines *maskirovka* as a "form of support for combat operations, its purpose being to conceal the activities and disposition of friendly troops, and to mislead the enemy with regard to the grouping and intentions of such troops." *Dictionary of Basic Military Terms* (Moscow: Voyenizdat, 1975), Officer's Library Series, published under the auspices of the U.S. Air Force (Washington, D.C.: U.S. Government Printing Office, undated), p. 118.

45. Among the Soviet strategic nuclear forces, only ICBMs are thought to be maintained at day-to-day levels of readiness allowing for prompt response to surprise attack. ICBMs which could be readied for launch on tactical warning or launch under attack within several minutes account for 80 percent of their ICBM launchers, or 95 percent of their ICBM warheads. About 20 percent of Soviet ballistic missile submarines are on station at any one time, and another 20 percent in port could contribute to LUA if they survived. Apparently no Soviet strategic bombers are maintained on air or ground alert. Hence Soviet prompt response is heavily dependent upon ICBMs, which include about 90 percent of the warheads available on day-to-day alert. See Meyer, "Soviet Nuclear Operations," in *Managing Nuclear Operations*, ed. Carter, Steinbruner, and Zraket, p. 494. The Soviet SS-18 Mod 4 force deployed in 1986 was estimated by the Pentagon to have the capability to destroy 65 percent to 80 percent of U.S. ICBM silos while retaining 1,000 unexpended SS-18 warheads for subsequent attacks. See U.S. Department of Defense, *Soviet Military Power: 1986* (Washington, D.C.: U.S. Government Printing Office, March 1986), p. 25.

46. Roger Beaumont, *The Nerves of War: Emerging Issues in and References to Command and Control* (Washington, D.C.: AFCEA International Press, 1986), p. 52.

47. Donald C. Daniel and Katherine L. Herbig, eds., *Strategic Military Deception* (New York: Pergamon Press, 1981), pp. 5–6.

48. For elaboration of these points, see Earl F. Ziemke, "Stalingrad and Belorussia: Soviet Deception in World War II," in *Strategic Military Deception*, ed. Daniel and Herbig, pp. 243–76, esp. pp. 247–54. Soviet operations in manchuria also provide illustrative material; see Lieutenant Colonel David M. Glantz, *August Storm: The Soviet 1945 Strategic Offensive in Manchuria* (Fort Leavenworth, Kansas: U.S. Army Command and General Staff Colelge, February 1983), esp. p. 165.

49. Ziemke, "Stalingrad and Belorussia: Soviet Deception in World War II," pp. 250–51.

50.   See Michael I. Handel, *Perception, Deception, and Surprise: The Case of the Yom Kippur War* (Jerusalem: Hebrew University of Jerusalem, 1976).

51.   Benjamin S. Lambeth, "Uncertainties for the Soviet War Planner," *International Security* 7 (Winter 1982–1983): 139–66.

52.   On the limitations of deterrence as understood from the standpoint of rationality theories, see Patrick M. Morgan, *Deterrence: A Conceptual Analysis* (Beverly Hills, Calif.: Sage Publications, 1983), 2d ed., esp. pp. 79–102.

53.   Condoleeza Rice, "The Making of Soviet Strategy," in *Makers of Modern Strategy*, ed. Peter Paret (Princeton: Princeton University Press, 1986), p. 675.

54.   Carl von Clausewitz, *On War*, ed. and trans. Michael Howard and Peter Paret (Princeton: Princeton University Press, 1976).

55.   Raymond L. Garthoff, *Detente and Confrontation* (Washington, D.C.: The Brookings Institution, 1985), p. 780.

56.   In 1941 the Soviet General Staff planned for advance deployment of their forces in European Russia in five military districts from the Barents to the Black Sea. Three of these were "special" districts, meaning that they were operational groupings able to fight for a limited time without mobilizing additional reserves. Actual frontier defense was assigned to the NKVD "frontier commands," which were not under the operational command and control of the Red Army. Moreover, lack of preparation in signals and communications throughout the Soviet armed forces was notable. See John Erickson, *The Road to Stalingrad* (New York: Harper and Row, 1975), Vol. I, pp. 68–73.

57.   Rice, "The Making of Soviet Strategy," p. 671.

58.   A. A. Sidorenko, *The Offensive* (Moscow, 1970), translated and published by the U.S. Air Force, Soviet Military Thought Series.

59.   See Hines, Petersen, and Trulock, "Soviet Military Theory from 1945–2000: Implications for NATO," pp. 117–37.

60.   My use of the term perspective is comparable to Michael Howard's "dimensions" of strategy; see his "The Forgotten Dimensions of Strategy," in *The Causes of Wars*, Howard (Cambridge, Mass.: Harvard University Press, 1984), pp. 101–15.

61.   On Western usage of the term operational, see Richard Simpkin, *Race to the Swift* (New York: Brassey's, 1985), pp. 23–24.

62.   John G. Hines and Phillip A. Petersen, "Changing the Soviet System of Control," *International Defense Review* 3 (1986): 281–89.

63.   Rice, "The Making of Soviet Strategy," pp. 664–65; and Simpkin, *Race to the Swift*, pp. 37–39.

64.   David M. Glantz, USA, "Soviet Operational Formation for Battle: A Perspective," in *Selected Readings in Military History: Soviet Military History*, Vol. I (Fort Leavenworth, Kansas: U.S. Army Command and General Staff College, January 1984), pp. 2–12, esp. p. 3.

65.   Colonel A. Yekimovskiy and Colonel A. Tonkikh, "Red Army Tactics in the Civil War," in *Selected Readings in Military History: Soviet Military History*, Vol. I, pp. 48–57.

66.   Ibid., p. 49.

67.   See Hemsley, *Soviet Troop Control*, pp. 169–74, for an excellent discussion of pertinent problems and Soviet approaches. Additional perspective on Soviet approaches can be gleaned from V. V. Druzhinin and D. S. Kontorov, *Concept, Algorithm, Decision* (Moscow, 1972), translated and published under the auspices of the U.S. Air Force. Soviet command system weaknesses are discussed in F. W. von Mellenthin, R. H. S. Stolfi, and E. Sobik, *NATO under Attack* (Durham, N.C.: Duke University Press, 1984), pp. 75–96, esp. pp. 83–93. According to these authors: "Given the long history of frictions and

ambivalence in Soviet military command, it is clear that the Soviet military commander is constrained in his capacity for independent judgment and action to a degree that could be fatal in a high-intensity conventional war" (*NATO under Attack*, p. 91).

68. Gorbachev noted in 1987 that "Clausewitz's dictum that war is the continuation of policy only by different means, which was classical in his time, has grown hopelessly out of date. It now belongs to the libraries. . . . A new dialectic of strength and security follows from the impossibility of a military — that is, nuclear — solution to international differences." Mikhail Gorbachev, *Perestroika: New Thinking for Our Country and the World* (New York: Harper and Row, 1987), p. 141. For operational implications see Colonel Stanislaw Koziej, "Anticipated Directions for Change in Tactics of Ground Troops," *Przeglad Wojsk Ladowych* (Review of the Ground Forces, a polish military journal), September 1986, pp. 5–9, trans. Dr. Harold Orenstein, Soviet Army Studies Office, Fort Leavenworth, Kansas.

6

Winning War and Peace

James E. Toth

This chapter addresses the ending of war. The usual approach is to study how wars begin in order to gain insight on how better to deter them. That notwithstanding, wars happen. Few nations in this day and age seek it; it usually is adopted as a better policy than the other choices in evidence at the time. Should a major war occur, it is the last battle — rather than the first — which will shape the future fortunes of the contesting nations. And the success of that last battle will depend in large measure on preparations made before the conflict begins. This chapter, then, is a conceptual exploration of the impact of conflict termination options on U.S. national security alternatives. The basic assumptions underlying the paragraphs that follow are that the Soviet Union will continue as the principal strategic threat to the United States, that rapprochement between the Soviet Union and the People's Republic of China will not occur in the near future, and that the United States will not initiate war.

POLITICAL UTILITY

In order to understand the circumstances under which wars are terminated, it is necessary first to review some general observations concerning the nature of war and its purpose.

There seems to be common agreement that war is a political act, that it is yet another aspect of man's social intercourse with his fellows, and that it is generally conducted to achieve some goal that is unattainable by more economic means. In the past, political and military theorists have assessed warfare in terms of motive, intensity, duration, and geography as well as other factors. Certainly a factor meriting consideration is the political utility of war. Once a policy of war is adopted, either by choice or by imposition, the nation must ensure that its resources are being employed wisely to achieve a politically useful conclusion.

Complete and Incomplete Wars

To begin with, has the war resolved the fundamental problems precipitating hostilities? Is the war as a political problem-solving effort complete or incomplete? If it is incomplete, then political and military strife can be expected to recur in due course.

An example of a complete war was the American Civil War, wherein the constitutional and economic issues precipitating conflict were resolved by a combination of military and political effort. Similarly, the results of World War II were essentially complete. In the case of Japan, the political leadership of the nation was overthrown by military action. Subsequently, the policies of the Japanese nation were modified by imposed institutional reform and eradication of the political and economic problems that had been perceived as threats to Japanese security and prosperity.

The points to be made here are that the basic underlying problems were solved, and they were solved by a combination of military and political measures. Similarly, the Third Reich was overthrown militarily, and Germany's future prospects as a world power were constrained by political division and alliance of the parts with the opposing European power coalitions. Again, the economic and political factors contributing to the rise of Hitler were carefully excised in the postwar reformation. Again, military endeavor of itself was only part of the equation.

There are also examples of incomplete wars, wherein decisive battles or campaigns considered at the time to have achieved victory were in fact unable to secure a stable and lasting peace. The First and Second Roman-Carthaginian or Punic Wars, the English-French clashes in the Hundred Years War, and more recently, the Arab-Israeli conflict all demonstrate that winning an isolated battle or campaign will not, of itself, ensure a stable peace until the underlying problems contributing to strife are resolved in one fashion or another. In essence, what history has termed wars in many cases are merely campaigns or phases of a protracted war with intervening periods of military quiescence.

There is yet another prospective obstacle to the attainment of postwar stability. The prosecution of a war may resolve the initiative problems and in so doing may create new frictions, provocations, or power imbalances that result eventually in a resumption of hostilities for different reasons. World War I and the Treaty of Versailles are generally credited with having sown the seeds of World War II. Similarly, the shifting power balance resulting from the World War II defeat and dismemberment of Germany, coupled with the attendant political and economic impoverishment of France and Britain, has drawn the United States and Soviet Union into competition.

Controlled and Uncontrolled Wars

There is another measure of a war's utility — the extent to which the conduct of that war supports the political requirements of the nation. That is to say, the conduct of war must be effectively controlled, for a war without proper direction may take a course of its own choosing and produce results inimical to national interests. Again, history provides examples. For instance, the Prussian contests with Austria-Hungary and France during the late nineteenth century were rigidly controlled by Bismarck to achieve limited objectives. Although the military campaigns were highly successful and would have permitted greater territorial conquests, Bismarck kept Prussian demands comparatively modest, with an eye toward postconflict stability in the European balance of power.

Another example of a controlled war effort was World War II. All things considered, the military operations of the allies were effectively subordinated to the political objectives agreed to by their national leaders. Unfortunately, the U.S. political objectives focused more on the defeat of Germany and Japan than the postwar political balance. The employment of military force in the Thirty Years War in Europe, however, was largely uncontrolled, as were the more recent events of World War I. In this latter contest, military action and its relentless consumption of national strength obscured and eventually destroyed the economic advantages of empires it was fought to preserve.

THE OBJECTIVES OF WAR

Having looked briefly at the underlying political nature of war, it is appropriate to continue with an examination of war objectives, which are separate and distinct, albeit supportive, of the political goals. The political ends specify the desired effect, that final state between the parties to the war deemed essential to the well-being of the nation. If the political objective is some derivation of the national desire for preservation (territorial, economic, ideological) and coercion of the policies of the opponent, the objectives of war must be those reasonably attainable goals that, when achieved, will provide a basis for realizing that political aim. Therefore, at the national level, victory must be defined as the achievement of the war objectives, which will vary in accordance with the political aim.

This is hardly a new revelation. Clausewitz states that, while in theory war serves to compel an opponent to our will and the aim of war is to disarm him, in actual practice, war need not be fought out until one party is overthrown. War is a continual assessment of probability, gain, and cost in which the ultimate value of the political objective precipitating conflict will determine the willingness to devote resources in its pursuit. And that assessment may change depending on successes, failures, and prospects for the future.[1]

Next, the selection of war objectives must focus on the fundamental strategic problem. There is a constant danger that a nation will dissipate its energies on manifestations of the problem rather than on the core problem itself. As an example, consider a prospective Warsaw Pact attack on Western Europe. Is our preeminent strategic problem the defense of Europe or the aggressive policies of the Soviet leadership and the circumstances that crystallized them? A wrong judgment on this basic point not only jeopardizes successful and stable termination of hostilities but also limits the strategic options available for problem solving.

What then are the general means for obtaining the objectives of war? There are two. The first seeks domination or the overthrow of the opponent's military strength and political policy. This generally requires total conquest and an imposed settlement. The second seeks concession — either political, geographic, economic, or military — of a limited goal without total conquest of the opposing nation. These courses, in turn, generally determine the nature of conflict termination to be sought.

The nature of conflict termination inevitably must be reckoned in the selection of war objectives and strategy. If the war is to be concluded by overthrow, then specific military, economic, and political efforts must be coordinated to achieve that end. If, instead, concessions are sought, the employment of national power will vary accordingly — for what is a negotiated conclusion rather than an imposed one.

OVERTHROW

The first option is overthrow, wherein one nation attempts to destroy the opponent's ability to resist in order to impose a settlement of its own choosing. This may be done by direct military action, subversive political action, or some combination of the two. The aim here is change of the offending policies of the nation in question. If that can be attained by internal change of policy or government, well and good. If the issues are such that the nation as a whole is united or the government in power cannot be dislodged, then military overthrow may be required. This approach requires either destruction of the enemy's military forces or disruption of their ability to operate. For example, Japan in World War II was defeated by a combination of these methods — destruction of expeditionary forces and naval power in concert with economic strangulation of the national industrial base that supported them.

Military overthrow, of itself, does not ensure a completed war. Consider the case of Napoleon's decisive defeat of Prussia at Jena and Auerstadt in 1806. Having failed politically to consolidate these military gains, Napoleon had occasion to regret this fact at Waterloo when Blucher's Prussian columns tipped the balance against the French. What ensures completion is careful political exploitation of ultimate military success. That must consider both near- and long-term possibilities and consequences.

Moreover, military overthrow may not be strategically desirable. While dictation of terms has its advantages, it should be kept in mind that the conquered nation has, in fact, become a dependent burden upon the conqueror. Whether for ravagement or reconstruction, the winner must make some disposition of the loser, and either course is not without its expense. The first cost is that of occupation, which, depending upon the extent of the nation and the relative docility of its inhabitants, can be an extended — perhaps continuing — drain on national resources and attention. The second is the impact on the defeated nation. The nation-state will continue to survive and, depending upon the character of its people, may even prosper. In some cases, wartime destruction has served as both political and capital catharsis, enabling vigorous regeneration of national strength without the encumbrance of outdated methods and an obsolescent industrial base. Germany (East and West) and Japan are current examples. The result is a prospective competitor 20 to 50 years hence that may have more efficient instruments of national power than does a conqueror, which advances by evolution rather than imposed revolution.

The nature of the limited objective for certain types of military action (e.g., raids, demonstrations) provides for their conclusion, but a strategic contest between powers with perceptions of vital interests in conflict does not — particularly when there is no decisive differential in power among them. That said, it may be useful at this point briefly to examine the prospects for overthrow of the Soviet Union after a major Warsaw Pact attack against NATO in Western Europe. At that turn of events, the policies and strategies of deterrence are functionally bankrupt; a war strategy will be required to direct national and coalition efforts toward an acceptable conflict conclusion.

The first problem is the selection of an appropriate war objective to support the political aim of overthrow. Few would argue against the judgment that the Soviet Union represents the center of gravity (Clausewitz's term) of the Warsaw Pact and that the Soviet Union's locus of national power is its military strength. Neutralization of that strength, then, must be the goal. Ultimately, that goal must be sought on the Eurasian continent, for that is where the Soviet military machine is anchored.

There are at least three continental strategic options. The first is a forward defense mustering strength early on in order to destroy the Soviet land and air forces in a head-to-head war of attrition on the axis of the Soviet main attack. The second defends at the point of the Soviet main attack while attacking on another axis into the Soviet Union itself, and the third is a classic Fabian strategy that seeks to dissipate Soviet strength before counterattacking. all three would feature global operations to assure free use of the seas and space and to tie down Soviet forces that might otherwise be brought to bear in Western Europe.

Assuming that the forces and support required for the first two options were immediately available and that their employment was successful, the result would be the pushing back of Warsaw Pact forces into the Soviet Union itself over shortening lines of communication. The situation is similar to that of 1812 and 1941 when invading armies pushed the Russians back into their expansive homeland. The problem is that there is no barrier to their continued retreat — even back to the Urals. So long as they maintain their forces intact and NATO lines of communication continue to lengthen, the task becomes more difficult and more expensive. From the point of view of a decisive blow against the Soviet center of military gravity, both strategies would require considerable time and almost endless resources. It would be impossible to mass the requisite military strength for these options early in the war. The first strategy would compound these problems by counterattacking the Soviets at their strongest point — the point where they have massed their forces for the initial attack of the war.

The third strategy accepts a Soviet overrun of at least a major portion of Western Europe before counterattacking. As a deterrent strategy, this approach is politically unacceptable because of the entirely reasonable unwillingness of any ally to accept the loss of part or all of its sovereignty — even temporarily — as a tenet of peacetime declaratory policy. However, as a strategy for war, it requires study.

Recall that in World War II, both the Japanese and German offensives expanded rapidly under their own momentum and limited opposition. However, they were not decisive in that they failed to destroy their principal opponents' ability to reconstitute military power, nor did they provide for any direct mechanism for terminating hostilities. In short, they ran out of strategic momentum. Once their initial territorial objectives had been achieved, their offensives ground to a halt, and their forces were widely dissipated to the requirements of occupation and conducting what could only be a strategically defensive war henceforth. The initiative was ceded to the opposition, and the fabric of military capability was stretched taut across many competing requirements — vulnerable to rupture at many points should a sharp force be applied.

For example, in 1944 before the Normandy invasion, some 45 percent of the German ground forces were scattered across Europe with 32 divisions in northern France, 8 divisions in southwest France covering the Bay of Biscay, 10 divisions in southeast France covering the Mediterranean, 18 divisions countering the Allied Italian campaign, 10 divisions protecting the Mediterranean and Adriatic coastlines of northern Italy, 28 divisions in the Balkans and Greece, 9 divisions in the Low Countries, and 18 divisions in Norway and Denmark.[2] Less than a quarter of Germany's forces in Europe were in position to participate in the defense against the Normandy invasion.

The same dilemma confronts the Soviets. Even if the Soviets were to occupy the whole of Europe, initial failure of the NATO land campaign does not mean a loss of the war. So long as control of the seas and space is held, eventual reconstitution of continental losses is possible. Actually, it is unlikely that the Soviets could take all of Europe; at the very least, Iceland, Great Britain, and Spain would probably remain as a toehold for a subsequent reintroduction of forces. Geographically, these territories block Soviet egress to the Atlantic, upon free use of which a NATO reintroduction would depend. If the United States and its remaining allies have the national strategic reserve capacity to mass forces in space and time before the Soviet industrial and manpower base can generate additional military strength, a military victory would remain possible.

As in the previous strategies, this option requires a massive investment of national power. However, the natural phasing of the strategy defers generation of the bulk of these forces until after the war has begun. By virtue of having lost much of the manpower and industrial resources of Europe, the United States and its remaining allies must bear a greater share of the burden.

There is a common assumption (held both in East and West) that large-scale war will inevitably escalate to nuclear exchange. Yet such an assumption fails to consider the wartime political decision-making process on either side — the cold, hard realities of which are considerably different from the polemics and posturing of peacetime policy. On the one side, at what point does the president of the United States feel that Soviet conventional gains are so great that the United States must expose itself to nuclear bombardment by launching a nuclear attack? How will such an attack regain lost territory? On the other side, the Soviets must ask equally hard questions. How long will it take to recuperate? Will a nuclear exchange decrease or increase national vulnerability?

In this latter regard, one of the problems confronting the Soviet Union is the residual power equation following nuclear exchange. While the United States enjoys good neighbors and oceanic insulation, the Soviet Union lies in proximity to the People's Republic of China with whom it disputes both territory and ideology. A nuclear exchange with its ensuing national destruction and expenditure of military strength might reduce the relative Soviet power advantage to the point that PRC military initiatives would be feasible. The alternative would be to preempt with a nuclear attack on the Chinese, which would place the Soviets squarely in the middle of a two-front war (war with NATO being our starting hypothesis).

Material destruction of itself will not achieve domination; it must be exploited with the means to impose a settlement upon the opponent. This requires a residual advantage in national power, either by preserving existing means or reconstituting them after attack. Therefore, preservation not only of a survival nuclear reserve force but also of the wherewithal for reconstitution becomes an imperative. Reconstitution requires material, transportation, and an industrial base, but most important it requires manpower, both in numbers and essential skills.

This point is not lost on the Soviets. From all indications, they are engaged in a broad civil defense program aimed at protecting essential leadership, economic functions, and large sectors of population.[3] And they have a survivable nuclear — and perhaps conventional — reserve. The United States has only a modest civil defense program. Therefore, U.S. recuperability would be largely a function of its dispersed national development and transportation network. Survival of industry, agriculture, and manpower has not been provided for. This is a vulnerability.

In waging nuclear war over time, the opponent's passive defense measures can be offset to a degree by destruction of his early warning capability. Without adequate warning, neither shelters nor evacuation measures are of any value. However, this will not affect anything beyond population protection measures. Industrial hardening and stockpiling — material and agricultural — will remain generally unaffected.

The old saw, "In the valley of the blind, the one-eyed man is king," has its strategic nuclear parallel: always retain a survivable reserve force in nuclear warfighting. Obviously, the nation with the last remaining salvo possesses considerable leverage. Therefore, neither side can afford to launch its last missile. This fact alone could extend the nuclear exchange and associated termination negotiation pending guarantees that both sides are down to their last bolt and are incapable of building more.

The extent of economic paralysis resulting from a drawn-out nuclear exchange is incalculable. Catastrophic confusion from nuclear damage, ongoing civil defense efforts, and damage repair will impede industrial and conventional military mobilization on both sides. As a result, the war may be expected to continue as long as neither side is able to demonstrate the clear capability to prevail.

All three strategies are equally susceptible to Soviet nuclear countermeasures. Except for clear-cut nuclear superiority, there do not appear to be nuclear warfighting options that would alter that fact. Again, nuclear weapons destroy, but they do not recover territory, nor of themselves do they stop wars. That must be done with either military or political exploitation of their effects. Their principal impact will be to add to the friction of war.

NEGOTIATED TERMINATION

The other choice is to wage war for concessions; these can be either offensively or defensively oriented, depending upon the political aim. By virtue of a policy that seeks a goal short of an imposed settlement, the nation has chosen a negotiated conclusion of hostilities. In that arena, both military and diplomatic efforts must function in harmony although, at any given time, the emphasis may shift from one sector to the other.

Certainly the goal of war for concessions is the negotiation of a settlement under advantageous conditions. This course does not seek domination or dissolution of the opposition; indeed, the continued existence of an economically and politically solvent sovereign state may be essential for a stable peace within the construct of the regional or international power balance. Rather, such a war seeks concessions aimed at removing or reducing the factors contributing to the conflict. These will either improve the aggregate national strength of the ascendant power or diminish the threat posed by the opponent. Objectives may be geographic, economic, or political — in this latter instance, for example, disruption of alliances or removal of a governing faction that has adopted a threatening policy. The key goal is a peace, which, while achieving the limited war objectives of the ascendant power, does not provoke a resumption of hostilities at a later time by the disadvantaged power — in other words, a completed war.

However, a nation may be obliged to negotiate a conclusion to hostilities in an effort to cut its losses. The ultimate goal remains that of preservation of sovereignty and other fundamental national values; should aggregate national power be flagging, the government may be obliged to seek the best agreement it can get before all negotiating leverage collapses. If unable to secure satisfactory terms either by force of arms or by negotiation, the nation may be required to sue for peace under the best conditions attainable, with the ultimate purpose of buying time to regenerate national strength for reconstitution of losses under more advantageous conditions. Russia took this course of action to end its participation both in the Russo-Japanese War and World War I; since then, the Soviet Union has recovered the losses it ceded in those contests and more.

However, such a strategy requires both constancy of direction and public support over extended periods of time — perhaps 10 to 20 years or more. Additionally, concessions granted to achieve peace may impede national reconstruction; trade patterns and alliances may be disrupted, and rearmament limitations with attendant supervision may be imposed. Therefore, the nation may have to achieve relative economic self-sufficiency and to develop the means for veiling the reconstitution of its military strength, at least initially. Certainly this was effectively done in Germany between World Wars I and II. With today's means of surveillance, the task would be most difficult but by no means impossible. It would be somewhat easier for a nation possessing the advantages of geographic expanse and relative isolation.

Implicitly, a war for concessions requires conflict termination through political negotiation. Accordingly, negotiation must be integrated into the strategy for such a war. Moreover, military effort must be supportive of the negotiations but capable — at least to the perceptions of the opponent — of continuing under its own right to achieve an imposed settlement.

Hans Morganthau has laid out four fundamental rules of diplomacy pertinent to wartime negotiation: crusades are unproductive; objectives must support the national interest and must be supported by adequate power; the opponent's interests and perspective must be taken into account; and compromise is necessary on issues not of vital interest.[4]

The historic evidence regarding the political utility of crusades underscores Morganthau's first point. As to the second, the importance of clearly understood political and war objectives cannot be overstated. Admiral C. Turner Joy, USN, Senior Delegate of the United Nations Delegation to the Korean Armistice talks during their first year had this to say:

> We learned in Korea that crystallization of political objectives should precede initiation of armistice talks. All personnel in the United Nations Command delegation were aware of the chameleon-like character of American political objectives in Korea. . . . Thus the political objectives of the United States in Korea weathervaned with the winds of combat, accommodating themselves to current military events rather than constituting the goal to be reached through military operations.[5]

Whereas the selection of war objectives for military overthrow will tend to focus on the destruction or neutralization of the opponent's center of gravity, objectives for a war of concession will be somewhat more complex. First, a necessary goal is the elimination of the destabilizing factors that precipitated the problem. In some cases, these are geographic or economic; in others, they may be a matter of national outlook highly resistant to change because of historic and ideological reasons. This latter may be very difficult to alter; the next best solution is to establish barriers that impede its disruptive influences.

Next, the war objectives should alter advantageously the relative balance of power between the competing nations and should seek advantages that may serve as *quid pro quo* in the eventual negotiating process. Whether at the marketplace or the negotiating table, one never gets something for nothing.

Negotiating power in war springs from two sources. First, there is the leverage that obtains from military success. Capture of enemy territory not only provides geographic advantage for military and economic purposes; it also provides trading cards for negotiation. Destruction of sensors, naval power, and long-range airpower not only stresses enemy resource apportionment during war; it also exposes the enemy to unhindered reinforcement of the theater of conflict by the mobilized industrial and manpower war potential of the United States.

Said another way, a prerequisite for successful negotiations is military achievement. Do not expect to accomplish by negotiation what cannot be achieved by coercive force of arms. If you are unable to wrest control of territory from the enemy, do not expect him to give it away at the peace table.

From time to time, it has been suggested that a "shot across the bow," either in terms of a nuclear demonstration or some other communication of U.S. resolve, will bring the Soviets to their senses in an attack on Europe.[6] However, it must be recognized that in preparing for such an attack, the Soviet decision-making process has estimated NATO military capabilities, no doubt assigning a "worst-case" value to the prospective Allied response, and has elected to proceed, demonstrating a willingness to bear the probable effects. Therefore, time given to launching such a warning and awaiting Soviet overtures for peace discussions merely delays the marshaling of an effective NATO counter — especially if the enemy responds with a similar "shot" in another location, even another theater, thereby extending the dilemma and further delaying the decision to proceed with war. The Soviets can be expected to negotiate conflict termination in productive terms only when they have already achieved their war objectives or when they believe they are on the edge of military disaster.

The second source of negotiating leverage is military potential. It is not only actual military defeat that forces the opposing nation to consider negotiation for conflict termination; it is also the threat of further harm, of further loss, of further advantage accruing to the other side should the contest continue. In this regard, it is essential to exercise some control over enemy perceptions by selective destruction of his reconnaissance and intelligence sensors. The normal tendency in the face of uncertainty is to overestimate ("worst-case") enemy strengths and to overlook his weaknesses and vulnerabilities. Negotiating successfully will be far easier if the opponent believes you are strong and have unlimited resources.

The length of time required to negotiate conflict termination appears to be a function of the actual power differential between the opposing nations, actual power being the capability to employ force effectively coupled with the apparent will to do so. A review of negotiating periods attendant to recent contests with the Communists (Cuban missile crisis, six days; Korea, two years; Vietnam, four years) tends to support that view. The overwhelming U.S. conventional and nuclear power won the day in 1962; the threat of U.N. war expansion ostensibly achieved the Korean armistice; and the expanded air war is generally credited with having brought the North Vietnamese to a negotiated agreement — such as it was.

There is always the danger that the opposing side will employ such negotiations or even armistice as a cover for force reconstitution in preparation for subsequent military initiatives. Admiral C. Turner Joy provided both warning and advice pertinent to this problem:

> The armistice effort in Korea taught this: never weaken your pressure when the enemy sues for armistice. Increase it. . . . Do not stop fighting until hostilities have ended, not if you want an armistice with the Communists of acceptable terms within a reasonable period of time.[7]

A nation must have a sufficient actual power advantage over an enemy to prevail in a war for concessions, just as it must in a war for overthrow. The difference is twofold: first, the objectives are more modest in a war of concession and therefore more easily attained than overthrow; second, military effort must be employed not only for military gain but also for negotiating leverage. If the power differential is not decisive, the nation must be prepared for a long conflict, including extended negotiation. If the nation desires to prevail and shorten the conflict, it must be able to mass national power decisively in time in order to influence both the military and diplomatic efforts.

CAPITULATION

The next termination option is simple capitulation. This is both a political and military act wherein hostilities are terminated by mutual agreement and control of the loser's military capability is ceded to the victor. Thus, the capitulating power becomes defenseless and subject to the imposed conditions for peace; it has succumbed to the opponent's strategy for overthrow.[8]

According to Paul Kecskemeti, the nation's decision to surrender or fight on depends upon the perceived threat to its core values, some of which may be dearer than life itself.[9] Clausewitz, however, believed that defeat in war was never absolute and that subsequent political remedies might be found to ease its burden.[10] Both writers were clearly influenced by the events of their time, Clausewitz by the Prussian reverses and ultimate triumphs in the Napoleonic Wars and Kecskemeti by the German and Soviet victories in the twentieth century, which sought to change the political and ideological foundations of conquered nations.

There is some question whether a nation possesses any negotiating leverage in capitulation. On the surface, it would appear that it does not; yet, when one considers that war and politics must continually assess both the merit and cost of their objectives, there may indeed be concessions that the ascendant power will be willing to grant to encourage surrender rather than a fight to the death. Indeed, pressing for unconditional surrender may create additional expenses in manpower, time, and other resources that outweigh further prospective gain. Consider the efforts to gain Japan's acceptance of the terms of surrender established at Potsdam. Had the allies remained unbending on the issue of the sovereignty of the emperor, the conflict undoubtedly would have required invasion of the Japanese homeland for final resolution. The cost would have been enormous.[11]

ARMISTICE

The last type of conflict termination is the armistice or truce. It differs from the other forms of negotiated settlements in that the parties entering into a truce recognize it as a temporary measure rather than a final resolution; "a truce then is a respite in wartime, not a peace."[12] In effect, it is a device to buy time pending negotiation of permanent settlement or resumption of hostilities. A nation would be wise to consider the advantages accruing to the opponent before proposing or agreeing to a truce. Further, the parties should agree only to what can be supervised.

In reviewing the various conflict termination options, two are of further value in considering the development of prewar national strategy: the overthrow and the negotiated settlement under advantageous conditions. Only these two alternatives provide the means for achieving political and war objectives established at the outset of hostilities. As the rigors of war modify these objectives and the resources available to achieve them, other termination alternatives may have to be considered.

CONCLUSIONS

There is, of course, no way of predicting the exact nature of a major military contest between the United States and the Soviet Union. However, in thinking through such a conflict to its alternative terminations, one may reasonably draw several conclusions which affect the development of U.S. national strategy.

First, conflict termination is a proper focus for strategists both in war and before. It keeps the eye on the essential objectives — political and military — necessary to control war toward a complete and advantageous conclusion and, one hopes, a more stable international balance in the aftermath. To base U.S. national strategy and defense posture primarily on suppositions of how war may begin is both expensive and futile; resources are continually and belatedly spent in response to perceptions of the opponent's prospective initiatives. It is a course leading to deception and delusion, and it cedes the initiative and freedom of action to the other side. It would appear far more useful to develop a strategy focusing on the wherewithal to end conflict advantageously, thereby evading the prewar artifices and deceptions of an opponent, while holding before him the reality of retribution for initiation of war.

Second, in war between the United States and the Soviet Union, both sides possess the wherewithal for massive mutual destruction while withholding a survivable nuclear reserve. That, coupled with the geography and resources of the principals, renders total conquest of one side by the other as highly unlikely. Therefore, prospective war would most probably be terminated by some combination of military action and negotiation.

Third, there is little hope that such a conflict will be short. Shot wars (e.g., the Austro-Prussian War, 1866 — seven weeks; Franco-Prussian War, 1870 — eight weeks) are possible only when the defender lacks the resources or geographic wherewithal to extend conflict pending a more favorable outcome. Such is not the case with either the Soviet Union or the United States. Without an appreciation for the uncertain duration of conflict — and this uncertainty increases with the scope and stakes of the war — the nation risks inadequate preparation. Merely keeping abreast of the opponent is not enough; a nation must amass war power sufficient either for military overthrow or for leverage to support a negotiated settlement. Mutual exhaustion, of itself, does not eradicate the requirement to resolve the precipitating issues. Unless these are solved in one fashion or another, the war is incomplete and will erupt again when both sides have recovered. That would appear to be the significant strategic lesson to draw from the Arab-Israeli dilemma.

Fourth, as the war will probably be of extended duration and considerable destructiveness, the United States will require strategic leverage to prevail by coercive force of arms. Fortunately, such elements of leverage exist, and their identity will be no surprise to any student of war or military history. They are

Well defined and pertinent political and war objectives. Once a policy of war is adopted, either by choice or by imposition, the nation must ensure that its resources — which are not endless — are being employed wisely to achieve a politically useful conclusion. This is the task of the president. Although he has many to advise him, he alone is ultimately responsible to the electorate.

Strategic and tactical excellence. The issue will be decided by employing capabilities rather than strictly qualitative and quantitative factors. In this regard, development of national strategic and military strategic expertise requires special consideration; the art and science of winning wars demands a broader perspective than that required to win battles or campaigns.

Security and deception in order to achieve economy of force, concentration, and surprise. Selectively controlling Soviet wartime perceptions of U.S. capabilities and intentions will require a coordinated global counterreconnaissance and counterintelligence capability as well as a sophisticated approach to deception.

An effective mobilization base capable of generating the wherewithal to mass national power in time for decisive employment. The cost of maintaining standing forces to defend against every prospective Soviet initiative is prohibitive. Standing forces should be long-leadtime items (ships, aircraft, and infrastructure) and forces necessary to respond immediately to limited contingencies. The bulk of the major war capability must be developed in the course of war. Only then will the U.S. electorate countenance such expenditures for national defense. This requires attention to manpower and industrial preparedness.

The ability to conserve forces, the national power generation base, and critical resources. Conservation requires more attention to a damage-limiting effort, particularly civil defense, industrial hardening, stockpiling, and preserving an adequate nuclear reserve.

Fifth, relative geographic insulation and a strong economic base equip the United States with the wherewithal to continue the war as long as necessary to weaken the Soviets before massing power in time to prevail. The first phase of any war will generally feature gains by the aggressor and losses for the defender. However, what is more important is winning the last phase of the war. If time is to be of use to achieve that end, it must be incorporated into the strategy.

Certainly any strategy pitting the industrial flexibility of the United States against that of the Soviet Union (and a long war does) gives an advantage to the United States. Even in terms of prewar deterrence, it is not the short, cataclysmic war that inspires the most dread; it is the prospect of a long, persevering, grinding war that is most destructive of a nation's social order. And, when good and sufficient cause is presented, it is the type of war that the United States can — and has — waged successfully.

Finally, the ability of a nation to prevail in such a contest depends on the preparations it has made before the fact. The attempt to stave off conflict by presenting the illusion of strength, or at least the high risk of initial failure by the attacker, is neither a new policy nor a particularly successful one. The Wall of China and the Maginot Line stand as mute testimony to that fact. Some 450 years ago, Niccolo Machiavelli counseled, "One should never risk one's whole fortune unless supported by one's entire forces, and therefore the mere guarding of passes is often dangerous."[13] That is reasonable advice even today.

NOTES

1. Carl von Clausewitz, *On War*, trans. O. J. Matthijs Jolles (New York: Random House, 1943), pp. 20–21.

2. B. H. Liddell Hart, "Marines and Strategy," *Marine Corps Gazette*, July 1960, p. 12.

3. *United States Military Posture FY 1986*, The Organization of the Joint Chiefs of Staff, p. 32.

4. Hans J. Morgenthau, *Politics among Nations: The Struggle for Power and Peace*, 6th ed. (New York: Alfred A. Knopf, 1985), pp. 584–88.

5. Admiral C. Turner Joy, USN (Ret), *How Communists Negotiate* (New York: McMillan, 1955), p. 173.

6. *Annual DOD Report, FY 1978*, p. 83.

7. Joy, p. 166.

8. Paul Kecskemeti, *Strategic Surrender: The Politics of Victory and Defeat* (Stanford: Stanford University Press, 1958), pp. 7, 11.

9. Ibid., pp. 13–14.

10. Clausewitz, p. 8.

11. Kecskemeti, pp. 194–206.

12. Hugo Grotius, *The Law of War and peace* (Roslyn: Walter J. Black, 1949), p. 421.

13. Niccolo Machiavelli, *The Prince and the Discourses* (New York: Random House, 1940), p. 178.

III

Low-Intensity Conflicts and the Soviet Challenge: Internal and External Dimensions

7

The United States and Unconventional Conflicts: Responses and Options

Sam C. Sarkesian

Over 150 years ago, Alexis de Tocqueville declared that the future of the world was in the hands of two nations.

> There are now two great nations in the world which, starting from different points, seem to be advancing toward the same goal: the Russians and the Anglo-Americans. . . . Their point of departure is different and their paths diverse; nevertheless, each seems called by some secret design of Providence one day to hold in its hands the destinies of half the world.[1]

True to de Tocqueville's insights, at the end of World War II the United States and the USSR emerged as the two central nations in influencing and determining the state of international security, and they remain so today. The fact that each superpower represents fundamentally different ideologies and political systems adds a particularly emphatic note to de Tocqueville's observation.

What is relatively new, but no less challenging, is *glasnost* and the Gorbachev era of the Soviet Union. On the one hand, the image of a peaceful and more "liberal" Soviet Union is emerging under the psychological campaign and public relations efforts of the Gorbachev team. On the other hand, Soviet strategy and its fundamental commitment to Marxism-Leninism retains the importance of continual conflict (not necessarily war) with the United States. Although the United States appears to be in a position to counter the Soviets and take initiatives in traditional areas of state-to-state relations and in strategic nuclear weaponry, it finds itself at a disadvantage in unconventional conflicts and in many relationships with the Third World. To be sure, the majority of Third World states seem to prefer close economic ties with the West. Nonetheless, the Soviet Union has found useful outposts in the Third World and bases for expanding its presence and influence. Given its historical record and its "active measures" strategy, the Soviet Union is likely to continue its policy and strategy, albeit in less visible form. What is not clear is the extent to which the Soviet Union and the United States are prepared to engage actively in unconventional conflicts in the coming decade. The experience of Afghanistan may well have convinced the Soviets that considerable influence and leverage can be gained through "active measures" rather than commitment of combat troops. The experience of Vietnam, on the other hand, may well have institutionalized in the United States a "Vietnam syndrome" in every Third World strategy. Nonetheless, unconventional conflicts are not likely to go away because of the presumed "peace is breaking out" phenomenon that emerged in 1988–1989.

The Soviet Union derives its advantage in unconventional conflicts and in dealing with the Third World from a number of sources. These are not limited to the secrecy associated with the closed Soviet system. Nor is it necessarily a reflection of more adept Soviet operational personnel. Although the soviet advantage includes these, it is also a result of a number of other factors resulting from the nature of the U.S. political system, the U.S. way of war, and the problems these create in policy and strategy.

These are best stated by de Tocqueville's observations of democratic foreign policy.

> The control of society's foreign affairs democratic governments do appear decidedly inferior to others. . . . Foreign policy does not require the use of any good qualities peculiar to democracy but does demand the cultivation of almost all those which it lacks . . . democracy finds it difficult to coordinate the details of a great undertaking and to fix on some plan and carry it through with determination in spite of obstacles . . . it has little capacity for combining measures in secret and waiting patiently for the result.[2]

What de Tocqueville concluded then is appropriate today. Indeed, it is clear that the United States finds it even more difficult to identify appropriate policy and undertake effective strategy in unconventional conflicts than in the whole range of foreign policy issues.

The issue of unconventional conflicts and strategy raises a number of troubling questions for the United States. How serious is the Soviet challenge? Should the United States respond? If so, how should it respond? What options and strategies exist for effective response? What are the best interests of the Third World?

CONCEPTUAL CONSIDERATIONS

Before we can begin to address these questions in some detail, there is a need to clarify the meaning and concept of unconventional conflicts. Some writers on unconventional conflicts insist upon skirting the issues surrounding concepts, policies, and U.S. politics regarding such conflicts. They presume these are clearly stated, understood, accepted, and interpreted by most Americans.[3] They further presume that concepts are simply intellectual exercises with little meaning to operational realities. But the fact is concepts are at the root of the problem facing the United States in unconventional conflicts. This is not simply a case of rhetoric. Concepts reflect the way problems are perceived and acted upon; they underpin policy and strategy.

Many U.S. analysts tend to conceptualize unconventional conflicts by such terms as low-intensity conflicts, special operations, guerrilla war, internal war, and small wars. Many also study such conflicts through conventional lens leading to distortions and incorrect diagnoses. All of this suggests that there are basic disagreements and differing perspectives within policy-making circles, the military, and the scholarly community. It is difficult to imagine how effective strategies and responses can be designed if there is lack of agreement, indeed, confusion, on just what it is the United States is supposed to protect and respond to.

Unconventional conflicts are not primarily small wars, nor are they military or intelligence measures specifically in support of tactical conventional operations.[4] Unconventional operations are also different from partisan operations, i.e., guerrilla forces operating under strict control of tactical commanders for the purpose of furthering the tactical success of conventional units.

Unconventional conflicts are designed to achieve a political goal without resort to overt aggression or the use of military instruments as primary in achieving that goal. Such conflicts are short of limited conventional war, political-military in content, and characterized by a mix of political, psychological, economic, and military means. The character of such conflicts has little to do with military order of battle or military strength. Additionally, the character of the battlefield and rules of combat are rarely determined by conventional armed forces; they are determined by the political-social character of a particular political system. What makes this especially complicated and complex is the fact that unconventional conflicts encompass terror, counterterror, revolution, counterrevolution, and the military and intelligence operations supportive of these strategies. In other words, in contrast to conventional wars of any magnitude, rarely are unconventional conflicts solely military in nature. Indeed, in the main, their final outcome usually rests on other than the capability of the military instrument.

In their most developed form, unconventional conflicts may be best described by their revolutionary component. Revolution is designed to overthrow the existing system in order to supplant it with a revolutionary one and establish a revolutionary order governed by a revolutionary elite. Some other aspects of unconventional conflicts, such as terrorism, may serve limited political purposes. Thus, in the larger sense, the purposes of unconventional conflicts range from very limited political goals to the overthrow of an existing system. Further, unconventional conflicts can be undertaken by groups challenging the existing system or by existing systems in response to threats or as a way to further their national interests.

In this respect, most, if not all, unconventional conflicts evolve from the instability and internal political dynamics of Third World states. This instability and propensity for internal conflict is best described by Heilbroner, who wrote years ago that "economic development is not primarily an economic but a political and social process. . . . The political and social changes required for economic development are apt to be revolutionary in nature."[5] In brief, instability and unconventional conflicts in Third World systems are, by and large, a result of struggles over control of the political system and all it suggests with respect to ideology, social order, and the character of the ruling elite. Although all unconventional conflicts are not necessarily triggered by the Soviet Union or its surrogates, they are likely to take advantage of the vulnerabilities such conflicts create in the existing system, including the specific Soviet goal of subverting the democratic nature of such conflicts. The Nicaraguan revolution of 1979 is an example of such subversion.

From the U.S. perspective, unconventional conflicts are also characterized by protractedness, operational ambiguity, and asymmetry. For the United States such conflicts are limited, but for the indigenous adversaries, these conflicts tend to be wars of survival and, as such, are total wars, with all that means in respect to effort, resources, and operational implementation.

The U.S. involvement in unconventional conflicts usually means operating in conjunction with third countries or with host regimes. In the larger sense, the Soviet involvement in unconventional conflicts may also include third states, but the nature of the Soviet system and its "grand" strategy are distinctly different from the U.S. system and strategy.

Thus, both the Soviet Union and the United States are involved in the Third World, not only in terms of traditional diplomacy and state-to-state relationships but in response to and initiation of unconventional conflicts. It is here that the Soviet Union poses a serious challenge to the United States.

The final point has to do with the definition of power projection. More often than not, most writers equate power projection only with the use of military power. As used here, the term is not simply the use of military power but the use of a variety of instruments and strategies to influence or shape the direction or orientation of a particular state, region, or group. Clearly, some of the most effective measures have little to do with the use of military power. They are more likely to be covert means and strategies employing psychological warfare and propaganda.[6]

THE NATURE OF THE SOVIET CHALLENGE

Over the past two decades, the Soviet Union has been active in Third World areas, particularly in trying to take advantage of internal instability and unconventional conflicts to further its national interests. Although there is a high degree of continuity in modern Soviet policy and strategy in dealing with the Third World, according to a number of scholars, they entered a new phase in the 1980s with the Gorbachev era. During the 1970s, Soviet power projections and expansion into Third World areas seemed to magnify with perceptions of U.S. indecisiveness and confusion.[7] Soviet decision makers appeared to believe that the impact of Vietnam and Watergate was debilitating to the United States.

Further, the Carter administration's ineffectiveness in dealing with the Soviet Union's power projection into a number of Third World areas had long-range implications, many of which are evident today in the attempts to establish Marxist-Leninist states in various parts of Black Africa, Central America, and the Middle East.[8] This Soviet power projection was pursued in spite of the Carter administration's attempt to create a high moral tone in U.S. foreign and security policy. Moreover, the Soviet Union's ability was enhanced by the neglect of U.S. human intelligence capabilities under Director of Central Intelligence Admiral Stansfield Turner. In the main, technological means were substituted for human means in the collection of intelligence. Yet, unconventional conflicts and the nature of the Soviet power projections into the Third World had more to do with the effectiveness of personnel on the ground and with a variety of strategies that were not easily susceptible to technological detection or analyses.

From the period 1975 through 1980, the Soviets not only projected their conventional military power into Third World areas but also supported the establishment of Marxist regimes in Angola, Ethiopia, and Mozambique. Additionally, they established close links with the new Sandinista regime in Nicaragua, a publicly declared Marxist-Leninist regime. But what was also a relatively new dimension was the use of Soviet surrogates and proxies. The Cuban military was deeply involved in Black Africa, and Eastern bloc countries became part of the overall Soviet penetration, presence, and influence in Third World states.[9]

The most visible and disturbing Soviet use of military force was its invasion and occupation of Afghanistan in 1979, to the shock of President Jimmy Carter. The Soviet use of Spetsnatz Forces in paving the way for the Soviet invasion was not lost on perceptive Western analysts.

Thus, in a matter of five years the Soviets had broadened their power projections from one almost totally focused on Europe and China, to a broad offensive extending to many parts of the southern hemispheres. Further, the Soviet Union established the basis for a "blue water" navy, magnifying its presence throughout the world.

Although some argue that Soviet power projections had diminished in the 1980s, following a policy of constraint and consolidation, a noted expert disagrees.

> The Kremlin did in fact employ its own military forces on regular occasions throughout the 1970s to influence and determine the course of events in the developing world. . . . Soviet use of military capabilities as an instrument of policy in the developing world during the 1980s has not diminished.[10]

Equally important, the Soviets were leaders in providing military assistance to the developing world in the 1970s, and they remain leaders in the 1980s. Although approximately 40,000 Cuban troops began withdrawal from Angola in 1989 flowing from the Namibia accord with South Africa, less visible forms of assistance and aid remain in place and are being expanded. Moreover, the Soviet-Cuban connection with Nicaragua and the revolutionaries in El Salvador seems to be well established. Indeed, quantities of HIND helicopters and armored vehicles from the Soviet Union gave visible evidence of the ties between the Soviets and the Sandinistas.[11]

A large body of literature provides compelling evidence of Soviet support for a variety of terrorists, although this may ease under Gorbachev. For example, in one of the more authoritative works on the subject, the author states, "This book is about war: the war which the Soviet Union is waging on the West — indirectly. In practical terms, international terrorism is power projection. It is the physical manifestation of a bid for power."[12]

In terms of the Soviet's "grand" strategy, unconventional conflicts and traditional forms of aid and assistance, as well as a variety of intelligence and political-psychological operations, are intermixed to maintain considerable pressure on the United States, the West, and Third World areas.[13] These active measures provide the Soviet Union with a degree of strategic flexibility that is difficult for the United States to counter. The Soviets have used diplomacy, public relations, psychological warfare (disinformation), mobilization of political fronts, and pseudo-peace groups with considerable skill, particularly since the ascension to power of Gorbachev, to place themselves on the side of peace. Anti-Western colonialism and an imperialist United States are key elements in the political-psychological campaign.

Soviet strategy is guided by the principles of conflict control and limitation. In the view of the Soviet Union, all means are acceptable short of direct confrontation with the United States. Further, no operations or involvement should be undertaken if there is a possibility of escalation leading to war. This strategy includes support of various revolutions and counterrevolutionary systems through a variety of proxies and surrogates and indirect methods common to unconventional conflicts. One authority concludes,

> During the remainder of this decade the United States will continue to encounter various low intensity challenges to its geostrategic, political, and economic interests in different regions of the Third World. Furthermore, the Soviet Union and its surrogates will continue to employ both political and paramilitary techniques to stimulate insurgency and terrorism.[14]

Reinforcing this campaign is the fact that the Gorbachev impact has influenced the thinking of some Americans, including some elected officials and policy makers who applaud the liberalization of Soviet politics. On reflection though, it may be best to heed the words of knowledgeable Soviet emigres. "As for the West, is it not embarrassing for people to be in such a hurry to applaud the Soviet Union for promising conditions that they themselves would not tolerate for a moment?"[15]

There is some agreement, nonetheless, that the Gorbachev era has brought with it important changes in internal Soviet politics. Further, these changes have had an important impact on Eastern Europe. It is also likely that the Soviet Union will follow a more accommodating foreign policy and a more cautious external policy posture. But, as one authority concludes,

> Preliminary indications are that Gorbachev is a follower of Andropov in policy toward the developing world as in other areas and that he will concentrate on internal economic development; but it would be foolhardy for anyone to predict with confidence the course of future Soviet policy.[16]

Even so, most feel that this will not lead to a political retreat, not even in Afghanistan, although, in 1989 Soviet forces did withdraw from Afghanistan. What all of this may mean is that the Soviets are seeking a period for consolidation and retrenchment. It is believed that this will be combined with a strategy to take advantage of targets of opportunity. Involvement in unconventional conflict appears to be part of Soviet long-term strategy and important to its policy goals.

According to one expert on the Soviet Union,

> In the Third World, rather than following a carefully drawn master plan, Soviet foreign policy seeks to hit targets of opportunity that promise to produce destabilizing ripple effects. Its overall guiding principle seems to be quite simple: the Soviet Union is committed to give support for political change everywhere in the world, except, of course, within its own realm.[17]

To be sure, the Soviets have had their failures such as in Egypt and in the Horn of Africa. Additionally, some consider the Soviet "migratory genocide" of the Afghans as a long-term strategic failure. With respect to the Soviet invasion of Afghanistan, some basic disagreements remain. While some argue that such an invasion was an aberration of Soviet policy, others argue that with respect to the Third World, "The lesson is unchallenged; the Soviets may enact this scenario elsewhere."[18]

The fact remains, given the nature of the Soviet system and its ability to maintain a degree of strategic flexibility, even under Gorbachev, such failures can be set aside, disguised, or concealed, at least publicly. Additionally, the Soviet Union has rarely hesitated to cut its losses and withdraw, if conditions warrant.[19]

To what end have the Soviets attempted to project their power in the Third World through unconventional conflicts? There appear to be at least three major purposes.[20] First, Soviet policy is to discredit the West and, in particular, to reduce or eliminate the presence and influence of the United States. Second, Soviet presence and the establishment of Marxist-Leninist regimes serve as strategic conduits for the extension of Soviet power and in fulfillment of the first purpose. Further, such regimes can serve as strategic bases for challenging the United States over a wide range of security issues.[21] Third, and finally, Marxist-Leninist regimes are likely to impose a political and social order with a certain set of values that are in direct contradiction to democracy and pluralism as known in the West. Even for some systems that have taken some steps in this direction, the China syndrome — brutal repression of pro-democracy forces in 1989, may well signal the limits of openness. Thus, the Soviet Union perceives that it has made a cumulative gain in its struggle with the United States. Further, the imposition of such a political order adds to the legitimacy of Marxist-Leninist ideology and reinforces the Soviet's presence and influence.

However, there are a number of constraints to Soviet power projections.[22] In broad terms these include external power relationships with the United States and its allies, internal issues, and Third World nationalism. All of these are important considerations, but the most pressing and threatening to the Soviet Union is the U.S. role. Interestingly enough, in the Gorbachev era, Soviet domestic economic problems add a particularly important constraint. But as noted earlier, the intensity of domestic constraints and the impact of *glasnost* on Soviet foreign policy directions and pursuits is not yet clear. One fact does seem clear, and that is the Soviet need for Western technology and financial support.

As a superpower, the USSR has legitimate interests in the Third World. As one writer notes,

Any assessment of the Soviet military role in the Third World has to take into account that some of Russia's activities are no different from that of other great powers and would be no different if the Soviet Union were a "capitalist" state . . . to grant legitimate involvement to one of the superpowers but not the other is somewhat hypocritical.[23]

Yet, it seems somewhat misguided to argue that Soviet policies, be they interventionist or otherwise, are no different from those of other powers. In our view, to equate the Soviet closed system, even under Gorbachev, with the open system of the United States, regardless of policy and strategy, is a gross distortion. The constraints and limitations imposed by open systems on its external operations is quantitatively and qualitatively different from those of closed systems. One need simply to point to the role of the U.S. Congress and the U.S. media in contrast to the role of the new Supreme Soviet and the Soviet media.

One Soviet expert puts it this way:

But what distinguishes the Soviet Union's performance in the world arena is its proven ability to totally consolidate all its efforts. In comparison with pluralistic Western nations, the Soviet Union has the advantage of a clenched fist over an open hand in promoting its foreign policy goals.[24]

Yet, Soviet involvement in the Third World must be analyzed carefully and cautiously. Much evidence suggests that Soviet power projections into the Third World are primarily a secondary effort and, indeed, may simply be diversionary. As one authority argues,

Although Soviet power projection forces have grown in recent years, the focus of Soviet doctrine and procurement continues to be on the "core." Heavy tank and motor rifle divisions suited for conventional warfare, rather than light divisions designed for rapid deployment to remote areas, continue to receive priority.[25]

Still, the Third World offers targets of opportunity for furthering long-range Soviet goals. Moreover, it is an article of faith in the Soviet Union that the United States and the West are extremely vulnerable in Third World areas and in responding to unconventional conflicts.

Finally, Soviet policy driving its strategy tends to be based on a zero-sums perspective. Whatever the United States loses, the Soviets gain; whatever the United States gains, the Soviets lose.

Underpinning all of this is a pragmatic dimension in which the Soviet Union will temporarily downplay ideology and conflict with the United States to achieve a particular goal for long-range benefits. In late 1987, for example, the Soviet Union developed friendly relations with Iran and established itself in the Persian Gulf. Thus, the Soviet Union legitimized its presence in an Islamic area, even while conducting a brutal campaign against a Moslem majority in Afghanistan.[26]

In contrast to Soviet policy and perceptions of the external world, Americans have a view that too often reflects self-images and an idealistic lens that distort the realities of international security issues and vital interests. Before examining U.S. strategy and responses to the Soviet Union, we need to review characteristics that flow from U.S. political culture.

U.S. POLITICAL CULTURE

The way Americans perceive the external world, their own system, and their individual character evolves from a unique political culture. This uniqueness is a result of the particular circumstances under which the United States was founded, settled, and expanded. Continental expansion, virtual isolation from Europe, and the view that Americans were "divinely ordained" for a special mission on earth shape the way Americans see themselves and, in the main, form the basis for their expectations. Thus, there is a religious as well as secular dimension to the political culture characteristic of the contemporary United States.

These are important determinants of U.S. policy, strategy, and capability in unconventional conflicts. Not only do mind sets evolving from the U.S. political culture perceive the world through "American lenses," but they make it extremely difficult to grasp the essence of unconventional conflicts.[27]

In this respect, the U.S. public is largely untutored in the nature of unconventional conflicts.* This untutored public extends into vast portions of the Congress and throughout large parts of the federal bureaucracy. The U.S. government, including the military, perceives conflicts of any type through conventional

---

*The concept of "untutored public" should not be construed as pejorative. This simply suggests that unconventional conflicts are complex, difficult, and often ambiguous and ambivalent affairs. This makes it quite difficult to clearly identify purposes, strategy, and the nature of the adversaries involved. Similarly, it is difficult to identify clearly the intent of the Soviet Union given its closed system (even under Gorbachev) and its ability to undertake a variety of secret initiatives.

The nature of the U.S. political system adds to the problems. The sharing and decentralization of power between branches of government, combined with a number of ambiguous legal and policy areas, invite disagreement and has lead to historical struggles between the executive branch and Congress. Since the end of the Vietnam War, Congress has reasserted itself into national security and foreign policy even though the first term of the Reagan administration blunted this reassertion, albeit temporarily. The War Powers Resolution, the various restrictions on intelligence activities, oversight of intelligence operations, and the Iran-Contra hearings are but a few examples of Congressional assertion and continuing conflict with the executive branch over national security policy. The continuation of Congressional assertion into matters of foreign and national security policy in the Bush Administration was well illustrated by the 1989 hearings and eventual rejection of John Tower as Secretary of Defense.

Further, the commitment to openness and free play of ideas creates an environment inviting debates and disagreements over policy and strategy. Openness demands a large degree of access to information by the public and the media. Yet, the very nature of unconventional conflicts often requires a degree of secrecy as well as implementation of special and covert operations. All of these tend to be discomforting, at the least, to notions of democracy.

The role of the media in the policy process is important in open systems in influencing public attitudes and in setting the public agenda. As is common knowledge, the role of a free press in open systems is well established and virtually sacrosanct. In the United States, the media, by and large, represent a particular political predisposition generally left of center of the political spectrum.[29] As such, most of the media elite tend to view U.S. involvement in unconventional conflicts from a particularly critical perspective. Indeed, many in the media are also untutored in the essence of unconventional conflicts. For most media elite, involvement in unconventional conflicts is perceived to be undemocratic. Thus, for example, much negative news was broadcast regarding U.S. support of the Duarte regime in El Salvador and in support of the Nicaraguan Freedom Fighters, but for many years little was said of the Soviet genocide in Afghanistan or the human rights violations of the Sandinista regime or of Castro's Cuba.

At the same time, there are those who identify all unconventional conflicts as crises. It is a short step from here to advocacy of the dispatch of U.S. armed forces to solve the "problem." Bordering on the precipitous, such advocacy adds to the confusing array of voices trying to shape U.S. strategy.

There are, to be sure, more complex and difficult political issues associated with making foreign and national security policy. But these few observations suggest that in times of unclear enemies and when important changes in policy and strategy are contemplated, it is difficult for any administration to develop consensus within the untutored public and among Congressional political adversaries. The problem is made more complex by the existence of interest groups who often advocate and lobby for policy in direct contrast to U.S. policy and strategy.

Those involved in U.S. policy making and conflict analysis add to the difficulties. There is a tendency on the part of many U.S. analysts and policy makers to compartmentalize Soviet policy and strategy initiatives, making it difficult to grasp the totality of Soviet strategy. The term "low-intensity conflict," for example, used by policy makers, both civilian and military, has a particularly military connotation. Applied to Soviet strategy, such a perspective lacks insights into the total dimensions of such strategy. The totality of Soviet strategy encompasses support not only for revolution, counterrevolution, and selected terrorist groups but also for a variety of nonmilitary means from military aid and assistance to diplomatic, political initiatives, and psychological warfare (all of these are part of Soviet active measures). Moreover, the Soviet Union's centralized and closed system underpins organizational structures and their functioning. This allows a central focus to organizational and operational implementation of strategy. Thus, the KGB, the Spetsnatz forces of the GRU, and the international arm of the CPSU can operate and implement a total Soviet strategy from a central point. The fragmented organizational structures and pluralistic power system in the United States have difficulty matching this focus.

Because of the persistence of the Vietnam syndrome, many Americans have difficulty developing a realistic understanding of the nature of the Soviet challenge and the essence of unconventional conflicts. Many in military and civilian circles tend to view all unconventional conflicts in terms of the Vietnam experience. Thus, involvement in Central America is viewed by some as another Vietnam, regardless of the geostrategic and political-psychological differences. Underpinning such views is the conviction that unconventional conflicts are no-win situations for the United States and that involvement will result in another Vietnam-type defeat.

These factors are part of the U.S. way of war. In the main, Americans see conflicts in terms of black and white.

Accordingly, wars begin by formal declarations or by bombing of U.S. battleships as occurred at Pearl Harbor in 1941. Wars are ended by formal signing of peace treaties as occurred on the U.S.S. Missouri ending the conflict with Japan. In brief, wars are fought against clearly identified enemies who are evil and who must be defeated absolutely. Thus, the policy is clear, the strategic goals are clear, and the U.S. people are mobilized to undertake a crusade against evil adversaries.

As Henry Kissinger wrote years go, "Our feeling of guilt with respect to power has caused us to transform all wars into crusades, and then to apply power in the most absolute way."[30]

In contemporary terms, rarely do conflicts begin and end neatly and precisely. There are many "shades of gray" to unconventional conflicts. But for most Americans, such matters fall outside the normal view of war. What makes matters even more complex is that Americans tend to categorize governing instruments the same way — the military is used only in time of war.

Adding to the difficulties, unconventional conflicts most often occur in Third World areas. Many Americans claim knowledge of the Third World, but few have developed the sensitivities and the language capability to understand and appreciate Third World cultures and their diversities. Moreover, a general lack of understanding by those along the entire political spectrum regarding the political dynamics and institutional instability created by the drive for "development" in the Third World tends to establish "either/or" positions. Those on the right tend to view all instability and unconventional conflicts as a Soviet design. Those on the left tend to view all revolutions against established non-Soviet regimes as nationalistic and democratic. And those in the center are presented with a confusing, ambiguous, and ambivalent set of principles and perceptions.

All of these complex external forces and issues, combined with the nature and character of the U.S. political system, present the U.S. public with a maze of policy views, directions, and alternatives. The result tends to undermine any common perspective and perpetuates a diversity of views, reinforcing a variety of political and psychological clusters making it difficult for any administration to develop a U.S. consensus on unconventional policy and strategy.

> Today, public-policy circuits appear to be dangerously overloaded. In frustration, many Americans now seek simple solutions to complex problems. They turn to repressive censorship, align themselves with narrowly focused special-interest groups, retreat into nostalgia for a

world that never was, succumb to the blandishments of glib electronic soothsayers, or — worst of all — simply withdraw completely, convinced that nothing can be done.[31]

U.S. POLICY

The conclusion by a group of distinguished scholars is a clear statement of broad policy goals that Western governments should adopt.

It is beyond dispute that the primary obligation of Western governments must be to defend their vital interests, to maintain a military balance, to protect and advance democratic and pluralistic values in the world, and to seek to strengthen the international system against the chaos and violence that threaten it.[32]

These policy goals have been stated in one form or another by a variety of U.S. presidents since the end of World War II. During periods of bipartisan consensus when disputes over policy and executive branch-Congressional disagreements usually stopped at "the water's edge," national security policy remained primarily in the hands of the president. Indeed, throughout history this generally has been the case, at least until the Vietnam War.

In the current period, while there may be some agreement among policy makers and members of Congress about the broad guidelines for U.S. national security policy, there is a great deal of serious disagreement regarding unconventional conflicts and the nature of the Soviet challenge. Thus, while many in Congress as well as in the executive branch may agree on broad policy goals, there are deep divisions over their specific application and strategic implementation. Part of this is a result of Congressional reassertion into policy making and strategy, and part is a result of the attempt by presidents to maintain and expand executive flexibility in national security issues. Further complications result from disagreements within the federal bureaucracy over policy and strategy and the fact that the U.S. military concentrates its efforts on mainstream issues and conventional skills.

Compounding the problem is the lack of a global vision regarding unconventional conflicts and the Third World. Only with the Reagan Doctrine (support of anti-Marxist revolution) combined with the Nixon Doctrine (self-help by those faced with Marxist-Leninist revolutions) was such a vision first articulated in rudimentary form. But this did not get beyond its initial phases and in light of the fallout of the Iran-Contra hearings in 1987, the Reagan Doctrine lost much of its credibility. Further, this doctrine did not develop the consensus required for the degree of political resolve, national will, and staying power for the protracted nature of unconventional conflicts. It is clear that the United States still lacks a reasonably effective and cost-effective strategy to deal with unconventional conflicts, not only to respond to possible Soviet active measures, but also to regional power struggles that affect U.S. national security interests.[33]

In any case, U.S. policy parallels the policy goals and obligations of Western governments stated earlier. These include protecting its vital interests, advancing democracy, seeking peaceful resolution of disputes, and helping establish an international order committed to democratic and pluralistic values. The problem for the United States has been, and continues to be, in interpreting these goals, developing domestic support, and translating them into strategic guidelines with respect to Soviet power projections and unconventional conflicts. As a result, policy either tends to be rhetorical or borders on the incoherent.

STRATEGIC GUIDELINES

Policy incoherency in unconventional conflicts leads to difficult strategic problems that are magnified by the apparent confusion regarding strategy as a concept. Some debate this matter, particularly within military and academic circles. As pointed out earlier, a number of academicians and policy makers presume that strategy can be designed with little reference to U.S. political culture and mind sets. They see little relationship between the domestic political environment, strategy, and operational capability. In our view, these academicians and policy makers are not only incorrect; they distort the concept of strategy to a narrow military dimension that is, in the main, the basis of U.S. weakness in unconventional conflicts.[34]

Strategy is more than the application of power to achieve national interests. It requires the application of intellectual analyses and insights. Strategy cannot be frozen in time and space. There must be a constant assessment of strategy and its application in specific circumstances. This requires knowledge not only of U.S. capabilities but also of the political-social and internal character of adversaries and allies. This process relies on a keen sense to assess and appreciate the intentions and strategies of adversaries and potential adversaries. In operational terms, effective U.S. strategy must be an effective intermix of a variety of instruments evolved from U.S. political culture.

In the context of U.S. political culture, strategy has been defined in a variety of ways such as political strategy, military strategy, and economic strategy. In the classical sense, strategy was defined as generalship and the ability to succeed in a clash of arms. In the contemporary context, "grand" strategy has evolved as "the coordinated employment of the total resources of a nation to achieve its national objectives."[35] But strategy is more than the design for the use of instruments and resources. In the words of one authority, it "is the use of power, but it is an exercise of the intellect rather than of pure muscle. Where the United States has failed to think and act strategically, it has been due to serious intellectual shortcomings."[36]

Another authority writes,

Perhaps the first step toward understanding U.S. strategy should be the realization that it can never be a static set of objectives, but must involve a dynamic process of defining, evaluating, and integrating the diverse interests and values of the American people. As a result, there may never be a definitive resolution. Instead, issues will continue to reassert themselves; problems will be dealt with, but rarely will they be solved with finality.[37]

It is this combination of the intellectual dimension with the need for flexibility and a dynamic process of analysis that many writers tend to overlook or ignore. They simply rush into issues of "how to do it," totally sidestepping the most difficult and important part of strategic thinking. Intermixed with the conceptual confusion over the meaning of unconventional conflict, is it any wonder that the United States has had such difficulty in defining what it is to achieve, how to go about doing it, and how to develop the necessary national will, political resolve, and staying power to respond to the Soviet Union in the realm of unconventional conflicts?

It is clear, however, that the United States cannot simply respond to Soviet initiatives or to those of other Communist regimes if it is to achieve its policy goals. In other words, the United States must develop a strategy of purpose that is not solely reactive. There must be policy initiatives and strategy designed to further U.S. policy goals in their own right.

Although the United States faces disadvantages in developing effective strategy in response to the Soviet Union, this is not to say that there are no reasonable options. Nor is it to suggest that the United States, or any open system, cannot develop an effective political-military posture in unconventional conflicts.

A litany of recommendations has been advanced, in this respect, ranging from public education to organizational changes. Many of these have been examined in a variety of studies.[38] Rather than review these here, suffice it to say, there is a need for an educated public, a more educated and sophisticated Congress, a more responsive and educated federal bureaucracy, and a U.S. military attuned to the challenges of unconventional conflicts. These are difficult enough to develop with respect to understanding unconventional conflicts. The design of effective strategy is no less difficult.

FIRST PRINCIPLES

One dimension of U.S. unconventional conflict strategy includes a series of principles that should guide the design of any involvement in unconventional conflicts. These First Principles include eight concerns.

First, unconventional conflicts cannot be viewed as a separate dimension isolated from the conflict spectrum or from the "grand" strategy of the United States.

Second, U.S. involvement must be shaped by the nature and character of indigenous political rule and system legitimacy. Appropriate strategic purposes must be aimed at the political-psychological and socioeconomic component of the indigenous system. This involvement must be based on an effective intermix of political, psychological, economic, and military means, depending on the strategic goal and the area in contention. U.S. strategy must never be conceived solely in military terms. The approach must be designed primarily as a measure for developing an effective and legitimate indigenous governing system.

Third, U.S. involvement must be designed to avoid the "Americanization" of the conflict. All visible efforts at regaining the initiative and restoring stability should rest with the indigenous system. U.S. involvement must remain low visibility (not necessarily low involvement) to ensure that the system being supported, or the groups being supported, remain primary instruments and credible to the indigenous environment.

Also, there may be instances in which visible U.S. support may be the "kiss of death" to indigenous leaders. Such support may erode the indigenous leader's legitimacy and image of independence while undercutting the ruling group's nationalistic credibility.

Fourth, determined efforts must be made to limit conflicts and avoid escalation. These efforts require a great deal of diplomacy with adversaries, antagonists, and allies, even while engaged in conflict. Further, the U.S. posture must be such that adversaries recognize the futility (or unacceptable risk) of broadening the conflict, and indeed, this U.S. posture must convince the adversaries to seek some political accommodation.

Fifth, strategic withdrawal must always be an option after initial involvement in unconventional conflict. Thus, there must be a constant reexamination of the strategy and identification of the best course that serves U.S. interests.

Sixth, conventional military forces are neither trained nor postured to engage effectively in unconventional conflicts. Rarely should they be used, except as a last resort strategy and only under clear strategic goals and vital interests that require direct U.S. control of the area. Effective involvement in unconventional conflicts requires an organizational structure and operational capability designed specifically for such conflicts. For the United States, this means Special Forces organization with the necessary training, planning, and doctrine to engage in unconventional conflicts. This military component must be committed to support a U.S. civilian structure designed especially for unconventional conflicts.

Seventh, an effective strategy for unconventional conflict must rest on clearly stated policy goals and strategic purposes. Although policy and strategy cannot be prisoners of public opinion polls or referenda, the requisite U.S. staying power requires understanding and support of the people.

Eighth, the intelligence function is critical for success in unconventional conflicts. This requires an effective intelligence system that spans both military and civilian components. Equally important, the intelligence function must not only collect necessary information; it must be capable of active measures such as penetration of an adversary's intelligence and political network, identification of its weaknesses, and the ability to exploit them.

The United States has found it difficult to follow these First Principles. Historically, successful engagement in unconventional conflicts has required a degree of sophistication and finesse that seems to escape the United States for reasons apparently inherent in the system and the U.S. way of war. Moreover, even when the U.S. military has successfully engaged in unconventional conflicts, it has soon forgotten the elements of success.[39] Lacking an institutional memory of such conflicts and persistent in its pursuit of conventional skills, the U.S. military has rarely been prepared for unconventional combat. Nor has it been able to provide the strategic or doctrinal sophistication to succeed.

The United States has needlessly handicapped itself in countering covert aggression by failing to develop and maintain the requisite professional expertise and other capabilities to deal with this threat. Specifically it has failed to acquire and sustain sufficiently professional capabilities for counterinsurgent, paramilitary, and special operations.[40]

There are some military professionals and civilian policy makers who are aware of such weaknesses. They are at the forefront in trying to develop a more effective U.S. strategy and organizational capability for unconventional conflicts.[41] Yet, these efforts have been frustrated by well-established institutional positions and conventional mind sets.

Although the First Principles should govern any U.S. involvement in unconventional conflicts, they create dilemmas in their operational implementation. For example, many consider U.S. involvement in unconventional conflicts to be low-cost and reasonably effective strategies, but there may well be high domestic political costs. Often such involvement requires covert operations and a high degree of secrecy. Moreover, there is no assurance that U.S. support of one group or another will be successful. The exposure of U.S. involvement and possible failures give political adversaries in the United States ample opportunity to challenge the credibility of U.S. policy. Exacerbating the problem is the fact that, in the main, the U.S. public tends to be unforgiving of failure.

Further, U.S. support of one group or another often is a choice between lesser evils. Thus, it is possible that none of the groups struggling against each other in a particular Third World area is "democratic" in the Western sense. However, it may well be the best strategy to support the group that is non-Marxist, even though lacking in democratic substance, in the hope that it will be more susceptible to U.S. influences moving it toward openness.

This point was well made years ago by Charles Burton Marshall. He wrote,

> For some people, it is hard to affirm commitment to a military cause except on a premise of unequivocal good arrayed against unmitigated evil. In combined efforts, this notion requires postulating an immaculate ally. The trouble is immaculate allies are fabled rather than real.[42]

Moreover, the United States is in a position of moral leadership that may well require it to be a counterbalance to

Soviet power projections. Moral leadership brings with it moral obligation and may necessitate support of groups opposing Marxist-Leninist regimes. The U.S. role as a superpower and its position as the central nation opposed to Marxist-Leninist systems makes its presence felt in one form or another in most parts of the world. In brief, the United States cannot distance itself from Soviet power projections through unconventional conflicts even if only on moral grounds. Therefore, to argue that it is immoral to support anti-Marxist revolutionaries is absurd. Such an argument is tantamount to accepting and legitimizing the establishment of Marxist-Leninist regimes that have "stolen" revolutions, especially when these regimes are supported by external Marxist-Leninist systems.

There is also a great degree of truth in the proposition that support of anti-Marxist revolutionaries not only raises the costs of Soviet power projections but also blunts, and may preclude, the extension of Marxist-Leninist revolutions. The preoccupation of the Sandinistas, for example, with the Nicaraguan Freedom Fighters may have prevented the Nicaraguan regime from exporting its Marxist-Leninist revolution. Moreover, the fact that the Nicaraguan Freedom Fighters have continued to exist for a number of years, most recently within Nicaragua itself, challenges the notion that the Sandinistas are totally effective in governing. Similar points can be made with respect to Savimbi's UNITA and the Mujahideen in Afghanistan. In terms of Afghanistan, one authority notes that resistance to the Soviet intervention has been accomplished at a low cost to the United States.

> Over the last four years, while we have made a single $15 million payment to Jonas Savimbi's UNITA, the Soviets have provided more than $2 billion in military assistance to the Communist regime in Angola and its 35,000 Cuban mercenaries.[43]

The same author points out that the U.S. assistance to the Mujahideen was "helping tie down well over 100,000 troops in Afghanistan."[44] There are other examples in Southeast Asia as well as in parts of eastern Africa. Indeed, it is probable that U.S. involvement in these conflicts has been, in no small measure, the cause for adversaries to seek "peaceful" solutions. For example, there seems to be some direct correlation between the supply of U.S. Stinger missiles to the Mujahideen and the Soviet decision to withdraw from Afghanistan. The use of Stinger missiles — a ground to air missile, caused considerable casualties among Soviet armed helicopters.

In any case, there must be a systematic and conceptual base upon which to build U.S. response to Soviet power projections and, more important, to develop strategy that is not a prisoner of Soviet initiatives. Such a strategy must anticipate potential threats to U.S. vital interests and design operational programs to blunt such threats. These, in turn, must be based on the larger view of U.S. policy underpinned by the recognition of the soviet challenge in the Third World. This is true even if this challenge is secondary to major Soviet concerns elsewhere. Further, both the United States and the Soviet Union as superpowers have legitimate interests in many parts of the world. Such interests do not necessarily lead to military intervention or evolve into unconventional conflicts. Indeed, such confrontations may be best resolved by the indigenous system in the Third World area or by "normal" diplomacy.

CONCLUSIONS

After all is said and done, the ascension of Gorbachev to power in the Soviet Union and the apparent changes taking place within Eastern Europe and in the Soviet Union cannot go unnoticed throughout the Third World. Some in the Third World are convinced of the obsolescence of Marxist-Leninism, others place their faith in economic forces compelling major changes in the Soviet Union. Still others fear a China syndrome emerging from the demands of Soviet nationalities and the historical ethnic animosities in the Caucasus. Yet, as of this writing, it has not been demonstrated that *glasnost* and the concept of a liberal democracy has been extended to Soviet national security and foreign policy and its outposts in the Third World.

It is also clear that the U.S. cannot simply respond to the Soviet policy. The interests and policies of regional powers and the challenges of Third World issues cannot be resolved simply because of the apparently more friendly and accommodating relationships between the U.S. and USSR, and European *glasnost*. The U.S. must deal with Third World issues and unconventional conflicts with policies and strategies in their own right. And until proven otherwise, this must include the possibility of involvement in unconventional conflicts, particularly in the Southern hemisphere. And to be reasonably effective, such involvement will need to be through an indigenous system and primarily by political-economic strategies that benefit indigenous systems and peoples.

Finally, the United States cannot simply wait for an unconventional conflict environment to evolve. Involvement before such conflicts develop (preventive phase) is the most effective and least costly strategy. But this requires a sophistication and maturity in national security policy that has yet to be demonstrated by the United States. As Clausewitz observed, ". . . in strategy everything is simple, but not on that account very easy."[45]

In light of the long historical involvement of the United States in unconventional conflicts and its more recent experience in Vietnam and Central America, however, it is not too much to expect (or ask), that the coming decade will see sophistication and maturity in U.S. response to Third World issues and unconventional conflicts. What makes this particularly important is the Gorbachev phenomena, assuming it lasts, which provides opportunities to resolve and respond to issues and conflicts in the Third World beyond what could have been imagined but a few years ago. It is time that the United States "Seized the Moment."[46]

NOTES

1. J. P. Mayer, ed., *Alexis de Tocqueville, Democracy in America*, trans. George Lawrence (Garden City, N.Y.: Anchor Books, 1969), pp. 412–13.

2. Ibid., pp. 228–29.

3. Response to the author's book, *The New Battlefield: The United States and Unconventional Conflicts* (New York: Greenwood Press, 1986), by some individuals reflects this perspective.

4. See the discussion in *The New Battlefield*, Chapter 2. The use of such terms as "small war," in the view of this author reflects a conventional perspective that ignores the essence of unconventional conflicts.

5. Robert L. Heilbroner, *The Great Ascent: The Struggle for Economic Development in Our Time* (New York: Harper & Row, 1963), pp. 17–18, 20–21. The lack of understanding of Third World political changes and the socio-economic environment, and the presumption that external forces make no difference in unconventional conflicts have led some scholars to develop what is being called cognitive model building assessments. Model building and classroom templates rarely capture the human dimension of unconventional conflicts. Additionally, without some understanding of the U.S. way of war and the fact that Third World modernization creates an environment extremely susceptible to unconventional conflicts, such scholars tend to develop a sterile approach to these conflicts. Indeed, to argue that too much is made of the "trauma of modernization" seems to reveal a lack of understanding of the sensitivities and challenges within the Third World arena. See, for example, D. Michael Shafer, *Deadly Paradigms: The Failure of U.S. Counterinsurgency Policy* (Princeton: Princeton University Press, 1988). The use of the term "counterinsurgency" reveals the author's approach. Indeed, after criticizing the lack of progress in addressing what he calls "counterinsurgency," the author fails to add anything new to the analysis of such conflicts.

6. See, for example, the discussion in Rajan Menon, *Soviet Power and the Third World* (New Haven: Yale University Press, 1986), pp. 74–88.

7. The assessment of Soviet policy is categorized into phases by many authorities. See, for example, Menon, pp. 1–18; and Alex P. Schmid, *Soviet*

Military Interventions since 1945 (New Brunswick: Transaction Books, 1985), pp. 73–85.

8. Uri Ra'anan, Francis Fukuyama, Mark Falcoff, Sam C. Sarkesian, and Richard Shultz, Jr., *Third World Marxist-Leninist Regimes: Strengths, Vulnerabilities, and U.S. Policy*, Special Report (Washington, D.C.: Pergamon-Brassey's, September 1985).

9. Alvin H. Bernstein, "Insurgents against Moscow," *Policy Review* 41 (Summer 1987): 28.

10. Daniel S. Papp, *Soviet Policies toward the Developing World during the 1980s: The Dilemmas of Power and Presence* (Maxwell Air Force Base, Alabama: Air University Press, December 1986), p. 157.

11. Bernstein, p. 27. See also Uri Ra'anan, "Political Aspects of 'Protracted Warfare'," paper delivered at the annual meeting of the American Political Science Association, September 5, 1987, Chicago, Ill.

12. Roberta Goren, *The Soviet Union and Terrorism* (Boston: George Allen & Unwin, 1984), p. 1.

13. Soviet theoreticians and policy makers do not accept the concept of unconventional conflicts. They feel that such a concept is an imperialistic notion derived from Western interventionist policies. Considering such notions as a pseudo-science, the Soviets define such matters in terms of wars of national liberation and local wars. For an excellent view of Soviet perceptions, see Daniel S. Papp, *Soviet Perceptions of the Developing World in the 1980s: The Ideological Basis* (Lexington, Mass.: Lexington Books, 1985).

14. See Richard Shultz, Jr., "Countering Third World Marxist-Leninist Regimes: Policy Options for the United States," in *Third World Marxist-Leninist Regimes*, Ra'anan et al., p. 125.

15. Vasily Aksyonov, Vladimir Bukovsky, Edward Kuznetsov, Yuri Lyubimov, Vladimir Maximov, Ernst Neizvestny, and Aleksandr Zinoviev, "Is 'Glasnost' a Game of Mirrors?" New York *Times*, March 22, 1987.

16. Francis Fukuyama, "Military Aspects of U.S.-Soviet Competition in the Third World," in *East-West Tensions in the Third World*, ed. Marshall D. Shulman (New York: W. W> Norton, 1986), p. 207.

17. Vadim Medish, *The Soviet Union*, 2d rev. ed. (Englewood Cliffs, N.J.: Prentice-Hall, 1985), p. 323.

18. Jiri Valenta, "The Soviet Invasion of Afghanistan," in "The Soviet Invasion of Afghanistan: Three Perspectives," Vernon Aspaturian, Alexander Dallin, and Jiri Valenta, ACIS Working Paper No. 27, Center for International and Strategic Affairs, September 1980, p. 18. For one of the most detailed accounts, see J. Bruce Amstutz, *Afghanistan: The First Five Years of Soviet Occupation* (Washington, D.C.: National Defense University Press, 1986). See also Gerard Chaliand, *Report from Afghanistan* (New York: The Viking Press, 1982); and John W. Coffey, "The Afghan Slaughter," in *This World: A Journal of Religion and Public Life* 16 (Winter 1987): 110–23.

19. See, for example, Papp, *Soviet Policies toward the Developing World*; and Bruce D. Porter, *The USSR in Third World Conflicts: Soviet Arms and Diplomacy in Local Wars, 1945–1980* (Cambridge: Cambridge University Press, 1984).

20. For a detailed examination, see Papp, *Soviet Policies toward the Developing World*, pp. 27–38.

21. Bernstein, p. 28.

22. For a detailed examination, see Papp, *Soviet Policies toward the Developing World*, pp. 38–46; and Menon, pp. 238–54.

23. Schmid, p. 151.

24.   Vadim Medish, *The Soviet Union*, 3rd ed. (Englewood Cliffs, N.J.: Prentice-Hall, 1987), p. 322.

25.   Menon, pp. 249–50.

26.   See Bernstein and Amstutz.

27.   For a detailed discussion on these issues, see the author's two volumes, *America's Forgotten Wars: The Counterrevolutionary Past and Lessons for the Future* and *The New Battlefield*. It is unfortunate that some academics and policy makers try to examine strategy while ignoring the importance of U.S. politics, political culture, and domestic political attitudes. This is not only a dangerous perspective; it also distorts the concept of strategy to the point of sterility. Indeed, one book reviewer argued that U.S. politics and the relationship between Congress and the executive branch are irrelevant to strategic considerations! Fortunately some analysts recognize the important linkage and consider it primary in examining strategy.

28.   Fukuyama, p. 210.

29.   For an analysis of the media elite and their political predispositions, see Sam C. Sarkesian, "Soldiers, Scholars, and the Media," *Parameters* 17 (September 1987): 77–87.

30.   Henry A. Kissinger, *Nuclear Weapons and Foreign Policy* (New York: W. W. Norton, 1957), p. 427. See also Charles Burton Marshall, "Morality and National Liberation Wars," *Southeast Asian Perspectives*, No. 4, December 1971.

31.   Malcolm G. Scully, *The Chronicle of Higher Education*, November 25, 1981, pp. 1, 12.

32.   Shulman, p. 224.

33.   Bernstein, p. 19.

34.   See note 19.

35.   Bruce Palmer, Jr., "Strategic Guidelines for the United States in the 1980s," in *Grand Strategy for the 1980s* ed. Bruce Palmer, Jr. (Washington, D.C.: American Enterprise Institute, 1978), p. 73.

36.   Gregory Foster, "Missing and Wanted: A U.S. Grand Strategy," *Strategic Review*, Fall 1985, p. 23.

37.   Terry L. Heyns, "Introduction to Key Issues in National Strategy," in *Understanding U.S. Strategy: A Reader*, ed. Terry L. Heyns (Washington, D.C.: National Defense University Press, 1983), p. 13.

38.   See, for example, Shulman; Heyns; and William A. Buckingham, Jr., ed., *Defense Planning for the 1990s* (Washington, D.C.: National Defense University Press, 1984).

39.   The concept of forgotten wars and forgotten lessons is discussed in the author's book *America's Forgotten Wars*. For example, the Vietnam War is listed as a forgotten war, not because Americans do not remember it, but because the U.S. military and others have "forgotten the lessons of unconventional conflict evolving out of Vietnam. Yet, there are many academicians, civilian policy makers, and military professionals who do not seem to be able to grasp the essence of this view. They are glued to conventional concepts and narrow based perspectives that see conflicts only in terms of 'World War II' syndromes."

40.   Stephen T. Hosmer, *Constraints on U.S. Strategy in Third World Conflicts* (New York: Crane Russak, 1987), p. 152. Yet, one authority argues that,

> American prospects on the periphery in the contest for the Third World are not as poor as many have supposed. The rules by which the Great Game is played do not inherently favor the Russians. The United States did poorly at this competition in the 1970s because we ceased to believe that it made any difference and found it rather unseemly in any case, thus shunning the tools that were available to

us (David C. Hendrickson, *The Future of American Strategy* [New York: Homes & Meier, 1987], p. 186).

41. These include a number of senior officers of the U.S. Southern Command and most professionals in U.S. Special Forces units.

42. Charles Burton Marshall, "Morality and National Liberation Wars," *Southeast Asian Perspectives*, No. 4, December 1971.

43. Bernstein, p. 28.

44. Ibid. See also Amstutz.

45. Anatol Rapoport, ed., *Clausewitz, On War* (Baltimore, Md: Penguin Books, 1968), p. 243.

46. "U.S. Interests in the 1990s: Seize the Moment," The American Assembly, Columbia University. Report published by the Seventy-sixth American Assembly, April 20–23, 1989, Arden House, Harriman, New York.

8

The Soviet Navy in the Third World

Roger Hamburg and John Allen Williams

INTRODUCTION: MILITARY INTERVENTION IN THE THIRD WORLD

Considering the costs of miscalculation, it is hardly surprising that the major powers exercise great restraint in their relations with one another. Rarely will a great power pose a military challenge to the core interests of another. Although the widespread dispersal of nuclear weapons since 1945 may have made the world a more dangerous place, large-scale war between the major powers has also been avoided.

The most likely area of potential military conflict is the Third World. To be sure, the more powerful countries do occasionally challenge one another there, but indirectly. For example, the United States fought in Vietnam against an enemy supplied in part by the Soviet Union, and the situation was reversed as the Soviet Union struggled in Afghanistan against a Mujahideen resistance supplied in part by the United States. U.S. and Soviet interests in the Third World are also furthered by other forces acting as proxies (as well as furthering agendas of their own), such as the Cubans in Angola and the Contras in Nicaragua.

Frequently it is the Third World countries that are in conflict. The Iran-Iraq war claimed hundreds of thousands of lives and proved most difficult to stop. India and Pakistan are still not resigned to sharing the South Asian subcontinent peaceably. Vietnam continues its domination of the Indochinese peninsula. In many cases there is some great power involvement, but the underlying dynamic is not the East-West struggle. U.S. and Soviet participation has generally been indirect and incidental, with the arguable exception of the U.S. Navy's operations in the Persian Gulf.

But frequently major powers intervene directly in the affairs of Third World countries, in struggles that may or may not relate to conflicts with other major powers. To date it has been primarily the Western powers that have done this. The United States intervened in Guatemala in 1954 to unseat leftist President Arbenz. The British and French cooperated with the Israelis in 1956 to try to seize the Suez Canal from Egypt after it was nationalized by President Nasser. U.S. Marines landed in Lebanon in 1958 in support of a pro-Western government there. U.S. troops also intervened in the Dominican Republic in 1965 and in Grenada in 1983. British forces recaptured the Falklands/Malvinas Islands from Argentina in 1982. French forces assisted the military of Chad in repulsing Libyan troops in 1987.

In contrast to the interventions of the Western powers, the Soviets have been comparatively inactive. With the major exception of Afghanistan, large-scale military actions with Moscow's own forces have been limited to preserving her East European buffer. Given the brutality of such intervention when it has occurred, one suspects that this relative inactivity is not due to Soviet squeamishness about using force when thought necessary. The explanation is more likely to lie in the Soviets' perceptions of their national interests and the instruments available to further them.

Our purpose here is not to make moral judgments about military intervention but to describe Soviet interests and naval capabilities for intervention in the Third World and to predict future developments. We begin with some ideological considerations about the importance of the Third World for the Soviets.

IDEOLOGICAL CONSIDERATIONS

Not surprisingly, Soviet perceptions of the Third World are shaped by ideology, including the Soviet view of internal "contradictions" in the Third World and the need for assistance in accelerating the historical process.

U.S attempts to intervene in the Third World are seen as interference with a "natural, law-directed process." U.S. opposition to revolutionary movements and Soviet-supported regimes creates sharp centers of tension. Regional conflicts are kindled by "imperialist reaction." The United States uses crises as a pretext to prop up reactionary regimes, preserve access to raw materials such as oil, and keep the Soviet Union out. There would be no tension if the "imperialists" did not create it by attempting to suppress national liberation movements and seeking to reestablish their former control.

Revolutions develop out of contradictions within society. Depending upon regional and international conditions, these contradictions may not become manifest but remain in latent form indefinitely. Once having occurred, revolutions must defend themselves and protect their new society from both internal and external class enemies. The Soviets seek easing of tensions, but long-term and deeper tendencies cannot always prevent the surprise appearance of a threat. In the Soviet view, Soviet assistance to victims of aggression (Angola, Ethiopia, Vietnam, Iran) is compatible with a desire to settle such conflicts peacefully.[1]

PROBABLE SOVIET NAVAL OBJECTIVES
IN THE THIRD WORLD

With its primary emphasis on land power and those naval capabilities useful in the direct defense of the homeland (and ensuring the survivability of the submarine-based strategic retaliatory forces — the SSBNs), the Soviet Union has been less concerned until relatively recently with building a "blue water" navy that could challenge the U.S. Navy for influence in the Third World.

Increased Naval Presence

In the 1960s opportunities were utilized to deploy naval forces in noncontiguous areas in the Mediterranean, Caribbean, and Pacific Ocean. To quote Admiral Gorshkov:

Friendly visits by Soviet seamen offer the opportunity to the people of the countries visited to see for themselves the creativity of socialist principles in our country, the genuine parity of the people of the Soviet Union and their high cultural level.

In more specific military terms,

Further growth in the power of our navy will be characterized by an intensification of its international mission. While appearing within our armed forces as an imposing factor in regard to restraining imperialist aggression and ventures, at the same time the Soviet navy is a consolidator of international relations.[2]

Gorshkov stresses this "sea presence." It can win friends and demonstrate Soviet power. It can be deployed in a time of crisis to reinforce client states psychologically, threaten Soviet enemies, and signal Soviet intentions to oppose U.S. moves, as in the October 1973 war in the Middle East. Naval forces can demonstrate resolve without the irreversible signalling of commitment provided by ground forces. Bolstering existing (if modest) naval forces or adding them where none previously existed can have major psychological effects. Navies, in Gorshkov's view, can surprise, intimidate, and lower the morale of the enemy and thus secure objectives without fighting.[3] Further,

> The Soviet navy, in the policy of our party and state, acts as a factor for stabilizing the situation in different areas of the world, promoting the strengthening of peace and friendship between the peoples and restraining the aggressive strivings of the imperialist states.[4]

Contribution to General War

Soviet thinking since the early 1980s has considered the possibility that a general war with the United States might not become nuclear but instead might have the character of an extended conventional war. This war could well extend over a protracted period and include the Third World as important theaters.[5] The increased Soviet interest in the Third World may be accounted for in part by a perceived need to create an expanded defense perimeter as the second phase of a world war in which they were victorious in Europe but unable to agree on peace terms with the West.[6]

Access to Port Facilities

The Soviet Union has been able to gain political influence from still modest naval assets in the Third World. The Soviets work by a process of accretion, usually establishing a naval presence in "operations in support of state interests," as in the Mediterranean in 1958 as the Soviets became active in Egypt; in the Caribbean in the 1960s, reflecting increased Soviet influence in Cuba; in the Indian Ocean in 1969, after operations in Somalia; in West Africa in 1970, after operations in Guyana; and most significantly in 1979 in Vietnam.

The Soviets focus on access to one or two nations in an area to gain influence and access to port facilities. After gaining such access, they can interact more frequently and intensively in the area. Permanent access to a port facility, as in Vietnam, brings significant benefits. Supplies need not be shipped from Soviet ports. Regional ports can repair and maintain Soviet ships. This makes possible an increase in the Soviet naval force in a given area that could not be accomplished without access to such ports. Larger forces mean more extensive naval operations, greater reaction to crises, more port visits, and more extensive influence. A naval presence helps deter actions adverse to Soviet interests, even in the absence of combat operations. This pattern occurred in the June 1967 war in the Middle East and recently in the Caribbean Sea where the Soviets can test U.S. defenses and show support for Cuba and other "progressive" states.[7]

Vietnam is the best example of this accretion strategy. Here Soviet capabilities and a strong political intention to counterbalance Japan, the People's Republic of China, and the United States, as well as break out of encirclement, came together and coincided with the interests of the local state. It exemplifies what Gorshkov implied: there is only one exclusively land theater — Europe — and except for it the navy would play the dominant role.

There is a large air and naval presence at Camranh Bay, Da Nang, and the South China Sea. The Soviets have foreign basing rights at Camranh — major air and naval facilities and a standing naval presence of 30 ships and submarines in the South China Sea. There is a buildup of SS-20 intermediate-range ballistic missiles and the likelihood of a larger, mobile SS-25 missile, which could threaten Australia (although negotiations may affect these missile deployments in ways not yet apparent). The Soviets have used Badger bombers (possibly to be replaced by Backfires with longer ranges) and have flown reconnaissance missions in the vicinity of U.S. bases at Clark and Subic Bay in the Philippines. They have also conducted amphibious missions 100 miles from the Chinese border in the vicinity of Hanoi.

These forces could be used in combat operations in the South China Sea in the initial stages of a general war.[8] They could be used to protect Soviet ballistic missile submarines and could deny unimpeded use of the sea (sea denial) to U.S. cruise missile forces and carrier battle groups. They could also intersect sea lines of communication (SLOCs) to South Korea and Japan. At a minimum, they could require a substantial diversion of United States naval forces.[9]

The Defense of Overseas Assets

Defense of distant assets will become increasingly important as the Soviets acquire allies and client states abroad. Especially important will be protecting the growing Soviet merchant fleet that carries cargo via the Indian Ocean between the Soviet Union and ports in the developing world and between the Black Sea and Pacific ports of the Soviet Union. The utilization of the fishing fleet often means the use of facilities in the developing world, much to the distress of Western navies.[10]

Intelligence Collection and Reconnaissance

Soviet merchant fishing and naval vessels monitor the operation of U.S. and other Western naval units. They follow U.S. missile tests and attempt to track U.S. fleet ballistic missile submarines. (There is no public evidence that attempts to trail SSBNs have ever been successful.) Operating areas included the Mediterranean in the 1960s, the Indian Ocean in the 1970s and 1980s, and the South Pacific in 1985. Moscow has major intelligence gathering sites in Cuba, Algeria, Libya, Ethiopia, South Yemen, and Camranh Bay, Vietnam.

Diversion of U.S. Naval Strength

Soviet deployments create uncertainty in the United States in a wartime situation, especially because U.S. naval forces have more ambitious sea control functions than the Soviet navy. The latter practices sea denial, including local sea control in areas contiguous to the Soviet Union. An example of attempted sea denial is the Cuban and Soviet naval presence in the Caribbean, which preoccupies U.S. units and detracts from the U.S. ability to project forces closer to the centers of Soviet power and to the Middle East and Persian Gulf. As Admiral Gorshkov said, enemy forces can be "pinned down" in secondary sectors so that they would be "paralyzed or constrained in their operations" and "hampered from interfering in an operation."[11]

Assertion of Global Power Status

Asserting global power status involves emulating the post-World War II U.S. ability to intervene globally, which in Soviet eyes made the United States a true superpower. The key function is still defense, with the external perimeters advanced. In the Soviet view, the United States has carriers and powerful amphibious power. Washington operates in close proximity to Soviet shores in the Mediterranean, the Sea of Japan, the Sea of Okhotsk, and off the shores of the Kamchatka Peninsula. The U.S. Navy is designed to strike at land- as well as sea-based targets. In the U.S. view, this compensates for Soviet advantages as a land power with internal lines of communication. The Soviets respond,

So it was only natural for the USSR to respond to the U.S. Navy's growing strike capability and its moving closer to the Soviet frontier by providing the Soviet navy with ships, aircraft and weapons capable of countering the threat posed by American naval forces. To defuse a potential threat from American aircraft carriers, ships armed with long-range missiles and amphibious forces, and to discover their intentions in good time, a Soviet naval presence must be maintained in those parts of seas and oceans from which the United States threatens or may threaten the Soviet Union.[12]

SOVIET NAVAL CAPABILITIES

An understanding of the prospective role of the Soviet navy in the Third World must include an appreciation of geography. The Soviet Union is a continental power with interior lines of communication and is almost autarkic in its resource self-sufficiency.[13] Militarily it has significant concerns near home, and it has little necessity to move beyond its borders. The four Soviet fleets are widely separated geographically and are restricted by ice and/or U.S. allies nearby. The Northern Fleet, whose job it could be to prevent the resupply of Europe, must travel past NATO member Norway to get to the shipping lanes and must pass through choke points guarded by the submarines of the United States and possibly other nations. The Baltic Fleet could provide amphibious support to the northern flank of a NATO-Warsaw Pact engagement but would face severe difficulty reaching the open ocean. The Black Sea Fleet has similar problems getting to the eastern Mediterranean. The Pacific Fleet, the Soviets' fastest growing and arguably the most powerful, is restricted by occasionally ice-bound bases and the presence of U.S. bases in Japan and Korea — in addition to the considerable forces of Japan.

Even in areas adjacent to the Soviet Union, Soviet naval forces are basically reactive. There is no effort or present capability to conduct offensive operations deep into the Mediterranean. The Black Sea Fleet cannot project naval power far into the Mediterranean in a war, but it could launch anti-SLOC operations with naval air units stationed in Syria and Libya and complicate and confound U.S. forces. It cannot conduct far-ranging offensive actions. Without major air or surface naval units, it must rely solely on submarines for the latter.[14]

At present the Soviets can deny the United States unimpeded access to areas where it was not previously challenged. Moscow can display naval power, react to local incidents, and oppose weak opponents at sea. It could use the navy in a strategic war, but it cannot at present fight a long conventional war at sea or oppose superpower intervention locally. But the significance of a "sea denial" capability should not be minimized, and an actual clash at sea always carries with it the possibility of escalation to a nuclear exchange, with Soviet naval forces acting as tripwires.[15] This is analogous to U.S. ground forces in Berlin, or other areas where the Soviets are stronger, that deter attack by their presence more than by their military capability.

Aircraft Carrier Development

The key indicator of Soviet intentions and future capabilities in the Third World may be the degree of development of aircraft carriers capable of handling high-performance aircraft. Without organic air power, fleets must rely on land-based aircraft for reconnaissance, self-defense, and land attack. Soviet naval aviation can be very potent, especially close to the Soviet homeland, but it is no substitute for deployable aircraft that can accompany a fleet wherever it sails. The U.S. Navy assumes the utility of such ships not only for power projection against the Soviet Union but also for actions in the Third World.[16]

The attack aircraft carrier is the indispensable naval force type for gaining and maintaining sea control beyond the effective range of land-based planes. If the Soviet fleet is to evolve into a sea command force, it will need a consistent and successful aircraft carrier program.[17] But there are major imponderables about the Soviet carrier construction program, Soviet operations and tactics, and the prospective missions of the carriers.

Work continues on the new nuclear-powered carrier, the *Tabilisi*, being constricted at Nikolayev on the Black Sea, and the aircraft for its air wing are under construction. The ship's flight deck configuration is not yet confirmed, however, and may be only a "ski jump" flight deck designed for relatively low-performance short takeoff and landing aircraft.[18] Such planes would have air-to-air and ground support mission capabilities, but they would be no match for the best Western fighters. Additionally, the Soviets lack underway replenishment ships for sustained combat in Third World operations. Soviet naval aviation will remain primarily a land-based force.[19]

There is also the question of Soviet tactical control in deploying carriers and the navy's relationship to the other services. In a Western navy, a carrier helps make a battle group self-sufficient with its own surveillance, defense, and attack capabilities. Would the Soviets permit such independence, the equivalent of "operational maneuver groups," in Europe? Soviet army and political leaders have been reluctant to realize the importance of sea supremacy for ground and naval operations. Gorshkov has complained in his writings of interference from other elements of the Soviet defense establishment in naval operations, and it is unlikely that this interference would cease in war. Even Gorshkov himself, while stressing the value of a surface fleet for a sea presence, was "strangely quiet regarding their strategic role in wartime." And in Soviet-assisted operations in Angola, Ethiopia, and Vietnam, the navy protected the flanks of the ground forces in traditional fashion. It was not an independent force in its own right.[20]

Even if such carriers are built, their mission would not necessarily be the same as for Western carriers. Soviet naval officers, in evaluating sea supremacy in World War II, contend that it is merely a "condition for successful conduct of major operational tactical missions." Soviet carriers when built would protect Soviet submarine bastions against NATO antisubmarine warfare and parry attacks from U.S. carrier aircraft and cruise missiles. In this sense they would seek a limited form of sea control rather than provide a focal point for power projection forces. The Nikolayev Black Sea shipyard can produce about one such ship in a four-year cycle. At this rate, by the turn of the century there would be only one carrier for each of the major Soviet fleets (or they might choose to operate two or more carriers together for mutual support as the United States does). This is no counterpart to the U.S. Navy's desired projection force of 15 carriers.[21]

Future Soviet carrier effectiveness is limited by several factors, including absence of a large Soviet attack carrier, the slow progress in building one, and the plans and doctrine to make it an effective instrument of intervention. There are also questions about the degree of decentralization the Soviet political authorities would tolerate as well as the political and army conservatism about any independent major naval mission.

Limited Naval Infantry

The Soviet naval infantry, or marines, is very small — only 20,000 men — and split among the four Soviet fleets. There are also doubts in Western quarters about Soviet ability to lift the entire marine force simultaneously, even with the use of the merchant marine. Many of the amphibious ships are at least 30 years old, and there has been no indication of large production runs of the newer, more capable ships like the *Ivan Rogov*. The lack of sea-based, organic tactical air power persists. Moscow does not have the present capability of going beyond the effective reach of land-based air power and taking casualties. It cannot mount large landings in the face of strong opposition, particularly opposition from the air.[2]

Despite the limitations noted, the Soviets use their resources with significant international political impact. Larger, more capable ships are being built. The first full-size aircraft carrier is being built at the Nikolayev shipyard on the Black Sea, a progression from the helicopter carrier of the late 1960s — whatever the final configuration of the flight deck. A limited number of more capable landing craft with larger capacity are being built, enabling Moscow to move forces further inland. The merchant fleet has a number of "roll on, roll off" vessels, staffed with regular naval officers, to aid Soviet clients. The Soviets have also developed two hospital ships in the Soviet fleet to permit the treatment of large numbers of casualties in remote locations. The Soviet hospital ship *Ob* is being deployed off the African coast to treat Cuban army personnel fighting in Angola.[23]

POSSIBLE FUTURE DEVELOPMENTS

Decline in Domestic Political Influence of the Soviet Navy

In actual deployment terms, there was a decline in the political use of the Soviet fleet in the late 1970s, contrary to Gorshkov's writings. There has been a corresponding stress on the use of naval forces in direct support of ground operations within continental theaters of operation like the Norwegian Sea. This may have reflected a debate on the use of the Soviet navy within defense circles, with writers like Admiral Stalbo, who supported the ambitious Gorshkov view of the naval mission, under attack. Some complained that Gorshkov and his supporters had overstepped naval prerogatives by dealing with policies that should be dealt with only by the higher political leadership. State sea power, for example, should be handled at a "higher level of science," not at the navy level.[24]

More Joint Operations

In an interesting parallel with current U.S. concerns, Admiral V. N. Chernavin, a nuclear submariner who replaced Gorshkov as naval chief of staff, noted the need for joint operations rather than an independent naval role. Joint efforts by all services should be conducted in all theaters. Others argued that Gorshkov and his supporters had neglected military, political, and economic factors in weapons development in their haste to give the navy a major role in the Soviet defense establishment. In December 1985, it was argued at a major naval training conference that some naval commanders had failed to understand the need for intensified combat training and had increased the number of sea exercises. Engine capacity was overused, fuel was overconsumed, and there was a premature aging of equipment.[25]

Construction Cutbacks

The future of major surface ship construction is in doubt with Admiral Gorshkov's retirement as navy chief of staff, although he was elected to the Party Central Committee at the Twenty-seventh Party Congress in March 1986. (He has since died.) The Soviet navy is still primarily a land-based air and submarine fleet. Many observers feel that surface ships are vulnerable to modern weapons. It is expected that cutbacks in naval construction will be reflected mainly in surface warships.[26]

CONCLUSION

The Soviet Union has not interposed its own forces to stop "imperialist forces" from intervening to stifle the "natural process" of national liberation movements or the independence of Soviet-assisted clients. The navy has had little direct influence on events in Afghanistan, the Middle East, or the Far East. Similarly, it has had a negligible impact on the situation in Poland.

At times, Soviet writings suggest that there is support for building the kind of naval forces with power projection capabilities to put teeth into Soviet rhetoric opposing such Western intervention in the Third World. The Soviets continue to monitor the use of Western navies and their past history as instruments of coercive diplomacy and direct intervention — tacitly approving it for their own future use.[27]

The Soviet Union will support existing commitments in Angola, Ethiopia, Vietnam, and — to a lesser extent — Central America. However, we are unlikely to see dramatically increased Soviet naval deployments in the near term, even to such important Third World areas as the Persian Gulf. Soviet willingness to seek and support new commitments will depend upon successful restructuring of the Soviet economy and its view of the global correlation of forces and the direction and significance of internal developments in Western states.

At present, however, the halcyon period of Gorshkov-Brezhnev naval expansion seems to be over. Even if external developments warrant it and the state of the Soviet economy releases resources for naval construction, it would require a major change in Soviet maritime doctrine and tactics for the Soviet navy to play the major power projection role in the Third World that Gorshkov seemed to advocate for it.

NOTES

1. Soviet sources quoted in Roger Hamburg, *Soviet-American Crisis Interaction: Patterns and Prospects*, unpublished manuscript, Harvard University, Center for International Affairs, pp. 225–26, nn. 18–20; "Pravda Assails U.S. Emphasis on Regional Conflicts," Joint Publications Research Service (JPRS), *USSR International Affairs*, UIA-86-015, p. 28; "USSR General Military Problems: Regional Conflicts and Imperialism's Plans," JPRS, *USSR Report: Military Affairs*, UMA-86-043, pp. 3, 8, 10; Robert S. Litwak and S. Neil MacFarlane, "Soviet Activism in the Third World," *Survival* 29 (January–February 1987): 34–35.

2. Admiral Gorshkov quoted in Norman Polmar and Norman Friedman, "Their Missions and Tactics," *U.S. Naval Institute Proceedings* 108 (October 1982): 36–37.

3. Andrew W. Hull, "Their Airborne Forces," *U.S. Naval Institute Proceedings* 108 (October 1982): 54; Roger Hamburg, "The Soviet Union and Low-Intensity Conflict in the Third World," in *Low-Intensity Conflict and Modern Technology*, ed. David Dean (Montgomery, Alabama: Air University Press, 1986), pp. 49–50.

4. Polmar and Friedman, p. 37.

5. James M. McConnell, "The Irrelevance Today of Sokolovskiy's Book *Military Strategy*," *Defense Analysis* 1 (1985): 247.

6. Michael MccGwire, "Soviet Military Objectives," *World Policy Journal* 3 (Fall 1986) 671–80.

7. Commander Bruce W. Watson, "The Soviet Navy in the Third World," in *Soviet and Other Communist Navies: The View from the Mid-1980s*, ed. James L. George (Annapolis: Naval Institute Press, 1986), pp. 251–69.

8. Although Clark and Subic Bay are only a few minutes' flight time from Camranh Bay, the reverse is also true. Whether the Soviet forces there would be a factor beyond the initial phases of a war is a matter for speculation.

9. Alvin H. Bernstein, "The Soviet Pacific Fleet," in George, pp. 238, 240–43, 246–47. Admiral Ronald J. Hays, Commander-in-Chief, Pacific Forces, stated that Soviet Badger bombers had made "threatening" reconnaissance flights from the Camranh Bay base in the direction of U.S. forces in the Philippines. Remarks at "Pacific Basin Security: Impact of Political and Soviet Change toward the Year 2000," symposium sponsored by the National Defense University and U.S. Pacific Fleet, Honolulu, Hawaii, February 26, 1987.

10. Don Shannon, "Fishing Fleets Expand Soviets' South Pacific Role," *Los Angeles Times*, September 1, 1986, p. 9.

11. Hamburg, "The Soviet Union and Low-Intensity Conflict," p. 49; Daniel H. Papp, *Soviet Policies toward the Developing World during the 1980s: The Dilemmas of Power and Presence* (Montgomery, Alabama: Air University Press, 1986), pp. 160–61; Gorshkov quoted in *Soviet Strategy in Latin America*, Robert S. Leiken, The Washington Papers 193 (New York: Praeger, 1982), p. 69.

12. *Whence the Threat to Peace*, 4th ed. (Moscow: Military Publishing House, 1987), pp. 76–77.

13.   For a more detailed discussion of Soviet navy capabilities and a comparison with the U.S. Navy, see John Allen Williams, "Missions and Forces of the U.S. and Soviet Navies," *Armed Forces and Society* 10 (Summer 1984): 507–28.

14.   Alan G. Maiorano, "Black Sea Prophesy," *U.S. Naval Institute Proceedings* 111 (January 1985): 62–64.

15.   Hamburg, "The Soviet Union and Low-Intensity Conflict," p. 51, and n. 49, p. 68. See also Polmar and Friedman, p. 35. Soviet sea control is not parallel to the Western concept. While wishing to protect their own coastal shipping from Western naval attack, the Soviets see the sea as a jungle with most warships subject to rapid destruction.

16.   The British were able to recapture the Falklands/Malvinas Islands in 1982 without high-performance aircraft. They were extremely professional, to be sure, but also very fortunate. Had they one or more *Nimitz* class aircraft carriers with the appropriate air wings, their losses would have been far smaller.

17.   Robert W. Herrick, "Roles and Missions of the Soviet Navy: Historical Evolutions, Current Priorities, and Future Prospects," in George, pp. 33–34.

18.   Robert C. Toth, "Soviets Seen Cutting Navy's Global Reach," Los Angeles *Times*, October 22, 1987, p. 1. The Soviet carrier may be a nuclear-powered equivalent of the British *Invincible* class antisubmarine warfare aircraft carrier, which was fortunate to survive the 1982 war with Argentina. The lack of high-performance aircraft capability of the new carrier is particularly interesting in view of a 15 percent decline in out-of-area deployments for the Soviet navy in 1987. It is not clear whether or not this is in response to the U.S. Navy's more offensive "forward maritime strategy" that calls for U.S. naval operations in Soviet waters under certain conditions.

19.   Report of Secretary of Defense Caspar W. Weinberger to the Congress on the FY 1988/FY 1989 Budget and FY 1988–1992 Defense Program, January 12, 1987, p. 37; *Soviet Military Power, 1987* (Washington, D.C.: U.S. Government Printing Office, 1987), pp. 86, 87.

20.   Watson and Dunn, *The Future of the Soviet Navy: An Assessment to the Year 2000* (Boulder, Colorado: Westview, 1986), p. 26.

21.   Hull, p. 56; A. D. Baker III, "The Aircraft Carrier," *U.S. Naval Institute Proceedings* 111 (December 1985): 53.

22.   Roger W. Barnett, "Commentary," in George, pp. 185, 186; Kenneth R. Whiting, *Soviet Air Power* (Boulder, Colorado: Westview Press, 1986), pp. 167, 168.

23.   Papp, pp. 161–65; Barnett, pp. 186–87.

24.   This echoes criticisms of the U.S. Navy for developing its Maritime Strategy, rather than letting the national command authority take the lead — a criticism the authors believe is ill-founded in view of the need for strategically sound planning as force structures are determined. Agreement with the process, of course, does not necessarily imply agreement with all the results.

25.   MccGwire, pp. 110, 112; Robert C. Suggs, "The Soviet Navy, Changing of the Guard," *U.S. Naval Institute Proceedings* 109 (April 1983): 37, 38, 40; *Gorbachev's Modernization Program: A Status Report*, paper presented by the Central Intelligence and Defense Intelligence Agencies for submission to the Subcommittee on National Security Economics of the Joint Economic Committee, Congress of the United States, March 19, 1987, p. 30.

26.   Watson and Dunn, *The Future of the Soviet Navy*, pp. 45–46.

27.   See Soviet citations in Hamburg, "Lessons Learned in 'Imperialist' Intervention," in *Soviet-American Crisis Interaction*, p. 50.

IV

Resources, Power Rejection,
and the
Global Soviet Challenge

9

Soviet Military Power and American Defense Resources: Competition and Scarcity

Lawrence J. Korb

INTRODUCTION

In early 1985, Caspar Weinberger projected that the Department of Defense (DOD) would need about $440 billion in budget authority in FY 1989. On November 23, 1987, his successor Frank Carlucci ordered the armed services to reduce the projected 1989 budget to $290 billion. This means that between February 1985 and November 1987 the Pentagon lost $150 billion or about 35 percent of its projected buying power. If Congress deals with the FY 1989 budget as it dealt with the budgets of the last few years and reduces the requested budget by about 5 percent or another $15 billion, the FY 1989 budget will be $275 billion, $65 billion or nearly 40 percent below the projected level. Moreover, it will mean that the defense budget will have decreased by about 13 percent in real terms since FY 1985. In real terms it will be back to the level that existed in FY 1983, the first full year of the Reagan buildup.

It is clear that DOD has entered a new period of budget austerity, and the decade of the 1990s will probably be like the decade of the 1970s when defense spending declined by 20 percent in real terms. What is not clear is what this era of constrained budgets will mean for U.S. security interests and what impact it will have on the military balance with our principal adversary, the Soviet Union.

To answer these questions, it is important to understand first how and why DOD came to its present predicament; to look at trends in Soviet military spending and Soviet military power; and to analyze the current state of U.S. military capability.

THE REAGAN BUILDUP

Many have labelled the decade of the 1970s as the "decade of neglect" of U.S. military capabilities. While this is a debatable hypothesis, U.S. defense spending declined markedly in both absolute and relative terms.[1] Real defense spending declined by 20 percent from 1970 to 1979 and, as indicated in Table 9.1, the share of the federal budget and GNP devoted to defense dropped from about 40 percent and 8 percent respectively to below 23 percent and 5 percent. At the same time Soviet military output increased significantly so that by the mid-1970s it was 25 percent higher than that of the United States. The Soviet invasion of Afghanistan and the seizure of U.S. hostages in Iran forced Americans to assess the implications of the deteriorating military balance. Public support for increases in defense spending, which had been at 10 percent at the beginning of the 1970s, jumped to 71 percent by the end of the decade. In the 1980 presidential campaign, both candidates supported substantial real increases in defense spending.

In 1981, newly elected President Reagan began his defense buildup. After adding $36 billion or 25 percent to Carter's FY 1981 budget, President Reagan called in January of that year for an annual 7 percent growth rate over FY 1982–1986. Reagan and his defense secretary, Caspar Weinberger, achieved their goals almost completely. Between FY 1980 and FY 1985, the defense budget increased by more than 50 percent in real terms. This brought the defense budget in FY 1985 to $286.8 billion. In real

TABLE 9.1
Defense Expenditure as a Percentage of Federal Spending and GNP for Selected Years

Fiscal Year	DOD Outlays as a % of Federal Outlays	DOD Outlays as a % of GNP
1960	45.0	8.2
1970	39.4	7.8
1975	25.5	5.6
1976	23.6	5.2
1977	23.4	4.9
1978	22.5	4.7
1979	22.8	4.7
1980	22.5	5.0
1986	26.4	6.2

Source: Annual Report to the Congress, FY 1987, Caspar W. Weinberger, Secretary of Defense, 1986, p. 315.

terms this was higher than the Vietnam War peak. By 1985, the defense budget accounted for 6.2 percent of the GNP and about 26 percent of federal outlays.

As will be discussed below, the Reagan buildup did not proceed in the most cost-effective manner. Nonetheless, the expenditure of $2.0 trillion in the FY 1981–1988 period bought a substantial amount of military capability in both the strategic and conventional force areas.

All three legs of the strategic triad were modernized. Deployment of Peacekeeper (MX) missiles in hardened Minuteman silos began. The Poseidon nuclear-powered ballistic missile submarine (SSBN) force began to be replaced with Trident submarines, and the B-1B bomber was introduced as a penetrating bomber and carrier for air-launched cruise missiles (ALCM). Development and testing began on several new strategic weapons systems such as the Trident II (D-5) missile, the Stealth bomber, and the Midgetman ICBM.

U.S. general purpose forces were also modernized across the board. More than 10,000 tanks and other armored vehicles were purchased for the army and marine corps, and more than 3,000 aircraft were procured. The number of deployable ships in the navy grew from 479 in 1980 to 570 by 1987.

Total active duty military personnel grew by more than 100,000 or 5 percent from 2,040,000 to 2,152,000 during the same period, while selected reserve strength grew by more than 200,000 or 25 percent. The number of civilian employees increased by more than 100,000 or 13 percent. More important, the caliber or quality of the armed forces improved dramatically. Whereas in 1980, only 68 percent of those joining the armed forces possessed a high school diploma, by 1987 it was 93 percent. Similarly, those scoring average or above average on the Armed Forces Qualification Test jumped from below 70 percent to about 95 percent.[2]

The full impact of the Reagan buildup is outlined in Table 9.2. As that table indicates, the number of strategic warheads increased by almost 27 percent; main battle tanks went up by 17 percent; combat vehicles, by 32 percent; combat aircraft, by 10 percent; and attack submarines and major surface combatants, by about 15 percent. In addition to increasing in quantity, the Reagan buildup increased the quality of the forces substantially. For example, the new M-1 tank is far superior to the M-60; the F-15 much more capable than the F-4; and the Nimitz class aircraft carriers fare better than those of the Forrestal class.

TABLE 9.2
The Reagan Military Buildup

	1981	1987
Strategic Forces:		
ICBMs	1,054	1,000
Strategic Submarines	36	36
SLBMs	576	640
Strategic Bombers	412	398
Strategic Warheads	10,086	12,772
Land Forces:		
Division Equivalents*	20.7	21.3
Main Battle Tanks	11,975	14,016
Artillery†	9,104	9,455
Infantry Combat Vehicles	15,974	21,064
Attack Helicopters	1,072	1,479
Air Forces:		
Fighter/Attack/Interceptor Aircraft**	3,912	4,272
Cargo/Transport/Tanker Aircraft	1,580	1,604
Naval Forces:		
Attack Submarines	84	96
Major Surface Combatants††	210	237
Ocean Minesweepers	3	8
Amphibious Ships	67	60

* Includes independent brigades.
† Includes howitzers, MRLs, and heavy mortars.
** Excludes Navy Operational Conversion Unit aircraft.
†† Includes aircraft carriers, battleships, cruisers, destroyers, and frigates.

Source: "The Defense Monitor," The Center for Defense Information, Vol. XVI, No. 7, p. 5. (Their sources are: DOD, IISS, CRS, Air Force Magazine, and CDI.)

REASONS FOR THE DEFENSE SPENDING CONSTRAINTS

Upon his reelection to office in 1984 President Reagan and Defense Secretary Caspar W. Weinberger expected defense expenditures to continue to increase as they had during the first Reagan administration. As indicated in Table 9.3, they expected to get nearly $2 trillion over the FY 1986–1990 period, an average real increase of 6 percent, and expected the defense budget to grow to about $478 billion by FY 1990. Not only did DOD not receive anything near the anticipated Reagan-Weinberger increase, the defense budget began to decline in real terms. Moreover, their five-year program was slashed by more than $500 billion or over 25 percent.

There are essentially two reasons for the constraints the U.S. Congress placed on defense spending. Perhaps the most

TABLE 9.3
Trends in Department of Defense Five-Year Plans
(Budget Authority in Billions of Dollars)

	Fiscal Year					Total 1986–1990
	1986	1987	1988	1989	1990	
Administration request, February 1985	314	354	402	439	478	1986
Administration request, February 1986	278	312	332	354	375	1651 −335
Administration request, January 1987	281	282	303	323	344	1534 −452
With freeze plus inflation, 1988–1990	281	282	295	305	315	1477 −509

Source: Author and U.S. Department of Defense, *Annual Report to the Congress, FY 85–FY 89* (Washington, D.C.: U.S. Government Printing Office).

important reason for the turn-around in attitude toward the level of defense spending was the growth of the U.S. budget deficit. While the annual federal budget deficit in 1980 was only $74 billion, by 1985 it had increased to a phenomenal $212 billion. This increase of $138 billion or 186 percent in five years provoked serious soul searching on the part of Congressional leaders, as did the fact that Ronald Reagan accumulated more debt in his first administration than all his predecessors combined. This led to the passage in 1985 of the Gramm-Rudman-Hollings deficit reduction bill, which mandated a balanced federal budget by FY 1991.

A second reason for the decline in support for increased defense spending was the perception that the defense buildup in the first Reagan administration was badly mismanaged. Many people who hold that position point to the outrageous prices that the DOD paid for items like hammers, screwdrivers, and toilet seats. Others point to the fact that on average DOD paid twice as much in the 1980s for major items like planes, ships, and tanks than it did in the previous decade yet received fewer than 25 percent more units. Indeed half the Pentagon's 40 major procurement programs in the halcyon days of the defense buildup were purchased below minimum economic productive rates.[3] Thus, even though the United States and the USSR spent about the same amount on military procurement over the last decade, the Soviets procured substantially more weapons systems. The Russians acquired about five times as many tanks, artillery pieces, and surface-to-air missiles and about twice as many helicopters and fighters. Only in shipbuilding did the United States hold its own. Even assuming that U.S. equipment is more sophisticated than that of the Soviets, the vast differences in numbers of units procured makes it clear that DOD did not get its money's worth.

Others point to the fact that no overall strategy guided the Reagan buildup. Secretary of Defense Weinberger's hands-off management approach allowed each of the services to set its own priorities. As Senator Sam Nunn (D-GA), chairman of the Senate Armed Services Committee, put it, "you have a Navy strategy, an Army strategy, an Air Force strategy, and a Marine strategy."[4]

Not surprisingly these perceptions, plus the burgeoning deficit, led to a precipitous drop in popular support for increased levels of defense expenditure. Whereas in 1980, 71 percent of the people in this nation supported an increase in defense spending, that number dropped to 13 percent in 1986. More ominously, 30 percent of the population advocated defense spending cuts as the best way to reduce the deficit.

SOVIET MILITARY CAPABILITY

U.S. military power does not exist in a vacuum. One must also look at what our principal adversary the USSR has been doing in the field of defense. Two indices are normally used to assess the state of the balance: strategic nuclear and the conventional balance in Central Europe.

Table 9.4 outlines the nuclear balance. As that table indicates, each side possesses some advantages. The Soviets have more land and sea-based missiles than the United States (2,346 to 1,640) while the United States leads the Soviets in bombers (317 to 165). Overall the Russians have some 554 or 28 percent more delivery systems whereas the United States has 2,829 or 26 percent more warheads.

Analysis of the NATO-Warsaw Pact conventional force balance during the Reagan administration revealed that, in nearly every "bean" count, the Soviet Union and its allies had a substantial edge over the United States and its European allies, despite the Reagan buildup. The Warsaw Pact's advantage was particularly striking in the area of arms possessed by ground combat forces. In some cases the Warsaw Pact held a four-to-one advantage in offensive and defensive systems. The air balance also favored the Eastern bloc but not to the same degree. The naval balance favored NATO as did the total manpower situation, combining all alliance active duty and reserve personnel.

TABLE 9.4
The Soviet/U.S. Nuclear Balance

United States			Soviet Union		
System	Number Deployed	Total Warheads	System	Number Deployed	Total Warheads
ICBM			*ICBM*		
Minuteman II	450	450	SS-11	440	440
Minuteman III	527	1,581	SS-13	60	60
MX	23	230	SS-17	150	600
			SS-18	308	3,080
			SS-19	360	2,160
			SS-25	100	100
Subtotal	1,000	2,261		1,418	6,440
SLBM			*SLBM*		
Poseidon C-3	256	3,584	SS-N-26	272	272
Trident C-4	384	3,072	SS-N-8	292	292
			SS-N-17	12	12
			SS-N-18	224	1,568
			SS-N-20	80	720
			SS-N-23	48	480
Subtotal	640	6,656		928	3,344
Bombers			*Bombers*		
B-52G/H non-ALCM	119	1,428	Bear non-ALCM	100	200
B-52G/H ALCM	144	2,800	Bear H ALCM	50	1,000
B-1	54	648	Bison	15	60
Subtotal	317	4,956		165	1,260
TOTAL	1,957	13,873		2,511	11,044

Source: *The Military Balance, 1987–1988*, The International Institute for Strategic Studies, London, p. 225.

However, both of these balances do not measure quality, nor can they predict the outcome of any potential conflict. For example, not only does the United States possess more nuclear warheads than the Soviets, but U.S. weapons are more accurate than their Soviet counterparts. Similarly Warsaw Pact quantitative advantages are offset somewhat by the superior technology and younger age of NATO's weapons and by the fact that NATO's force readiness and manpower quality are higher than that of the Warsaw Pact.[5] In addition NATO is a defensive alliance with a far superior economic base.

Nevertheless, the United States is not in such a strong military position that it can become complacent. It must make some very judicious decisions if it is to maintain its current level of military capabilities. This is particularly true in the area of conventional forces where the recently concluded INF treaty and the decision of NATO not to modernize the Lance short range nuclear missile diminishes the reliance it can place upon nuclear forces to offset conventional disadvantages.

To deal effectively with the current situation of constrained defense budgets, the United States must take certain steps. These may be placed into five categories.

First, the Department of Defense must not exaggerate its current budget dilemma. It is true that the FY 1989 budget will be significantly below its projected level and some 13 percent below the peak level of FY 1985. However, spending for FY 1989 is not returning to the level of the mid-1970s. Rather, it will be at about the same level as FY 1983. In that year budget authority in real terms was 37 percent higher than FY 1980 and 50 percent higher than FY 1975, the low point of the "decade of neglect." More important, defense spending in FY 1983 was higher in real terms than it was at the peak of the war in Vietnam.

Second, the United States should not exaggerate the growth in Soviet military spending. When the Reagan administration came into office, it assumed that Soviet military expenditures were growing at the rate of 5 percent each year in real terms. However, by 1983 the CIA had reversed its estimates of Soviet growth downward to 2 percent a year. Moreover, the CIA found that over the past decade, the rate of Soviet military procurement had remained flat. During the 1979–1986 period, Soviet defense spending increased at an annual real rate of 2.1 percent less than half the growth rate of the United States.[6]

Third, the executive branch must accept the fact that we are entering an era of restrained budgets and must plan accordingly. Even after the passage of the Gramm-Rudman-Hollings deficit reduction bill in 1985, the Reagan administration asked for large increases in the defense budget annually and allowed the DOD five-year defense plan to project levels of growth similar to those of the early 1980s. As a result, Congress was forced to reduce defense spending by $80 billion in the FY 1986–1988 period to meet Congressional spending targets, and by December 1987 the five-year defense plan was underfunded by about $500 billion. Because of the budget compromise reached in the aftermath of the October 1987 stock market crash, the Reagan administration finally agreed to submit a realistic defense request for FY 1989. However, in order to accomplish that task, DOD was forced to adjust its proposed budget downward by $33 billion or 10 percent in a matter of weeks.

Fourth, within its budget DOD must give priority to supporting the force structure that it purchased in the first part of this decade. From FY 1980 through FY 1985, spending on procurement jumped by 92 percent in real terms while readiness spending, which is primarily in the operations and maintenance (O&M) account, increased by only 31 percent. During the FY 1986–1988 period, O&M funding grew by less than 1 percent a year, not nearly enough to support the larger force structure, and is actually some 30 percent to 40 percent below its projected levels.

Instead of giving priority to supporting the existing force, DOD has given priority to producing the next generation of weapons systems. Funding for research and development, which grew by 63 percent in the FY 1980–1985 period, has increased by an additional 25 percent in real terms even in the constrained environment of the last three fiscal years. This not only has made it difficult to purchase the spares and ammunition for the forces in being but also has driven up the unit costs of the current generation of weapons systems precipitously. For example, in FY 1988, DOD paid $67 million for each F-14D fighter and $60 million for each EA-6B electronic warfare plane because it purchased only six of each. Nonetheless it went ahead at a breakneck pace with the next generation of planes, i.e., the ATA, ATF, and Stealth bomber.

Fifth, DOD must reduce its force structure goals. Within a budget declining in real terms, DOD simply cannot afford to maintain a 600-ship, 15-carrier battle group navy, an 18-active-division army, and a 38-tactical air wing air force. Nor can it afford to modernize all three legs of the triad while simultaneously undertaking a large-scale strategic defense program (SDI). Maintaining such conventional forces and that kind of strategic nuclear program requires real growth in the defense budget of about 5 percent per year.

While these steps can assist DOD in obtaining the most capability out of its current level of defense expenditures, they are essentially short-term fixes. For the long term, DOD must establish some strategic priorities. It cannot continue the practice of the Weinberger era, which allowed each service to establish its own strategy. DOD has three choices.

First, it can adopt the navy strategy, espoused most recently by former Secretary of the Navy James Webb on January 13, 1988. It argues that we are more than a European nation, that our future as a nation is tied very closely to Asia, and that the United States also must pay more attention to security threats in its own hemisphere. Because of these assumptions, DOD should adopt a maritime strategy and give budget priority to the sea services (navy and marine corps) whose military capabilities are more applicable in Asia and the Western Hemisphere.

Second, DOD can choose the recommendations of the Commission on Long Range Strategy, which were made public on January 12, 1988. The commission, which was cochaired by then Undersecretary of Defense Fred Ikle and nuclear strategist Albert Wholstetter, accepts the premise of the Navy Department that the United States is concerned too much about the Soviet threat in Europe. However, the commission report argues that we need to give priority to developing highly mobile versatile forces, which would be supported by high technology weapons.

Third, the United States can go back to the policy of the late 1970s, which structured our conventional forces on being able to handle a European contingency plus a smaller conflict outside Europe. The premise of this strategy is that the problems outside Europe are primarily political and economic and that the main military threat to U.S. interests lies in the area of Central Europe.

Each of these strategies has obvious force structure implications, and each deserves close analysis. It is not clear which one should be adopted, particularly in light of the nuclear and conventional arms control proposals put forth by Soviet leader Gorbachev in 1988 and 1989. What is clear is that the United States cannot afford to continue the Reagan strategy of "horizontal escalation," which gave priority to everything and thus to nothing. The strategic choices that the Bush administration makes will have a great impact on the security we buy within our constrained budgets.

NOTES

1. For contrasting positions on this subject, see *International Security,* Fall 1975, pp. 5–69.

2. The accomplishments of the Reagan buildup are outlined in Caspar Weinberger, *Annual Report to the Congress, FY 1987,* February 5, 1986, pp. 43–54. See also Anthony Cordesman, "Threat Forces," in *American Defense Annual, 1986–87,* ed. Joseph Kruzel (Lexington, Mass.: D. C. Heath, 1986), p. 97–101; and Lawrence J. Korb, "Defense Manpower and the Reagan Record," in *The Reagan Defense Program: An Interim Assessment,* ed. Stephen J. Cimbala (Wilmington, Del.: Scholarly Resources, 1986), pp. 63–92.

3. Thomas William, "Effects of Weapons Procurement Scratch-Outs on Costs and Schedules," Congressional Budget Office, 1987.

4. Quoted in "Which Weapons Will Work," *US News and World Report,* January 19, 1987, p. 18.

5. Senator Carl Levin (D-MI), *Beyond the Bean Count,* January 20, 1988, pp. 20, 26, 36, 67.

6. Joshua Epstein, *The 1988 Defense Budget* (Washington, D.C.: The Brookings Institution, 1987), p. 1.

10

Commercial Warfare and National Security: Outlasting the Kremlin in a Protracted Conflict

John E. Starron, Jr.

INTRODUCTION

As we approach the year 2000, the United States and its allies are confronted with three major problem sets regarding the global resource base.[1] The first problem set deals with the relationship between global population (now approaching 6 billion) and available earth-bound resources. We can summarize this problem set by citing a 1980 "Report to the President":

> If present trends continue, the world in 2000 will be more crowded, more polluted, less stable ecologically, and more vulnerable to disruption than the world we live in now. Serious stresses involving population, resources, and environment are clearly visible ahead. Despite greater material output, the world's people will be poorer in many ways than they are today.[2]

Since the publication of that statement, we have seen widespread famine in Africa and the destruction of thousands of square miles of tropical rain forest, plus critical materials shortages.[3] Resolution of this problem set requires nothing less than global management of resources and establishing intergovernmental institutions (such as the International Natural Rubber Organization) to conduct this management. Unfortunately, few governments are prepared intellectually or concerned enough to devote the needed time, talent, and treasure to the task. This problem set is obviously important to U.S. national security, but we will consider it only incidentally in this chapter.

The second problem set deals with the effort of the Third World countries to replace the "old international economic order" (OIEO) with a "new international economic order" (NIEO).[4] Here, a host of governments have asserted the right to control the resources within their boundaries. Exploitation of those resources (whether petroleum, timber, minerals, or fish, for example) must accord with the interests of the host people. Past alienations of the resources, whether by treaty, contract, or conquest, are being called into question.

Two recent illustrations can help us gauge the success of this ongoing transformation. The governments of the Organization of Petroleum Exporting Countries (OPEC), a cartel created in 1960, have finally repatriated their oil and natural gas resources, through indigenization or nationalization with or without compensation to the previous foreign owners.[5] Presently, OPEC is composed of 14 countries located on three continents; it controls about 60 percent of the world's petroleum reserves. Saudi Arabia, which can produce a barrel of petroleum at less than half a cent, is the most influential member of OPEC. The cartel has twice demonstrated its monopolistic power. With the Law of the Sea Treaty entered into force in 1979 the community of States, with the glaring exception of the United States, has restricted the future private exploitation of seabed resources. Although also of vital concern to U.S. national security, we will deal with this problem set only tangentially here.[6]

The third problem set entails the conflict over resources between the Communist bloc and the Western camp.[7] This is but a component of a broader spectrum of conflict between the two superpowers and their respective allies. We know that national power is ultimately founded on geography, technology, demography, and ideology. Since World War II, the Soviets have expanded territorially in Eastern Europe and thereby acquired additional territory, resources, and people. The final outcome of the relocation of the boundaries eastward and the incorporation of previous sovereign States into the Soviet empire has yet to be determined. Moreover, as of the summer of 1989 the results of Gorbachev's reform are still unclear. But, that resource concerns are part of the Soviets' grand strategy is indicated from Moscow's drive for self-sufficiency, its commercial linkages within the COMECOM, its exploitation of Afghan mineral resources, and from such statements as, "Our aim is to gain control of the two great treasure houses on which the West depends: The energy treasure house of the Persian Gulf and the mineral treasure house of central and southern Africa."[8] While there are changes underway which have reduced the hostile feelings between East and West, are we sure the favorable trend will continue?

The purpose of this chapter is to deal with this third problem set, to review briefly this arena of actual and potential conflict between the Communist bloc and the Western camp, to identify and discuss offensive and defensive material policy options, and to offer a course of prudent action to protect the interests of the United States and its allies from the hazards of commercial warfare.

Our thesis is that there is a plausible case for Soviet-sponsored commercial warfare against the United States and that, therefore, U.S. policy makers and security analysts should account for this potentiality when formulating political or grand strategy. Prudent policy makers cannot do otherwise.

NATURE OF COMMERCIAL WARFARE

We can define commercial warfare as deliberate hostile actions by an aggressor State against the trade and commerce of a target State for the purpose of crippling the target State's capability to support its military forces or to sustain its population. An aggressor State can direct hostile action against the production or sale of commodities and resources as well as against the transport of raw materials. Commercial warfare is an indirect, low-intensity, low-risk conflict. A traditional "state of war" does not exist and generally no military forces are involved.

Since time immemorial, families, communities, tribes, nations, and later, States have exchanged goods and services. Originally unorganized, the exchange system eventually became formalized with times, location, and conditions of exchange mutually agreed by all parties. As with all social relationships, some attempt to take personal advantage of the situation, to profit by the misfortune or ineptitude of others. Gradually, there were movements away from direct exchange (where buyers and sellers could confront each other) to indirect exchange (where middlemen position themselves between buyers and sellers in order to benefit from the transaction). At least one common characteristic in all exchanges has been various forms of conflict.[9] Here, we need to distinguish conflict from competition. Commercial competition, not a common phenomenon, is an activity in which two or more agents compete in a marketplace under which there is full disclosure of all facts and conditions, and there is no coercion to exchange.

In modern times, trade and commerce have become highly complex and complicated activities requiring the time and talents of governments to keep them both efficient and equitable. Indeed, a host of institutions (for example, the Customs

Service), professionals, and rules are now involved in international commerce, and governments, as the instrument of sovereignty, have come to play major roles to protect the national interests. Today economic theologians speak glowingly of the global commercial system, and they place great value on the continued movement toward commercial interdependence and on the annual quantitative increases of exchanges between States. Although the protagonists for more commerce between States emphasize the advantages of such endeavors (and there are many), few researchers articulate the disadvantages (and there are many). Put more bluntly, what are the national security implications for the United States of offshore dependence on strategic and critical materials? For the United States, this critical question dates from the aftermath of World War I when officials became concerned about the lack of self-sufficiency in many raw materials.[10]

SCOPE OF COMMERCIAL WARFARE

When we try to ascertain the motivation and probable conduct of a totalitarian political system, we rarely have the opportunity to find explicit statements of policy followed by concrete programs that operationalize that policy.[11] In the ideal case, words and deeds do match. More likely, however, there is a great disparity between what dictatorial regimes say and what they do. Consequently, the security analyst, if true to his craft, must identify the opponents' capability to cause harm, to determine and extrapolate trends, must project likely outcomes, and finally must assess the national security implications of all this. In this case capabilities speak louder than words. This process, called threat assessment, requires a unique combination of knowledge and imagination on the part of the analyst.

Notwithstanding Gorbachev's current protestations of accommodations with the United States and his proposals for arms control, some security analysts are still seeking demonstrable evidence of a stand down of Soviet inspired global subversive and hostile activities against the West. Clearly, Soviet deeds still do not match Moscow's words. We can only conclude prudently that the theologically based struggle between Marxist-Leninist communism and the "capitalist world" continues, that the Soviets' strategic objective is the same — the destruction of capitalism, but that the strategy may have changed, from direct, high-intensity, and high-risk conflictual forms (such as conventional war in Europe) to indirect, low-intensity, and low-risk conflictual forms. The probability is rather small that the Soviet Union will engage the United States in either a nuclear

COMMERCIAL WARFARE AND NATIONAL SECURITY • 243

war or a direct, conventional war unless Moscow calculates that it has overwhelming strategic advantage. Most likely, it appears to be the Soviet strategy since World War II, in fostering their world revolution, to choose limited objectives using surrogate forces in conventional war activities to battle the archenemy. The wars of national liberation in China, Korea, Cuba, and Vietnam were manifestations of this approach. But even at this lower level of conflict, the chance for mistakes that could lead to escalation or contagion is still too great. Thus, of necessity, the Kremlin needs to move further down the spectrum of conflict to forms that are more subtle and less likely to alarm governments and populations but that can still debilitate the enemy. The potential for indirect, low-intensity, low-risk conflict, such as insurgency, terrorism, and commercial warfare, is apparent. Unfortunately, many in the West do not want to contemplate commercial warfare as a form of conflict. To borrow from Herman Kahn, this is to think the unthinkable! It challenges the dogmatic idealist's view of how the world should work. It questions open market-based free trade, which every government "should" be for, and it reassesses the reality of how international commerce actually transpires. Lastly, it subjects the few direct benefactors of trade and their special interests to intense analysis with the valuative criterion being "in the national interest."

We do not feel obligated to show that commercial warfare has taken place. The historical record is replete with incidents. Analysts have described many incidents involving petroleum, natural rubber, cobalt, and grains, for example, since World War II. In both World Wars an important impetus for the growth of the German chemical industries was to develop substitutes (such as synthetic rubber, synthetic fuels, and nitrates) for critical war-making materials.[12] This was a defensive policy against resource denial. A major purpose behind submarine warfare practiced by both sides during both World Wars was to interdict the flow of materials of the other side. This was an offensive materials policy to deny resources to the enemy. In the late 1950s, the Eisenhower administration devised an elaborate administrative apparatus (called COCM) to deny strategic commodities and technologies to the Soviet Union and the PRC.[13] Much of this early effort was done covertly. More recently, the Arab oil embargo against the United States (1973–1974) was an act of commercial warfare even though we elected not to call it such. One can also argue that the 1979–1980 petroleum price increases fostered by OPEC, which sent commercial shocks throughout the world, was at least an unfriendly act. Admittedly, we find it difficult to distinguish between peaceful commerce and commercial warfare, and therein lies the advantage to our potential enemies.

The U.S. commercial system (based on the notion of open trade) is more vulnerable to commercial warfare than the Soviet self-reliant oriented commercial system. In addition, the United States continues to be increasingly dependent on offshore sources for strategic and critical materials. This provides an aggressor State with many "targets of opportunity" in terms of access and movement of materials. Even with stockpiles, strategic conditions place the Soviet Union in an ideal offensive position and the United States in an awkward defensive position. Moscow has the initiative, and we can only respond. The prudent course of action for the United States is to make arrangements to either lessen or compensate for our material vulnerabilities.

DIMENSIONS OF COMMERCIAL WARFARE

Let us look briefly at selected dimensions of the problem set of commercial warfare.

Case of Eastern Europe

Moscow's relationship with communist Eastern Europe is instructive.[14] The Soviets base their relationships not on an open market approach where individual "firms" seek their advantage but rather on centrally coordinated exchange of goods and services. Indeed, an intergovernmental agency called the Council for Economic Mutual Assistance (COMECON) provides the administrative structure for the exchanges. While the Soviets seek self-reliance in the resource area, they appear to deny the same opportunity to their Eastern European allies. The general tendency is for the Eastern European countries to provide resources and markets and for the USSR to be the manufacturing center. The exception to this general scheme is natural gas, which the Soviets now have in superabundance and which they use to exchange (indirect barter) with both Eastern and Western Europe for technology and foreign monetary exchange. We have here an effort to integrate the economies of the Eastern European States with that of the Soviet Union in order to influence their behavior. For strategic planners, Eastern Europe can be viewed as an extreme case for economic interdependence that limits political behavior. In the summer of 1989, it is too early to judge the impact of President Bush's visit to Poland and Hungary on the strength of their commercial linkage to the USSR.

Case of Albania

Not all communist States desire to be placed in a position where Moscow can threaten the continued flow of commerce if one is being uncooperative in other arenas.[15] Even some communist States (for example, Albania and the PRC) treasure their independence and are willing to suffer great deprivations to maintain it. For example, after major disagreements in the international communist movement, Moscow withdrew its aid from Albania in 1981. The Soviet objective was to discipline the Albanians for their role in the dispute over the nature of communism. But the Party of Labor of Albania or PLA (the Albanian Communist Party) reacted, after a period of time debating what course to follow, by moving toward a national policy based on self-reliance. The thrust of the self-reliance program was to prevent economic coercion by Moscow.

For the Albanian, self-reliance meant:

"'Internal factors' should be the driving force in socialist constructions." Internal factors center on priority to heavy industry and the predominance of the domestic market over specialization in the global economic system.

Autarchy is not the objective, but "commercial exchanges on an equal basis with other countries" is permitted.

Sincere socialist aid is acceptable, "but such external resources should have an impact on the economy through the 'internal factors.'"

It "should be practiced on all levels and in all branches of the economy."

It "implies a policy of strict savings aimed at avoiding waste in manpower, raw materials, energy or financial resources."

It "requires a strong commitment to research on and development of an indigenous scientific and technological capacity."[16]

Obviously, this is a difficult road to socialism!

The self-reliance policy became both an approach to economic development and a means of defending the State from external pressures. Today, "Albania is probably the most self-reliant country in the world." It has "managed to establish an economic structure relatively independent of a continuous supply of foreign inputs." Interestingly, the 1976 Albanian constitution declared prohibitions against taking credits and loans or forming joint ventures with companies or countries of a "bourgeois" or "revisionist" character.[17] For strategic planners,

Albania can be viewed as an extreme model for self-protection from commercial warfare.

Case of Japan

In attending to the current struggles between the commercial, social, and political forces and the resulting trends around the world, we must be conscious of those forces and trends which could alter the geostrategic balance of power between East and West. Perhaps the most vulnerable State to commercial warfare is Japan, the second largest commercial power. Fundamentally, Japan has a throughput economy, and she depends heavily for her prosperity not only on offshore sources of raw materials but also on foreign markets in which to sell her products. Much of Japan's behavior prior to World War II is explainable in terms of requiring secured sources of materials.[18] The East Asia co-prosperity sphere of pre-World War II days was a conceptualization, almost realized, of regionalizing a commercial regime whereby Japan served on the manufacturing center and other States provided resources and markets. By this arrangement all members would prosper, but Japan's prosperity would be at a higher level. Today, Japan is still highly dependent on offshore sources for materials, and particularly petroleum and natural gas, the energy needed to fuel her growing economy. Japan currently looks to the Persian Gulf area for her petroleum, to Indonesia for her natural gas, and to Austria and Canada for her coal. But, the Persian Gulf is often a region of conflict. The sea lines of communication are long and sometimes hazardous, and Japan has no navy to protect them. She depends on the United States to guard her lines of commerce with the rest of the world as well as her access to Middle East oil. For the strategic planners, Japan can be seen as an extreme model of vulnerability to resource denial.

COMMERCIAL WARFARE AND NATIONAL SECURITY POLICIES

The Soviets appear to deal with the problem of resources more rationally and comprehensively than the West. In our strategic assessment of Soviet acquisition of critical resources, we can identify at least four approaches which we list in order of apparent Kremlin preference. The evidence for these come from Soviet behavior and outcomes, rather than from publicly announced policy.

Self-reliance

First, the Soviets prefer to practice self-reliance.[19] The Soviets' great territorial extent gives them the best opportunity to possess the minerals and other natural resources within their borders needed for superpower status. The self-reliance approach necessitates major efforts to explore, develop, and exploit the natural resource base of the country. When nature does not provide a particular resource, such as natural rubber, then a program is implemented to produce synthetics. A case in point is the Soviet synthetic rubber industry.[20]

The Soviets face two major difficulties in achieving self-reliance. The first is the high latitude of their country, which provides relatively less land with the proper climate for agriculture. Attempts to bring marginal lands into production result in expected, periodic crop failures. The second is that the industrial heartland of the USSR is generally west of the Urals whereas a good portion of the mineral and other natural resources is found east of the Urals, in Siberia. To traverse the vast mountain ranges and to cross the mighty rivers of Siberia requires inordinately high investments in the construction and maintenance of transport systems. The Kremlin's desire for warm water ports on the world ocean is not without logic. In addition, the Soviets opened the 3,100-kilometer Baikal-Amur Mainline railway in September 1984 to access better vast mineral and timber-rich regions into the economy.

Incorporation

Second, and of interest to contiguous regions and States in Eurasia, is incorporating territory into the USSR by either conquest or treaty. The incorporation approach has been the fate of Estonia, Lithuania, and Latvia and parts of Germany, Romania, Finland, and Poland. Like other areas of Central Asia, Afghanistan appears also to be destined for incorporation. Afghan natural gas from two major fields near the Soviet border is already being transported through large-diameter pipe to the Soviet Union. There are reports that the Soviets are developing the high-grade chrome ore deposits as well as the rich iron ore reserves at Hajijak.[21] The process of Soviet imperialism continues. Soviet troop withdrawals make it an indirect process rather than a direct one.

Communization

The third approach for resource acquisition is to install a communist government in a target country and thereby bring about the exchange (barter) of Soviet aid and assistance for local materials. Examples of this approach are sugar and nickel from Cuba and natural rubber from Vietnam.[22] Both Cuba and Vietnam are accessional members of the Council for Mutual Economic Assistance, which "promotes coordinated economic planning and trade specialization." The ultimate goal of CMEA is "full economic integration."

Trade

The fourth approach, and the least desirable, is for the Soviets to visit the markets and trade for what they need. Here, the Soviets appear to use their monopsonistic leverage skillfully. Besides technology, grains from the West to compensate for bad crop years is an important item.[23] Moreover, Moscow is seeking with some success to "market" its vast natural gas surpluses in Western Europe and Japan. Little imagination is required to see the potential for mischief if these arrangements come to pass.

We need to stress here that the acquisition of resources is not always the primary motivation behind moves to incorporate contiguous territory or to communize offshore States, but potential resource acquisition is a consideration.

COMMERCIAL WARFARE AND RESOURCE STRATEGY

As mentioned above, a State's strategic material condition, either the one presented by geography or the one of choice, will determine whether a State's policy will be, from a commercial warfare standpoint, offensively oriented or defensively oriented. For purposes of comparison, we will outline both orientations briefly and use the United States as an illustration.

Defensive Materials Policy

The objective of a defensive materials policy is to minimize the potential adverse effects resulting from a natural or elective dependence on offshore sources for essential raw materials. In this case, the processes for defensive policy making (that is, goals, strategies, and priorities) would involve at least five steps:

Identify those industries within the United States that contribute to civil-essential or defense-related production of goods and services.

Identify those strategic and critical materials used by the above industries for which the United States is dependent on offshore sources.

Inventory the domestic availability of these dependent materials from both private and public stocks.

Determine the materials that are in a significant deficit condition over the short term (1–5 years) and the long term (5–20 years).

For each of the above materials, prepare, fund, and implement a program to overcome the deficit condition of the strategic or critical material.

The White House Staff together with the Bureau of Mines provides us part of this strategic assessment as part of the "National Indicators System." We have adapted some of their information in Table 10.1 The table highlights only three of the six industries reported. We find similar situations with the electronics industry, the machine tool industry, and steel making, plus others.

Traditional defensive strategies embodied in a program for a specific material could include conservation, recycling, stockpiling, substitution (such as composite materials or titanium), exploration for additional domestic sources, diversification of offshore sources, and materials research.

Clearly, a defensive materials policy is a national effort of some importance. It involves the systematic collection of data on a global scale. It involves the development of a national perspective on materials usage. It involves the development of a cadre of materials specialists (for each essential material) whose vision is beyond corporate or industrial needs. In the past, some of these defensive material strategies have been organized into specific programs. During World War II, for example, we built almost from scratch an aluminum industry and a synthetic rubber industry. A titanium metal industry was the outgrowth of a government program during the Korean Conflict. More recently, under the provisions of Title III of the Defense Product Act of 1950, as amended, a guayule rubber program is underway in the southwestern part of the United States.

Offensive Materials Policy

An offensive policy for commercial warfare has similar concerns as that of the defense. Here, the strategic goal is to

TABLE 10.1
Strategic Assessments of Essential Industries

Industry	Area of Use and Critical Materials
Chemicals	Raw Materials: 　Chromium 　Cobalt 　Titanium Catalysts: 　Titanium 　Platinum
Energy	Superconductors: 　Columbium 　Titanium Batteries: 　Nickel Nuclear Power: 　Cobalt 　Chromium 　Nickel
Transportation	Aircraft Parts: 　Cobalt 　Chromium 　Nickel 　Titanium Automobile Parts: 　Chromium 　Columbium

Source: Government of the United States, Bureau of Mines, *The Domestic Supply of Critical Materials* (Washington, D.C.: U.S. Government Printing Office, 1983), p. 12.

inflict measured damage on the resources and materials infrastructure of the target State. The intent is to weaken the target State's ability to wage higher levels of warfare. In this regard, at least five general strategies (means) are applicable:

to deny access by the target State to a strategic material,
to interdict the movement of a strategic material to a State,
to make more difficult (that is, more costly), the acquisition of a strategic material by a target State,
to prevent the sale by a target State of a commodity in a specific market, and
to make more difficult the sale of a commodity by a target State.

Admittedly, this offensive approach is not to the liking of most Americans unless confronted by unfriendly countries.

CONCLUSIONS

The practitioners of commercial warfare during "peace-time" are not able to inflict mortal damage on a target State. Rather, commercial warfare is a debilitating process wearing away the psychological and physical strength of a society. Whether conducted covertly or even overtly, commercial warfare is indirect, low-intensity, low-risk conflict. A target State, especially one industrialized, can usually accommodate itself to annual damages to their production base, but over the long haul, the accumulation of damage will have its effects. The modern day Soviets founded their communist theology on violent revolution, and they sustain it by conflict. In the contemporary world, direct, high-intensity, high-risk conflict, such as conventional war, is militarily inapplicable and places the existence of the Soviet Union in jeopardy. We believe that Moscow is seeking new forms of conflict (such as terrorism, insurgency, and commercial warfare), which will continue the theologically-required revolution, but at subtle and in more crafty ways. We must monitor closely the changes taking place in the Soviet Union today.

Generally, policy makers in the United States are conscious of Soviet intentions and U.S. material vulnerabilities. Our offshore dependence offers many targets of opportunity. The Congress has acted with legislation calling for national material policies with concern for defense needs. We do have a National Defense Stockpile and a Strategic Petroleum Reserve, but there were reports that the Reagan administration wanted to dispose of these assets for budgetary purposes.

What needs to be done? Fortunately, there are some low-cost programs that will provide an identification and alert system to provide early warning of potential danger. First, we need to have a clear and realtime picture of the extent of our material and raw material vulnerabilities. This requires the assemblage and analysis of data and information on all those essential materials (such as fuels, foods, feeds, fibers, medical plants, minerals, and industrial plants) for which we are now or will become dependent on foreign sources of supply. There are already studies which look at portions of this problem, but few take a comprehensive view from the prospective of U.S. national security. Probably the agency which has done the most on this topic is the Bureau of Mines.

Second, because many governmental agencies have responsibilities and interests in this area of commercial and resource warfare, we need to establish and staff a small high-level central office to coordinate and guide overall government defensive activities. This office would have to deal with foreign governments, international agencies, and private corporations at home and abroad. A likely host for the central office would be an expanded National Critical Materials Council, originally created by Public Law 98-373, the National Critical Materials Act of 1984.

There is progress toward better top-level management. The DOD is now the manager of the National Defense Stockpile (Executive Order 12626), and the secretary of defense now reports annually to the Congress on the state of that stockpile.

NOTES

1. This paper is a product of an ongoing study of global resources and national security policies designated on Project HOMER.

2. Government of the United States, Council on Environment Quality, *The Global 2000 Report to the President: Entering the Twenty-First Century*, Vol. 1 (Washington, D.C.: U.S. Government Printing Office, 1980), p. 1.

3. Carl K. Eicher, "Facing up to Africa's Food Crisis," *Foreign Affairs* 61 (Fall 1982): 151–74; Government of the United States, U.S. Interagency Task Force on Tropical Forests, *The World's Tropical Forests: A Policy, Strategy, and Program for the United States* (Washington, D.C.: U.S. Government Printing Office, 1980); and Nicholas Guppy, "Tropical Deforestation: A Global View," *Foreign Affairs* 62 (Spring 1984): 928–65.

4. Two excellent discussions of the NIEO are Robert L. Rothstein, *Global Bargaining: UNCTAD and the Quest for a New International Economic Order* (Princeton: Princeton University Press, 1979); and Stephen D. Krasner, *Structural Conflict: The Third World against Global Liberalism* (Berkeley: University of California Press, 1985).

5. An analysis of cartels is provided by Davis B. Bobow and Robert T. Kudrle, "Theory, Policy, and Resource Cartels," *Journal of Conflict Resolution* 20 (March 1976): 3–56.

6. Some useful background is provided by Finn Laursen, "Security versus Access to Resources: Explaining a Decade of U.S. Ocean Policy," *World Politics* 34 (January 1982): 197–229; Francis T. Christy, Jr., "Property Rights in the World Ocean," *Natural Resources Journal* 15 (October 1975): 695–712; Jack N. Barkenbus, "The Politics of Ocean Resource Exploration," *International Studies Quarterly* 21 (December 1977): 675–700; and Maharaj K. Chopra, "Asia and the Law of the Sea: Strategic Aspects," *The Journal of the United Service Institution of India* 106 (April-June 1976): 99–112.

7. For a review of this arena, see Werner Kaltefleiter, "The Resource War: The Need for a Western Strategy," *Comparative Strategy* 4 (1983): 31–49; H. Clayton Cook, Jr., "Soviet Economic Warfare and U.S. Maritime Policy: A Critique," *Conflict* 6 (1985): 201–27; and William J. Mazzocco, "Peaceful Coexistence and Petro-Warfare," *Conflict* 6 (1985): 239–54.

8. Quoted in J. Allen Overton, Jr., *The Resource War: It Can't Be Won without Being Waged* (Washington, D.C.: American Mining Congress, undated), p. 5.

9. A useful review of this point in John Conybeare, "Trade Wars: A Comparative Study of Anglo-Hanse, Franco-Italian, and Hawley-Smoot

Conflicts," *World Politics* 38 (October 1985): 147–72.

10. Grosvenor G. Charkson, *Industrial America in the World War: The Strategy behind the Line, 1917–1918* (Boston: Houghton Mifflin, 1923), p. 30.

11. The difficulty of interpreting Soviet motivation and behavior is analyzed by Richard Pipes, "How Vulnerable Is the West?" *Survey* 28 (Summer 1984): 1–33; see also Rebecca Strode, "Soviet Strategic Style," *Comparative Strategy* 3 (1982): 319–39.

12. Two recent examples dealing with this point are Arnold Krammer, "Fueling the Third Reich," *Technology and Culture* 19 (July 1978): 394–422; and Graham D. Taylor, "The Axis Replacement Program: Economic Warfare and the Chemical Industry in Latin America, 1942–44," *Diplomatic History* 8 (Spring 1984): 145–64.

13. A biased discussion of this policy is presented in Gunnar Adler-Karlsson, *Western Economic Warfare, 1947–1967: A Case Study in Foreign Economic Policy* (Stockholm: Almqvist and Wilsel, 1968).

14. Material for this section is drawn in part from Alan H. Smith, "Plan Coordination and Joint Planning in CMEA," *Journal of Common Market Studies* 18 (September 1979): 3–21; and M. M. Kostecki, "The Role of the CMEA's Foreign Trade Monopolies in Mineral Markets," *Resource Policy* 11 (September 1985): 201–12.

15. The major sources for this section are Berit Backer, "Self-Reliance under Socialism — The Case of Albania," *Journal of Peace Research* 19 (1982): 355–67; Elez Biberaj, "Albania after Hoxha: Dilemmas of Change," *Problems of Communism* 34 (November–December 1985): 32–47; and Tito Favaretto and Angelo Masotti Cristofoli, "Economic Relations between Italy and Albania in the Post-World War II Period," *East European Quarterly* 21 (March 1987): 119–34.

16. Berit Backer, "Self-Reliance under Socialism," p. 356.

17. Ibid., pp. 363, 366–67.

18. See, for example: Michael A. Barnhart, "Japan's Economic Security and the Origins of the Pacific War," *The Journal of Strategic Studies* 4 (June 1981): 105–24.

19. Philip R. Ballinger, "Probability of Continued Soviet Mineral Self-Sufficiency," *Resource Policy* 11 (September 1985): 160–76.

20. R. R. Lewis, "Innovation in the USSR: The Case of Synthetic Rubber," *Slavic Review* 38 (March 1979): 48–59.

21. Other minerals reported include beryl, fluorspar, lead, zinc, bauxite, lithium, tantalum, and nilbrium.

22. Richard M. Levine, "The Mineral Industry of the USSR," *Minerals Yearbook, 1984* (Washington, D.C.: U.S. Government Printing Office, 1984), preprint, p. 23.

23. Discussions of early Soviet grain purchases are in Dan Morgan, *Merchants of Grain* (New York: Penguin Books, 1980), pp. 47–51, 152–69.

V

Conclusion

The Soviet Challenge in the 1990s: Peaceful Offensive or Operational Entrapment?

Stephen J. Cimbala

The Soviet challenge in the 1990s and beyond will not come in the form of surprise nuclear attacks against North America. It is almost equally difficult to imagine that the Group of Soviet Forces Germany will come blowing through the Fulda Gap and across the North German plain with the objective of totally conquering Europe. These scenarios are now treated by U.S. and Soviet analysts as notional and highly improbable "worst case" scenarios.

If not those contingencies, then what? Perhaps it is preferable to start on the other end of the problem, addressing what it is that U.S. and allied military forces can be expected to do. We can define five very broad functions or missions: deterrence, reassurance, denial, retaliation, and control. Each of these is a politico-military mission or function. The policy apparatus of the state must be orchestrated to maximize available conventional or nuclear forces. If these are the generic missions to which U.S. and allied forces might be committed, how successfully are those missions going to be accomplished?

POLITICAL FUNCTIONS: DETERRENCE AND REASSURANCE

Deterrence is thought of primarily in nuclear terms, and this is especially unfortunate in view of the greater importance of the latter, compared to the former.[1] A failure of conventional deterrence is more likely to lead to nuclear war than a "bolt from the blue" attack by one superpower against another.[2] Conventional deterrence has a historical paper trail, and the trail shows that it is extremely volatile. Nations have attacked their opponents when the most competent intelligence appreciation would have suggested otherwise. And otherwise vigilant adversaries have been caught napping by the most outrageously designed surprise attacks.[3] Conventional deterrence, that is to say, can be shown to have failed under conditions such that academic and military observers would have predicted otherwise.

Conventional deterrence also implies a capability for denial of enemy objective without unnecessary escalation to the use of nuclear weapons. There is substantial debate about whether NATO now has these denial capabilities. However, there is less debate over the inadequacy of U.S. and allied denial capabilities in areas outside Europe. Even the U.S. Joint Chiefs of Staff during the Reagan administration estimated that defense spending would have to increase by some $750 billion, in addition to the Reagan program requested and funded during the president's first term, in order to support U.S. global military commitments. Former Secretary of Defense Caspar Weinberger ended, perhaps wisely, the custom of defining how many conventional wars the United States could fight simultaneously. The mismatch between U.S. conventional denial capabilities and those of the Soviet opponent in Europe is noted by many commentators. Perhaps this was a race that the United States need not have attempted to run, given the overwhelming advantages to the Soviet Union of interior lines, short-range communications, and available reinforcements for a war in Europe.

It might be argued, and was so argued by the U.S. Navy, that matching the Soviet ground forces in Europe was an unnecessary or unprofitable enterprise, compared to building maritime force structure for rapid and flexible global employment.[4] In this the navy was joined by civilian strategists and policy analysts who suggested that a maritime emphasis was more appropriate for a world-island nation leading the free world coalition and matching its resources against the Soviet Union, which dominated the Eurasian heartland.[5] Against this were those, including former Defense Department official Robert W. Komer, who contended that a continental emphasis was dictated by the need to avoid the "likelihood fallacy" of avoiding preparedness for war in Europe because other conflicts were more likely.[6] At one level, these arguments about strategy were guises for budgetary battles over force structure, which the navy largely succeeded in winning. At another level, the disagreements did reflect a continuing tension in U.S. strategic thought.

In the continental-emphasis school, general purpose forces, which were suited for making war in Europe, are by implication going to be transferable to almost any other contingency. Army divisions may be lightened so that they are more transportable in case of conflicts in the Third World, where not quite so much firepower may be necessary. But U.S. Army doctrine is to be globally applied. The Carter administration put this into practice by creating the Rapid Deployment Force (RDF) for the Persian Gulf and other outside-of-Europe situations, but the Carter concept of the force was "fustest with the mostest" and not necessarily dependent on sustainability for weeks or months of conflict. The Reagan administration turned RDF into Central Command and added force structure sufficient (on paper) to conduct war in Iran or elsewhere in the Middle East-Southwest Asia theater for the duration.

The point is not that the United States can forego some capability for rapid insertion of combat forces into austere areas, including the Persian Gulf, for it surely does. The issue is the relationship between U.S. conventional forces and deterrence. Is Central Command, which is essentially fighting a large conventional war in Iran or Saudi Arabia, the kind of force that is going to deter Soviet intervention in that area when the USSR would otherwise be inclined to attack? The question is almost never posed in this fashion because of the excessive concentration of deterrence studies on nuclear questions. Almost no nuclear attack by one superpower against another ever seems worth the cost of whatever benefit it is supposed to bring. Therefore, policy makers and analysts slip into complacency about how well deterrence is thought to work, almost automatically, although professional military people are less likely to.

Conventional deterrence is less durable than nuclear, and so it is likely to be tested. However, the smart opponent is not going to provide a test for which U.S. and allied forces have arranged their deployments and doctrines. Strategy, as Edward Luttwak has noted, is a dialectical business, with an opponent who is intelligent and aiming to turn the tables on your strategy by guessing what you are going to do and then doing the opposite.[7] Thus the canonical scenario for which the RDF/ Central Command was devised, a Soviet invasion of Iran with the objective of taking over the oil fields around Khuzistan, may never materialize. A more probable contingency might be the demise of the regime in Saudi Arabia, primarily if not exclusively from internal causes. It was not a Soviet invasion that toppled the Shah and his regime in 1978 and 1979, nor even the hint of Soviet assistance to fraternal revolutionary allies inside Iran. Instead, a coalition of clerical and lay religious zealots, left-wing opponents, middle-class intellectuals and business people, and others dissatisfied with the Shah came together with sufficient force to topple the Pahlavi dynasty.[8] Nor was the determinant in Iran an absence of U.S. military power, ready to be applied to the situation on short notice. Rescuing the Shah from his own indecision, and therefore the hesitancy of his own internal security forces and army until it was too late, was no more probable than rescuing Ferdinand Marcos in the Philippines or the tottering regime of Chiang Kai-shek in 1949.

Suppose the Soviets were to contemplate an invasion of Iran. As Joshua Epstein has shown, this would not necessarily be an easy undertaking for them, especially if their objectives included seizure of Iranian oil fields in the southwest.[9] The size of the U.S. Central Command forces may be less important for deterring a Soviet move of this sort than the speed with which a force of moderate size can be placed between Soviet invaders and the Khuzistan oil fields. Whether an apparent Soviet mobilization for an attack southward into Iran would result in a prompt decision-making process in Washington is unknown. Assuming that decisions could be rapidly taken and forces deployed in a timely manner, the tasking and rules of engagement for such forces would have to be very specific to the mission of repelling Soviet aggression. U.S. forces could not take sides in any Iranian civil strife that may have broken out or preceded the Soviet military invasion.

The potential insertion of U.S. forces into Iran and the possibility of a direct clash between U.S. and Soviet armies might be sufficient to deter any deliberate Soviet attack on Iran. However, the deterrence of internal subversion, which the USSR could subsequently exploit, is another matter. The question of deterrence has been applied even less to low-intensity conflict than it has to conventional warfare.[10] The United States has been skeptical of military intervention in the Third World since Vietnam, and this skepticism extends into the Pentagon itself. To the extent that such self-doubt is widely known to potential adversaries, low-intensity conflict seems to pay off as a strategy of modest risk. However, this may over-simplify the problem because the problem of low-intensity conflict or internal war may be less a military than a political problem.[11] By a "political" problem is meant one of legitimacy of the political institutions and leadership within a polity. Since Max Weber called it to our attention, we have known that leaders have essentially three pathways to legitimation: tradition, personal charisma, and rational-legal authority. In some contexts more than one basis for authority or legitimacy exists, in which case the governing elite or ruler is that much safer from being deposed.

In these situations of potential internal war, which might dislodge a regime to which the United States is friendly, the best deterrent might not be the threat of direct military intervention. Direct intervention smacks of gunboat diplomacy and U.S. imperialism. The United States is more likely to succeed in working with the existing government to strengthen its military and political capabilities. A caveat is that the United States cannot rescue a hopeless enterprise. Dictators like Duvalier in Haiti, Marcos in the Philippines, or the Shah in Iran who are determined to self-destruct must be permitted to do so, and the United States should be prepared to establish ties with political opposition in nations whose leaderships have irretrievably lost their legitimacy. This decision is sometimes hard, as the failure of U.S. intervention in Vietnam demonstrates.[12]

This brings us to the second function that military preparedness must perform, that of reassurance. Reassurance is explained by Michael Howard as the feeling on the part of democratic publics that their defense forces are in fact capable of defending them.[13] This might sound truistic, but it is a profoundly important observation. Western publics will withdraw support from policies and armies that seem not to be defending them in any necessary, visible, and obvious way. This behavior pattern may be laid at the door of very many causal agents, including family and school — but that is someone else's subject. For our purposes it is a political reality that must be faced by policy makers in the United States and its allies in NATO Europe.

During the first term of the Reagan administration, there was a public furor in Western Europe over the NATO-proposed deployments of 572 Pershing II and cruise missiles scheduled to begin in December 1983. Protest groups representing diverse ideological persuasions mobilized their forces and attempted to prevent the beginning of the deployments as scheduled. One of the common motivations that inspired the European protest against Intermediate Nuclear Force (INF) modernization by NATO was the felt lack of reassurance on the part of Europeans about the role of nuclear weapons in NATO's deterrent strategy. And this was a perfectly logical perception, shared by lay persons and experts on both sides of the Atlantic.[14]

NATO declaratory strategy is a political compromise reflected in the so-called "flexible response" doctrine formally promulgated in 1967. This compromise allows Americans to believe in a long fuse connecting conventional war in Europe with the ultimate engagement of the U.S. strategic nuclear deterrent. Most European governments, meanwhile, believe in a shorter fuse because of their belief that the Soviet Union is more deterred from starting any war if its leaders have to contemplate the very prompt engagement of U.S. strategic missiles and bombers. This makes the roles of theater nuclear weapons somewhat ambiguous. Theater nuclear weapons delivered by ground launched ballistic and cruise missiles, for example, are classified by range: intermediate-range missiles, shorter-range missiles, and so-called battlefield or tactical nuclear weapons. For purposes of the superpower agreement in December 1987, to eliminate the first two classes of ground launched missiles and their associated weapons, the remaining tactical nuclear weapons are those with ranges shorter than 500 kilometers.[15]

However, it is not clear that the weapons of shorter range are the least dangerous, if the objective is to provide a credible NATO deterrent based on conventional denial forces not dependent on early first use. The tactical nuclear weapons are those that are going to be overrun first by invading Soviet armies. Battlefield commanders will have to request "bottom up" nuclear release well in advance of the moment when their actual employment might be timely. There is no guarantee that the higher echelons of NATO policy making will respond with sufficient velocity to provide responsive guidelines for limited and selective employment of nuclear weapons. As Katherine McArdle Kelleher has noted, "The operational requirements of bottom-up release border on the impossible."[16] NATO is thankfully not entirely dependent upon this procedure, nor is the United States acting unilaterally in response to Soviet attack in Western Europe. Still, the NATO policy-strategy story for limited nuclear war in Europe is less than reassuring.

The difficulty of NATO governments in providing reassurance to their publics on this point, of the necessity for continuing modernization as well as arms control in theater nuclear forces, is not only due to the obvious destructiveness of nuclear weapons. There are additional and more subtle problems, which are recognized by military planners and expert analysts. One of these is the problem of peripheral control over nuclear weapons that are distributed among widely dispersed U.S. and other NATO general purposes forces in Europe. NATO, that is to say, does not have a nuclear force separately organized and commanded from its conventional forces, say a NATO "SAC" under joint European control. Such an organization was proposed during the Kennedy administration as the Multilateral Force, a fleet of nuclear armed surface ships crewed by mixed nationalities with weapons provided by the United States.[17] This proposal died stillborn, but it remains the case that NATO cannot offer a strategy for defending itself with forces that are separately organized as conventional only or nuclear only. This, in turn, influences Soviet calculations about what they can expect to accomplish once war has begun. Those Soviet calculations affect the probability that any conventional war in Europe can remain below the nuclear threshold, even if NATO wants it to.

If NATO cannot defend itself with a "conventional" force separately organized from a force capable of delivering theater nuclear weapons, then it cannot pose to Soviet planners a calculable risk. It poses the incalculable risk that however war begins, its expansion into something far more destructive cannot be precluded. For most of NATO's existence, this posing of an incalculable risk to the Soviet Union for any conventional war in Europe is what makes deterrence work, according to defense specialists in the member governments. However, once the Soviet Union achieved effective strategic nuclear parity with the United States and then began to improve its theater nuclear forces as well, this posing of escalatory risks no longer obviously worked to NATO's advantage. NATO could still credibly threaten to get engaged in an escalatory process over which it might then lose control, but it could not credibly threaten to dominate the process of nuclear escalation in Europe. Faced with this recognition, European leaders such as former West German Chancellor Helmut Schmidt began demanding modernization of NATO theater nuclear forces. This made more visible Europe's dependency on defending itself with nuclear weapons or relying upon them for deterrence, and in so doing undermined public reassurance.

Nor is NATO's policy and strategy dilemma the only illustration of failed reassurance. U.S. intervention in Vietnam failed because of the inadequate reassurance provided to the U.S. public and to prominent critics of U.S. policy that the war could be won, or some other sensible political objective obtained, at a tolerable cost. And again, as in the case of NATO declaratory policy for the use of nuclear weapons, the public was onto something genuine. What is common to both cases is that the public perceived no war-winning strategy in the traditional sense. Europe could not be defended with nuclear weapons without blowing it up in the process. Vietnam could not be defended at an acceptable price in domestic political upheaval and lost U.S. blood and treasure. In both cases the "man on the street" had a common wisdom coinciding with some uncommon strategic insights.

It might be the despair of policy makers and military planners that U.S. and NATO allied public opinion is so fickle and not presumptively supportive of governing elites' objectives.

To the contrary, it is the responsibility of governing elites to make the case for public consumption, in a democratic society. Michael Howard has referred to this as the societal dimension of warfare, and in this he is quite right, for it points to the fundamental basis of public support on which democratic foreign policies must rest.[18] And U.S. post-Vietnam experience in this regard is not encouraging. It might be thought salutary, and undoubtedly is so regarded by some parts of the political spectrum, that U.S. post-Vietnam inhibition against military intervention remains a public and elite fixation. Were there no challenges to U.S. security emanating from outside Europe and in a form other than conventional war, this fixation might be acceptable. But few experts on either side of the Atlantic would so argue, even if they would not attribute all of the "out of the area" threats to Soviet influence. Thus the U.S. and European societal dimensions of warfare must be mastered, else fortress Europa and fortress America will be isolated from their surrounding environments. To the risk of isolation, in not coping with threats originating outside Europe, is added the risk of division, between U.S. and European elite perceptions of the importance of support for one side or another in low-intensity conflicts or internal wars. U.S. and European differences over U.S. support for the regime in El Salvador and U.S. opposition to the Sandinistas in Nicaragua had the potential for spillback into Atlantic alliance unity during Reagan's first term. NATO Europeans did not prove to be very supportive of U.S. efforts to resupply Israel during the October war of 1973, and the United States was on the opposite side of its British and French allies during the Suez crisis of 1956. When Britain and Argentina moved toward war over the Falkland Islands in 1982, the United States initially attempted to strike a posture of neutrality and attempted to mediate. Later the Reagan administration sided with its NATO ally against Argentina and even provided Britain with vital intelligence and logistical support.[19] This U.S. support was, of course, welcome to Margaret Thatcher and the British public. It was equally distasteful to Latin Americans in its symbolic support for neocolonialism, despite the abhorrent internal conduct of the Argentine regime during the 1970s.

If the U.S. public is not reassured that military force is still useful apart from a repeat performance of World War II, neither are U.S. policy makers. Former Secretary of Defense Caspar Weinberger more than once suggested that he would be averse to getting U.S. forces into any conflict unless he had broad public and Congressional support, clear military and political objectives, and all the resources deemed necessary by military commanders to do the job. Arguably no wars ever fought by the United States met these criteria except World War II; certainly Korea and Vietnam do not. Korea was regarded by many Americans who lived through those years as a draw at best and a defeat at worst. Vietnam then and now is considered an embarrassment if most media and cinematic representations suggest public awareness. However, there is an important disclaimer here with regard to U.S. public reassurance about military intervention. Public opinion polls for decades have shown that a president who does *anything decisive,* including failure, receives an immediate surge of public sympathy. Even John F. Kennedy, having admitted that the Bay of Pigs operation was a fiasco, received a temporary boost in the Gallup poll shortly thereafter. Truman's intervention in Korea was initially popular, as was Johnson's commitment of U.S. forces in Vietnam in 1965. Truman and Johnson were victims of public hostility later, when continued fighting failed to proceed to an apparently favorable conclusion. In Korea, public perception of the conflict was confused by a change in military objective, and therefore political objective also, as MacArthur pursued the North Koreans across the 38th parallel and as far north as the Chinese border. Subsequently his forces were pushed back by Chinese intervention, and the United States was forced to settle for its original objective of restoring the status quo. During the U.S. military intervention in Vietnam, public confusion about political and military objectives contributed to hostility toward U.S. policy.

We have been suggesting that the functions of deterrence and reassurance are related, sometimes negatively. The potential for negative valence in this relationship between deterrence and reassurance is only that — potential. It is not foreordained. Policy makers and military planners have some leeway to shape public opinion and to build options into war plans and force structures. At one logical extreme, deterrence and reassurance are entirely opposed to one another. At another, they are entirely supportive of one another. These logical ends of the continuum are rarely apparent in practice. Most actual decisions of policy and war planning will have to cope with marginal trade-offs between the two. Soviet planners, in turn, will want to present challenges that force this trade-off, between deterrence and reassurance, to be as painful for the United States and NATO as possible. Obviously the Kremlin has decided that indirect aggression pays higher dividends, relative to the expected costs, than direct aggression, at least in areas of vital geopolitical interest to East or West.

The more difficult issues are those posed by Soviet gains that are not necessarily at the expense of the West, that is, gains that are not part of the zero-sum competition so familiar to game theorists. In a zero-sum game, one side's wins are by definition the other side's losses. In most Third World crises and internal wars, Soviet and U.S. or Western interests are not so obviously opposed. A gain for the USSR, say in the fall of a pro-Western Third World government to a declaredly Marxist one, is not an indisputable loss to the West. It is curious how rapidly Western analysts, who recognize that outcomes in the Third World do not always have this East-West, zero-sum character in theory, are driven to the zero-sum extreme in practice. Thus former U.S. UN Ambassador Jeane Kirkpatrick emphasized the distinction between authoritarian and totalitarian governments, in order to justify U.S. support for the former and opposition to the latter. But these distinctions are not meaningful in some Third World situations, and the authoritarians are not necessarily the United States' best allies just because they are less unsavory than the totalitarians. What Kirkpatrick and others were attempting to do was to isolate self-declared Marxist regimes, especially those who might ally their fortunes with the Soviet Union, from other regimes that were less clearly allied with Soviet foreign policy objectives.

This, too, presented a difficulty. It presented all declaredly Marxian regimes as isomorphic, regardless of the gap between rhetoric and reality characterizing their economies and societies. Some developing states have adopted a quasi-Soviet model as part and parcel of accepting more Soviet military and other assistance. But others have given little more than lip service to the Marxian or Leninist model of social and economic development. And the Soviet Union has acknowledged that it must support "just" wars of national liberation even when the most favorable outcome from their standpoint, a truly Leninist model of development and control, is uncertain. Thus the case studies of Soviet advancement in the Third World during the 1970s — Angola, Ethiopia, South Yemen, and Mozambique — were not of a piece with regard to the character of their regimes or their degree of commitment to supporting Soviet objectives outside their own national boundaries.

Public reassurance was not improved during the 1970s by U.S. policy makers' apparently poor grasp of the process of political revolution. U.S. history conditioned them to expect economic development and social change to progress in a linear fashion, along with the institutions of a pluralist democracy. In many developing societies this has not happened. More rapid social change has led to political deinstitutionalization, to a debilitation of the political process. More people may participate in political activity in some way, but they are not participating through legitimated political channels, such as established parties and interest groups. Instead, their participation is often anomic, dissociated from normal channels, and unaccountable. The public sector then becomes privatized, handed over through corruption and bribery to the most powerful political barons. The comparatively small number of landholding families that monopolized power in Nicaragua under Somoza provide one illustration of the result, a government or public sector that is nominally in charge but that is, in fact, a mechanism for through-put from the private to the public sector. The government of Panama was for many years under the de facto control of military officers who thrived on the Western Hemisphere drug trade and who, like General Noriega, had the actual power over the most important allocative and coercive decisions in their societies.

The U.S. Congress tends to expect that all social change in developing societies will follow the Western path, or should, if the policies followed by U.S. presidents and their State Departments are prudently chosen. In fact the probability that events in the developing societies will push most of them toward pluralist democracy, at least in the near term, is very slight. Faced with this unpleasant reality, the Congress, the media, and the White House react with predictable frustration. The left calls for large doses of economic aid and a hands-off military posture. The right demands that regimes exuding a Marxian odor be decapitated. U.S. intelligence agencies are given the impossible mission to forestall the establishment of any government hostile to U.S. interests in geographically important regions, such as Latin America. When they attempt to carry out this mission, they find that the attitude of Congress toward covert operations is ambivalent: Congress will tolerate an operation that is invisible or going well but will rapidly disengage its support from any operation that receives unfavorable publicity.

The problem of reassurance to the U.S. public about the need for intelligence and low-intensity conflict capabilities is larger than "no more Vietnams." Indeed, the Vietnam syndrome is mostly overrated. The more important issue is Americans' intolerance for ambiguity in foreign and defense policy, hence lack of patience with limited and protracted conflict. This problem of reassurance is related to the first political objective of deterrence. If the U.S. public cannot be reassured that military intervention in support of U.S. global objectives in the Third World is a viable alternative, then deterrence of low-intensity conflicts that are inimical to U.S. interest cannot operate. Low-intensity conflict seems to be at the opposite pole from nuclear war, in terms of the destructiveness of the weapons used by combatants. Yet there is a disturbing similarity, in terms of U.S. public and professional military expectations about the desirability and feasibility of the use of force. Nuclear war and low-intensity conflict are both felt to involve no-win situations for the U.S. armed forces and for the opinion and policy elites whose judgments will be called to account in such conflicts. The connection between force and policy in most scenarios of either type is insufficiently clear. No one can write a scenario for superpower nuclear war or for a sustained U.S. war in the Third World in which the benefits seem to exceed the probable costs.

MILITARY FUNCTIONS: DENIAL, RETALIATION, AND CONTROL

The political uses of armed forces have been discussed, and they are related to the primarily military functions of denial, retaliation, and control. Of course, political and military objectives for the use of force are not mutually exclusive. We shall see that, in the case of control especially the political and military casts are almost indistinguishable. However, we have grouped these as military functions because of the requirement that the armed forces must be able to do these things — denial, retaliation, and control — if they are to accomplish any missions at all. So the issue is not, for the moment, what that mission is and whether it was properly chosen. It is instead the question of whether military forces, relative to the political tasking they have received, can deny the opponent his objectives, retaliate in order to inflict punishment or accomplish other objectives, and remain contributory to the objectives set by policy, as opposed to some inherent organizational or bureaucratic imperative.

Denial and Retaliation

U.S. forces can be tasked with many denial missions relative to the arenas of possible conflict with the USSR or its surrogates. The most important case, although not the most probable, is Europe. For decades a large debate has surrounded the issue of the relative weights to be given, by the United States and its NATO European allies, to denial forces compared to retaliatory forces. In the early 1950s, NATO originally set force-building goals of 96 ground divisions deployed in Europe (36–40 in the highest state of readiness). These so-called Lisbon force goals were rapidly abandoned when it became clear that neither U.S. nor European leaders were interested in paying the bill for such large conventional forces. Moreover, the U.S. nuclear strategy under Eisenhower veered in the direction of the New Look (and, later, the New New Look), which emphasized the early nuclear retaliation by SAC in response to Soviet invasion of Western Europe.[20] Although the Kennedy administration brought about a change of emphasis in the direction of flexible response, noted above, flexible response did not realign the roles assigned to U.S. nuclear forces and allied conventional forces in Europe. The NATO conventional forces (capable of being armed with nuclear weapons under the proper political and military release) were to provide denial of immediate Soviet and Warsaw Pact objectives and to buy time for decision making with regard to initial nuclear use. Thus conventional denial and nuclear retaliation were regarded as complementary and mutually supportive missions for the deterrence of war in Europe.

As Samuel P. Huntington has pointed out, however, there is no logical reason why this must be so; it is only the convention born of historical precedent and the constraints of European domestic politics.[21] He has outlined a proposal for a conventional retaliatory offensive in Europe by NATO in the event of a Warsaw Pact invasion without nuclear weapons. Soviet forays into Western Europe would be met by NATO retaliation without nuclear weapons into Eastern Europe. This has some comical aspects when played out on sand tables, with a resemblance to the relationship between the French Plan XVII and the German Schlieffen Plan in 1914. The execution of both plans without any deviation would have resulted in the French and German armies passing one another, as in a revolving door. However, Huntington's proposal and the idea of conventional retaliation are more serious than this.

The importance of thinking through the issue of conventional retaliation, even if it is politically infeasible under present conditions in West Germany, is heuristic. Forcing the option of conventional retaliation onto the menu of scholarly discourse, if not NATO war plans, forces recognition of the relationship between denial and retaliation in NATO strategy. There is no stone table limiting conventional forces to denial missions, nor nuclear weapons to retaliatory ones.

Let us consider another approach to the use of conventional forces as retaliatory forces. This approach is embodied in the U.S. "Maritime Strategy" as articulated by the navy in order to develop professional consensus on a context for thinking about peacetime and wartime operations.[22] The U.S. maritime strategy includes among its components the creation of threats to the viability of the Soviet fleet ballistic missile submarine (SSBN) force during conventional warfare. The idea is that forward operations of U.S. attack submarines (SSNs) in the Norwegian and Barents Seas can force the USSR to dedicate more assets to the protection of its SSBN assets. Thus the Soviets will have fewer resources with which to contest U.S. and allied maritime supremacy in and across the Atlantic.[23] In addition, U.S. forward operations will create attrition in the Soviet SSBN fleet, which will cause Soviet leaders to fear the loss of their strategic nuclear reserve. This threat will, in the U.S. navy's estimation, prompt the USSR to cancel its conventional invasion of Western Europe. Critics have disputed whether this component is realistic or desirable, even if it is a realistic expectation that the Soviet calculus in favor of war termination can be influenced by strategic ASW operations without nuclear escalation.[24]

The issue here is neither to defend nor attack U.S. maritime strategy but to point to at least one service doctrine that took into account the possibility of conventional as well as nuclear retaliation in order to terminate war in Europe. The U.S. maritime strategy was thus a chessmate of the Huntington proposal for conventional instead of nuclear retaliation, although in the navy's case, ground and tactical air forces are the pawns holding the front of the board, while maritime forces strike decisively against the opponent's jugular. And the assumption of the U.S. navy is that the Soviet jugular in conventional war is its dispersed and bottled up maritime capability, relative to that of its Western opponents.

However, and to the detriment of those who would exclude nuclear weapons completely from either denial or retaliatory roles, neither the U.S. maritime strategy nor the conventional retaliatory offensive in Europe can be implemented without raising the risk of nuclear escalation. The maritime strategy — it has been faulted by critics precisely on this score — if implemented as described in declaratory policy, will result in inadvertent nuclear war.[25] Of this phenomenon there are two kinds. The first is inadvertent nuclear war growing out of misapplied rules of engagement that delegate significant discretion to commanders under limited conditions. The second kind of inadvertent escalation is that which is deliberately created by policy makers along the lines of the "threat that leaves something to chance," as Schelling has described it.[26] It would appear that the critics feel the U.S. navy strategy runs more of the first kind of risk of inadvertent war. U.S. attack submarines would find it difficult if not impossible to distinguish Soviet SSNs from their SSBNs, and it is not clear that the navy sees the distinction as one that is worth making in wartime. The very early surging of U.S. SSNs into the Soviet SSBN bastions in the Barents Sea and under the Arctic ice may risk confrontations that Soviet commanders might confuse with a surprise first strike.

Although the navy strategy cannot avoid the risk of nuclear escalation, the more pertinent question is whether the risk is acceptably posed or unacceptable from the standpoint of uncontrollable risks. The navy case is that the risk of escalation is posed in a manner that is controllable and acceptable according to NATO strategy. Moreover, the case for inadvertent nuclear war growing out of U.S.-Soviet maritime conflict has been questioned by several experts outside the navy who have no vested interest in doing so. Both Donald C. Daniel of the U.S. Naval War College and Tom Stefanick have concluded that a campaign of attrition against Soviet strategic ballistic missile submarines would not probably result in immediate escalation by the USSR to nuclear war, especially to strategic nuclear war.[27] One can make two sorts of arguments about why not. First, Soviet doctrine does not make automatic any response on their part to SSBN attrition, and, therefore, predictions of what they must do in response are very conjectural. They have many options other than nuclear escalation, on land or at sea. Second, the USSR may choose to absorb attrition of its SSBN force if the war on the Central Front is going according to their prewar game plan and if NATO has not yet used nuclear weapons against Soviet forces. There is every reason to believe that disarming NATO without nuclear escalation is the preferred Soviet strategy for war in Europe.[28]

The relationship between denial and retaliation in U.S. strategy is also posed acutely by the potential development and deployment of ballistic missile defense (BMD) technology. The Reagan Strategic Defense Initiative has provoked a debate in the defense policy community that is primarily pertinent to these two issues — on those occasions when the debate is pertinent to anything at all. The relationship between denial and retaliation was at first rejected by the administration, following the presidential cue to render nuclear weapons impotent and obsolete. This led to claims that the entire U.S. national territory might be defended against strategic ballistic missile attacks from the Soviet Union, if only the appropriate technologies could be developed and deployed in a timely manner. As the rhetorical dust settled, the Strategic Defense Initiative Organization (SDIO) rapidly conceded that a more feasible near-term objective (meaning the next several decades) was the selective defense of retaliatory forces and other important U.S. sites from any Soviet first strike. Thus SDI moved from the ambitious declaratory mission of comprehensive protection of the U.S. population to the more manageable task of technology development for point defense deployment options in the 1990s.

Of course, both superpowers have been through at least two cycles of air or ballistic missile defense deployments in the post-World War II period, as Herbert York has recently recapitulated.[29] Neither has been able to deploy any combination of defenses that changes the basis of strategic stability. The bases of stability have remained offensive retaliation and societal vulnerability. Although there is some question whether the USSR prefers a strategy of societal vulnerability of simply accepts mutual vulnerability as unavoidable, there is little doubt that Soviet leaders have acquiesced to the existence of mutual deterrence.[30] U.S. critics of SDI therefore argue that a basically stable balance of terror will be subverted by U.S. BMC deployments. This balance of terror is judged to be dependent not on denial capabilities but on retaliatory capabilities residing in offensive forces.

The Reagan strategic concept holds the reverse tenet: a transition to defense dominance in technology and ultimately in strategy, will be made possible by a mutually agreed U.S.-Soviet constraint on offensive modernization, along with virtually comprehensive strategic defenses.[31] Th Soviets have acknowledged an interest in limiting the growth offenses but have thus far expressed hostility to the Reagan vision of a defense dominant world, in general, and the U.S. SDI program, in particular. The Soviet view apparently includes ABM Treaty-limited deployment of defenses, together with offenses that may be modernized but constrained in numbers of delivery vehicles and diversified in terms of survivable launch platforms. The United States has had difficulty understanding Soviet arms control proposals in the 1980s because the Soviet Union is itself uncertain with regard to the evolution of its strategy-technology mix. The U.S. bean-counting approach to SALT and START, which sought to reduce the numbers of first strike capable systems, primarily heavy Soviet ICBMs, solved yesterday's problem of U.S. vulnerability but will not solve tomorrow's. Tomorrow's problem might be a combination of limited Soviet BMD, more survivable land and sea-based cruise and ballistic offenses, and a born again Soviet bomber force equipped with long-range air launched cruise missiles (ALCMs). The U.S. "window of vulnerability" might not be in the first half hour of war with the destruction of U.S. ICBM silos but in the postexchange period during which relocatable targets might not be detected and, therefore, not hit. The point is not that it would be a consolation to attack these more difficult targets if those improved postexchange counterforce capabilities weakened deterrence. Instead, the concern would be that U.S. capabilities of this sort, which were obviously inferior to those of their Soviet counterparts, would weaken deterrence.

The relationship between Soviet strategy and technology is even more clouded than the preceding discussion has suggested. Additional uncertainties are inherent in the debates that took place within Soviet political and military circles during the 1970s and 1980s about two issues: the role of nuclear weapons in Soviet military doctrine and strategy and the possibility of a new understanding of the relationship between offense and defense in Soviet force structure and employment policy for nuclear or conventional war.

A virtual bookshelf of material exists on these topics, and only the gist of Western concerns about Soviet doctrine and strategy on these points can be noted here. As to the first, the role of nuclear weapons, the Soviets during the 1970s apparently adjusted to NATO flexible response strategy by acknowledging that war in Europe might have a conventional phase, even a decisive one, and that nuclear escalation was not automatic. They also acknowledged the possibility of selective uses of nuclear weapons in one theater of military action or operations without necessarily and automatically expanding those exchanges into U.S.-Soviet territorial homeland strikes.[32] This was certainly a loosening of the rigidity of the one-variant war scenarios that formed the basis of Soviet declaratory doctrine during the Khrushchev years. As Michael MccGwire has noted, an important doctrinal shift took place in the mid-1960s, after which the Soviets made it a primary objective to avoid the nuclear devastation of Russia.[33] Therefore an optimal Soviet plan for any war between NATO and the Warsaw Pact excluded immediate nuclear escalation as not in the Soviet interest and, if possible, resolved the issues in the Soviets' favor while preventing or deterring NATO nuclear escalation. If the use of theater nuclear weapons proved to be unavoidable, then the USSR would, contrary to its earlier doctrine, attempt to limit their use to the specific military objectives at hand while seeking to otherwise control escalation.

The second issue, even more contentious among Western analysts and perhaps among the Soviets themselves, was the emergence of a declaratory doctrine of "defensive sufficiency" or "reasonable sufficiency" on the part of some prominent Soviet military and political writers. These doctrinal shifts were favorably noted in prominent U.S. newspapers, including the New York Times, and attested to by various U.S. experts on Soviet military doctrine and strategy.[34] It was less certain in this case, compared to the case of reduced emphasis on the early use of nuclear weapons in theater strategy, that any dominant consensus within the USSR had displaced an earlier and established view. Some U.S. experts viewed the Soviet doctrine as a larger context from which the 1987 and 1988 START proposals developed, at the behest of Gorbachev, in order to limit U.S.-Soviet arms competition in the short run. This would, in turn, permit retooling the Soviet economy in the direction of "postindustrial" high technology required for the next century of competition with the West in military capability and economic productivity. It seemed to have been foreshadowed in the 1970s, too, that Soviet wariness of NATO high technology conventional weapons, mated to conventional deep attack strategies, would provide to the West a preclusive defense without nuclear weapons in Europe. Soviet conventional force modernization would require some period of transition to operational art based on high technology forces and on improved strategic and theater command, control, and communications.

However, if the USSR had indeed decided to improve its ability to compete with U.S., NATO European, and Japanese high technology for civilian and military purposes, this was a decision having equivocal implications for the evolution of Soviet military doctrine and strategy. Soviet military doctrine has both sociopolitical and military-technical aspects.[35] The Kremlin leadership is able to change the first, at least nominally, more rapidly than the professional military is able, or willing, to adjust the second. The military-technical doctrine changes only after scientific innovation is diffused throughout the military bureaucracy, in the form of force structure and military exercises. This is especially the case for innovation of doctrine and technology in the ground forces, where tradition and the study of military history hold sway compared to experimental research and doctrinal faddism. Nor is the Soviet system of troop control necessarily receptive to military-technical innovation until there is some established expectation as to how innovations will be reconciled with the Soviet imperatives for centralized command and control. Centralized in this context does not mean inflexible, but it means that each level is adaptive within the mission assigned by its superior level.[36]

The implications of a doctrine of military sufficiency, should the USSR actually adopt and implement it, may be dramatic. The first implication is that the Soviet Union might be willing to accept a much smaller strategic nuclear force, which was adequate for second strike countervalue retaliation but less than adequate for flexible nuclear targeting or for counterforce attacks. Related to this is the possibility that if U.S. strategic nuclear offenses were similarly limited in their performance capabilities, then mutual agreement on limited BMD deployments, to strengthen deterrence by protecting retaliatory forces, might be had. Of course, there might be other and less expensive ways to protect retaliatory forces, including arms control and passive defenses such as hardening, dispersal, and mobility.

The second implication is that the USSR might be satisfied with theater forces deployed in Eastern Europe inadequate to support any preemptive attack against NATO forces and command systems. These realigned Soviet forces would be tasked for the defensive mission of repelling a NATO attack and not otherwise be capable of mounting preemptive attacks of their own. In this Western view of evolving Soviet doctrine for war in Europe, the USSR would accept the division of Europe into permanent spheres of influence. Not even the dissolution of West European and trans-Atlantic cohesion would tempt aggression so long as NATO was seen as strictly defensive in its intentions and capabilities.

This is a somewhat optimistic view of Soviet aims and ambitions in Europe, but it is not an impossible one given a convergence of certain very favorable developments. The first is a continuation of the U.S.-Soviet dialogue on strategic arms reductions. The second, related to the first, is the commitment by both sides to abide by the ABM Treaty (perhaps as amended) until well into the 1990s. The third is the creation of a reduced expectation on the part of NATO that the USSR has significant capability for conventional *blitzkrieg* in Europe. The fourth, related to the second, is that the U.S. SDI or the Soviet BMD program does not upset the applecart of offensive arms reductions and limits on strategic modernization. The fifth, and perhaps most important, is that crisis stability holds firm and that no situation outside Europe brings about a U.S.-Soviet confrontation to unravel previous arms and security agreements.

The third item on this list is more problematical from a military-technical standpoint, in the Soviet perspective. It is difficult to see how Soviet planners are going to rewrite their script for a rapid and decisive conventional war in Europe, preferably without nuclear escalation, into some alternative. Remember that the Soviets do not draw the same distinction between deterrent forces and warfighting forces that Western military analysts do. Conventional and nuclear forces for war in Europe (as opposed to intercontinental strategic nuclear war) are to be used in a combined arms philosophy, which is very pragmatically cast. It is designed to defeat the opponent's forces, to occupy the most important centers of political and military power in those parts of Western Europe under attack, and to deter further Western escalation with remaining Soviet nuclear and conventional forces.[37] The alternative to this strategy, from the Soviet perspective, cannot be appealing. They are either a protracted, global conventional war or a strategic nuclear war. In the first instance the economic long odds are against the Soviet Union because of its economic potential compared to that of the United States and its allies. The second case offers the Soviet Union the prospect of destroying itself on behalf of some nominal "victory" in the sense that more Soviet nuclear warheads might survive than U.S./NATO ones. The likely condition of Soviet and U.S. cities makes this point moot.

It will take some time to determine whether Soviet military planning and force structure, in addition to declaratory doctrine, are moving toward defensive sufficiency. Perhaps the political implications of this transition, if it takes place, are more important than the military. The political implications would include a freezing of the East-West division into a military detente, fulfilling the Harmel report with a vengeance. This would then leave to Western prime ministers and presidents less of a rationale for maintaining U.S. combat forces in Europe, and it might also provoke European conventional force reductions in NATO. Ironically, the denuclearization of NATO's theater defenses could be propelled inadvertently by SDI, whose technology spinoffs could include ATBMs (theater ballistic missile defenses) not dependent on nuclear weapons.[38] In a worst-case scenario for NATO alliance management, nuclear weapons of all ranges have been withdrawn from Western Europe, and U.S. conventional forces have been reduced in the misbegotten expectation that "Europeans can defend themselves." This worst-case possibility should not materialize, but it will challenge NATO political and military competency to stay abreast of Gorbachev's fast-moving arms control agenda. The USSR has clearly embarked upon a political strategy of reducing the threat to its security by arms control in the short run and by economic and technology restructuring for the long run. As hinted at previously, this strategy will require the management of some difficult and sensitive command and control issues on the part of Soviet political and military leaders.

Control

The relationships among denial, retaliation, deterrence, and reassurance are linked by the problem of control. Frequently defined as "command and control" or "command, control, and communications," this is actually a two-part issue. The command part has to do with leadership or goal setting. The control function involves monitoring and influencing subordinates' behavior in order to see that goals are accomplished. Command

and control are impossible to separate in practice, including the practical applications of military art and science.[39] As might be expected, given the preceding discussion, Soviet and Western views of command and control draw from different conceptual frameworks and historical traditions.

In the Soviet historical experience, the issues of command and control are certainly bound very closely together. The fledgling state that survived the Russian Revolution had to organize very quickly. One of the first issues that had to be decided was what kind of army the Soviet state would need to accomplish its objectives. There was a spirited debate on this, well into the latter 1920s and long after Lenin had departed the scene. Among other issues, one important matter was whether a people's army based on voluntary recruitment could suffice for Soviet needs, or, instead, a professional military officer corps loyal to the state would have to be developed. The latter view quite obviously prevailed, but it is nonetheless instructive to review the debates among Soviet military intellectuals, including Trotsky and Frunze, in order to follow the development of their thinking on these subjects.[40] The dilemma for the Soviet leadership was that a professional officer corps might not necessarily be a loyal one or that its loyalty might be to the Russian nation or Soviet state at the expense of the party and its leadership.

For the USSR to have solved this problem as effectively as it has done was no small accomplishment, but there were many bumps along the way. Loyalty of the officer corps to the party/political leadership was assured by penetration of the personnel selection system with Chekists of all descriptions.[41] Stalin's purges of the 1930s included the best of the officer corps and contributed directly to the Soviets' early disasters against Hitler's forces in 1941. The Red Army was rotted from within by incompetence and political toadying and had not time to pull up its socks before the Wehrmacht struck in June 1941.[42] The Winter War against Finland had been a preview of things to come. The Soviets' performance in the early stages of the war was as incompetent as the recovery of military effectiveness and the improvement in its performance throughout the conflict were remarkable. The Great Fatherland War was the seedbed of the Soviet armed forces of the present era. It influenced the Soviet military leadership in its thinking about all matters of military doctrine, military science, and military art.

As a result of prewar and wartime experiences, the Soviet leadership was better positioned after World War II to integrate its answers to the problem of maintaining troop loyalty and of preserving professional military competency. The integration took place at both theoretical and practical levels. At the theoretical level, there was no tension between the objectives of loyalty and competency. Such tension as might exist was the result of inadequate tutelage in the precepts of Marxist-Leninism, including the notion thereby derived that the commander was responsible for the political indoctrination and the combat performance of the troops under his command.[43] However, the extent to which the military zampolits are turned loose to hector the rank and file in daily or weekly sessions varies a great deal among units and their assigned missions. There is a largely ritualistic character to this among the masses of conscripts who populate the Soviet armed forces and whose rebellion the Party is not really worried about (although they might be if the misguided follow some rebellious leaders). Instead, it is the military leadership, and that at the topmost levels, that must be clearly subordinated to party objectives and political control. This is a matter of continuing vigilance to screen out those who are not suitably projective of their commitment to the party way of doing things, including the tasking of armed forces and the decision about when to use them and for what.

However, it would be a mistake to suppose that the members of the Soviet military leadership are a monolith on the issues that are most important to them professionally, including the study of military history and its applications to contemporary problems. Soviet military doctrine has undergone significant revisions on more than one occasion since the end of World War II, and the process continues even now. What is not debatable is the primacy of political objectives set by the Party leadership, although even here the officer corps has substantial influence. When former Soviet Premier Nikita S. Khrushchev attempted to reduce substantially the complement of Soviet ground forces in order to emphasize the role of nuclear weapons, he laid the cornerstone for his eventual dismissal. All that waited was the right occasion, which Khrushchev provided in the aftermath of the Cuban missile crisis of 1962.[44] Having summoned a loyal military clique to prevent his ouster in 1957, Khrushchev had become by 1964 unacceptable to the military leadership across the board. It was no coincidence that a military buildup followed Brezhnev's accession to power thereafter, nor that changes in force structure eventually did also.[45]

So the military bureaucrats and their allies in heavy industry have some significant political clout, but as interest groups instead of as authoritative policy makers. There is no state-within-a-state admissible in the Soviet vocabulary. The problems of control are more subtle. They have to do with crisis management, escalation control, and intrawar deterrence. That these are also potential problems for the United States is no surprise. It is sometimes said that the Soviet and U.S. or Western paradigms for thinking about strategy are so different that the very notions of crisis management and control of escalation are illustrations of Western ethnocentrism. Perhaps the labeling is ethnocentric, but the problems are not so easily dismissed. The control of crisis is a requirement imposed on Soviet and U.S. political establishments and on their supporting armed forces and command systems. The alternative to crisis management is the ruination of two large societies. Escalation control is the ability to limit the scope and destructiveness of conflict even after it begins. It applies to conventional as well as nuclear war between superpowers or their allies although its application to nuclear wars is obviously more conjectural. Intrawar deterrence is related to escalation control and is made possible by the preservation of, at least, a countercity retaliatory capability through all phases of a U.S.-Soviet conflict.

Crisis Management, Escalation Control,
and Intrawar Deterrence

Crisis management studies have flourished in the United States since the Cuban missile crisis of 1962. That specific crisis has been investigated by many historians, political scientists and others curious about the management of superpower confrontation.[46] Studies of that crisis and other less dramatic confrontations between U.S. and Soviet interests have revealed less than one might have supposed, given the volume of studies and the prestige of some of the authors. The Cuban crisis has been represented as a case study of successful U.S. decision making by the president and his key advisors (the "ExCom" or Executive Committee of the National Security Council, a cover title applied to the group). Khrushchev acquiesced to U.S. demands that the medium- and intermediate-range ballistic missiles in Cuba be dismantled and removed from that island. Kennedy used a technique of naval "quarantine" (blockade in all but name) to compel the Soviet leader to withdraw the missiles, allowing for the possibility of escalation to more dramatic and war-threatening moves if the quarantine did not work. Kennedy's decision making made effective use of limited pressure upon the Soviets combined with the credible threat of doing more if necessary. And U.S. military superiority at the strategic nuclear and conventional levels (in the Caribbean, where it mattered) was able to reinforce U.S. threats to escalate if Khrushchev did not relent.[47]

However, the Cuban case is less successful if it is understood, as it might reasonably be, as an instance of luck instead of crisis management. The truth was that the United States knew precious little about how the Soviet Union was making its decisions during this crisis. This lack of knowledge about Soviet decision making was revealed when Khrushchev sent two very different responses to President Kennedy in letters one day apart. The first response was conciliatory and suggested that the USSR might be willing to reach an agreement along the lines that the U.S. president had first demanded: the withdrawal of missiles from Cuba, along with a U.S. pledge not to invade Cuba. The second response caused U.S. policy makers to wonder who was in charge in the Soviet Union and to consider more seriously the possible necessity for U.S. air strikes against the missile sites.[48]

Kennedy and his advisors chose the "Trollope ploy" in which they ignored the second letter from Khrushchev and responded only to the first. This ultimately proved to be successful in helping to resolve the crisis on terms acceptable to Kennedy. Recently declassified transcriptions of tapes from meetings of the Ex-Com on October 27, 1962, reveal something very interesting about the successful use of this U.S. ploy to resolve the crisis. As some of the president's advisors grew more doubtful that the crisis could be resolved without further escalation, it was Llewellyn Thompson who argued that pessimism was unwarranted and that the "Trollope ploy" might still bear fruit.[49] Thompson's expertise on the Soviet Union contributed to his important insights in the deliberation of the ExCom. However, Thompson, too, was forced to rely upon conjecture instead of hard evidence about Soviet intentions and priorities.

The recently declassified transcriptions on Cuba also reveal some previously unfocused differences in perspective between President Kennedy and his advisors. Kennedy was apparently more prepared to play another diplomatic card, in the form of trading Jupiter missiles in Turkey for Soviet missiles in Cuba, than his advisors were. According to James G. Blight of Harvard University, who assisted McGeorge Bundy, Kennedy's Special Assistant for National Security and transcriber of the pertinent tapes on Cuba, "It was only the President who expressed strong and repeated enthusiasm for the merits of the trade."[50] Whereas the consensus among his advisors was fatalistic about avoiding war, Kennedy was still considering, and perhaps leaning toward, trading missiles in preference to an air strike, invasion, or other option that might involve direct U.S.-Soviet fighting and nuclear escalation.

The frustration for U.S. scholars then and now is that they do not have a credible account from the Soviet participants about Politburo decision making and about the Soviet view of their own efforts to implement those decisions. There is a U.S. and Western literature that attempts to interpret Soviet motivations for introducing missiles into Cuba, but these inferences are dependent upon reconstructed Soviet logic through U.S. conceptual lenses. Graham T. Allison has reconstructed what might have been the Soviet and U.S. logics of decision making pertinent to the Cuban crisis. He develops three models of decision making and applies each model as an explanatory tool for both sides: the rational policy, organizational process, and governmental politics models.[51] Each of these models adds another dimension to the understanding of the U.S. behavior, but they are not equally explanatory of the Soviet. This is not because one must use a Marxian model to understand Soviet behavior, as is sometimes wrongly supposed. The problem is a weak data base or an insufficient testimonial record from the Soviet participants, compared to the U.S. ones.

A second difficulty is that the unknowns inside the Soviet bureaucracy are compounded by the unpredictables in the maneuvering between the two sides during the crisis. Precrisis diplomatic communications did not reach the designated target with the appropriate message. President Kennedy clearly sought to communicate, in public and through private channels, his determination not to allow the emplacement of "offensive" missiles in Cuba. These signals either came too late or were not believed to be adequate indicators of what Kennedy would really do when the missiles were discovered. There is also the possibility that the Soviets engaged in wishful thinking that the missiles would not be discovered until they were ready for launch, thus presenting a *fait accompli* to the Americans. One wonders, if that were so, how the USSR expected to deter a U.S. conventional attack on Cuba with the threat of preemptive nuclear attack against North America. Given the strategic nuclear balance in 1962, a Soviet nuclear attack on North America would surely have resulted in the destruction of the USSR as a modern society with comparatively little devastation to the United States. Of course, "comparatively little" devastation would be unprecedented catastrophe by U.S. standards, and it might have been enough to deter the Americans, as President Kennedy's apparent willingness to consider a missiles-for-missiles trade suggests. This, however, is allegedly not how Soviet policy makers are supposed to reckon, according to their doctrine. They should not have expected Kennedy to be deterred by the absolute losses they might inflict upon U.S.

society but by the prospects for relative losses that the Americans or Soviets might have imposed on one another. However, even that perspective should have suggested caution to the Soviets, for their survivable strategic nuclear capability was greatly inferior to that of the United States, and the United States had recently and publicly declared it so.[52]

Khrushchev's own explanation that his motivation was to deter U.S. attack against Cuba (apart from the presence of Soviet missiles) reads as disingenuous.[53] After the abortive Bay of Pigs invasion of the preceding year, this was not a viable option for Kennedy without a pretext larger than the mere existence of the Castro regime. U.S. "rational policy" analysts, in Allison's terminology, would argue that the USSR simply sought to reverse an adverse nuclear balance by using essentially the same short-term improvisation as had the Americans in the 1950s. In the earlier decade, the United States had deployed Thor and Jupiter IRBM in Europe in the expectation of improving deterrence in the near term, while awaiting the subsequent development and deployment of U.S. land and sea-based strategic missiles (ICBMs and SLBMs) in the 1960s. Thus, it might be argued that the Soviets by placing missiles into Cuba sought to pose a threat to Americans, from medium-range delivery systems, analogous to the threat the Americans were presenting to the USSR from missile bases in Turkey. Something similar, in the way of responding to one threat with something analogous and proportionate, has been suggested as an interpretation of initial Soviet responses to the onset of NATO Pershing II and cruise missile deployments in December 1983. The USSR threatened to move some of their nuclear armed submarines closer to U.S. shores in order to present a comparable threat to U.S. command centers and other time urgent targets highly valued by the United States.

The problem with this rational policy model, of Soviet motivation prompted by a desire for presenting "analogous menace," is that it is more characteristic of U.S. than of Soviet reasoning about these matters. The USSR would be unlikely to place much emphasis upon posing of a symmetrical threat to U.S. interests, as opposed to its motivation for demonstrating an effective threat. Soviet historical experience does not suggest to its leaders that symmetrical threats are very effective. This does not exclude a Soviet interest in escalation control or intra-war deterrence. The USSR wants to avoid wars that may lead to undesirable political or military outcomes if it has diplomatic alternatives. If war cannot be avoided, the Soviets want to obtain the most favorable outcome possible, using force in the most efficient way. Sometimes "efficient" means a rapid and overwhelming concentration of offensive power at the decisive point of the opponent's vulnerability. At other times it means an approach that may permit a sliding scale of options, as the scenario unfolds. The Soviets have demonstrated this kind of adaptive flexibility in wartime conditions. As Colonel David Glantz of the U.S. Army Command and General Staff College, Fort Leavenworth, Kansas, has noted, they were forced to adapt their operational art of war and their force structure in order to drive the Wehrmacht from Russia during World War II. The early stages of that conflict forced upon Soviet military planners adaptive responses for the conduct of the operational defensive. Later stages required equally adaptive responses to the requirements of conducting deep offensive operations over extremely large fronts or groups of fronts.[54] These innovations in doctrine and strategy posed the problem of controlling large groups of forces on the offensive under fluid and uncertain battle conditions. Soviet capabilities in this regard defied the expectations of Western military strategists then and now.

NOTES

1. John J. Mearsheimer, *Conventional Deterrence* (Ithaca, N.Y.: Cornell University Press, 1983).

2. Richard K. Betts, "Surprise Attack and Preemption," in *Hawks, Doves and Owls: An Agenda for Avoiding Nuclear War*, ed. Graham T. Allison, Albert Carnesale, and Joseph S. Nye, Jr. (New York: W. W. Norton, 1985), p. 56.

3. For a discussion of this problem in a variety of contexts, see Richard K. Betts, *Surprise Attack: Lessons for Defense Planning* (Washington, D.C.: The Brookings Institution, 1982).

4. Admiral James D. Watkins, USN, "The Maritime Strategy," *Proceedings of the U.S. Naval Institute*, January 1986, pp. 2–17.

5. See Colin S. Gray, *Maritime Strategy, Geopolitics and the Defense of the West* (New York: National Strategy Information Center, 1986).

6. Robert W. Komer, *Maritime Strategy or Coalition Defense?* (Cambridge, Mass.: Abt Books, 1984) argues that the Reagan defense program has favored unilateralist maritime approaches to deterrence and defense compared to multilateral approaches.

7. Edward N. Luttwak, *Strategy: The Logic of War and Peace* (Cambridge, Mass.: Harvard University Press, 1987) emphasizes the dialectical character of all strategy.

8. The Iranian case was an all-round debacle. On the deficiencies of the Iran rescue mission during the Carter administration, see Richard A. Gabriel, *Military Incompetence: Why the American Military Doesn't Win* (New York: Hill and Wang, 1985), pp. 85–116.

9. For an insightful analysis, see Joshua M. Epstein, *Strategy and Force Planning: The Case of the Persian Gulf* (Washington, D.C.: The Brookings Institution, 1987).

10. A discussion of this appears in Max G. Manwaring, "Limited War and Conflict Control," in *Conflict Termination in Military Strategy*, ed. Stephen J. Cimbala and Keith A. Dunn (Boulder, Colo.: Westview Press, 1987), pp. 59–76.

11. The relationship between legitimacy and military posture in the context of low-intensity conflict is analyzed in Sam C. Sarkesian, *Beyond the Battlefield: The New Military Professionalism* (New York: Pergamon Press, 1981), Chapter 6.

12. Robert W. Komer, *Bureaucracy at War: U.S. Performance in the Vietnam Conflict* (Boulder, Colo.: Westview Press, 1986), Chapter 3.

13. Michael Howard, *The Causes of Wars* (Cambridge, Mass.: Harvard University Press, 1984), pp. 246–64.

14. On motivations for European antinuclear protest, see James E. Dougherty and Robert L. Pfaltzgraff, Jr., eds., *Shattering Europe's Defense Consensus: The Antinuclear Protest Movement and the Future of NATO* (New York: Pergamon-Brassey's, 1985).

15. See U.S. Department of State, *The INF Treaty: Negotiation and Ratification*, Current Policy No. 1039 (Washington, D.C.: Bureau of Public Affairs, U.S. State Department, February 1988).

16. The problem of bottom-up release is discussed in Catherine McArdle Kelleher, "NATO Nuclear Operations," Chapter 14, in *Managing Nuclear Operations*, ed. Ashton B. Carter, John D. Steinbruner, and Charles A. Zraket (Washington, D.C.: The Brookings Institution, 1987), p. 458.

17. On the MLF, see David N. Schwartz, *NATO's Nuclear Dilemmas* (Washington, D.C.: The Brookings Institution, 1983), Chapter 5.

18. Michael Howard, "The Forgotten Dimensions of Strategy," in *The Cause of Wars*, Howard, pp. 101–15.

19. See Richard Ned Lebow, "The Deterrence Deadlock: Is There a Way Out? in *Psychology and Deterrence*, ed. Robert Jervis, Richard Ned Lebow, and Janice Gross Stein (Baltimore: Johns Hopkins University Press, 1985), pp. 180–202.

20. Timothy Ireland, "Building NATO's Nuclear Posture: 1950–1965," in *The Nuclear Confrontation in Europe*, ed. Jeffrey D. Boutwell, Paul Doty, and Gregory F. Treverton (London: Croom Helm, 1985), pp. 5–43.

21. See Samuel P. Huntington, "The Renewal of Strategy," in *The Strategic Imperative*, ed. Huntington (Cambridge, Mass.: Ballinger, 1982), pp. 1–52 for discussion of the concept of conventional retaliation as related to the mission of conventional deterrence.

22. Watkins, "The Maritime Strategy," pp. 2–17.

23. An authoritative reference on this subject is Donald C. Daniel, *Anti-Submarine Warfare and Superpower Strategic Stability* (Urbana, Ill.: University of Illinois Press, 1986).

24. John J. Mearsheimer, "A Strategic Misstep: The Maritime Strategy and Deterrence in Europe," *International Security* 11 (Fall 1986): 3–57, esp. pp. 14–17, 45–54, on counterforce coercion and its potentially counterproductive effects.

25. Barry R. Posen, "Inadvertent Nuclear War? Escalation and NATO's Northern Flank," *International Security* 7, reprinted in *Strategy and Nuclear Deterrence*, ed. Steven E. Miller (Princeton: Princeton University Press, 1984), pp. 85–111.

26. Thomas C. Schelling, *The Strategy of Conflict* (Cambridge, Mass.: Harvard University Press, 1966), pp. 187–204, discusses the "threat that leaves something to chance."

27. For comments on the relationship between strategic ASW and war termination as outlined in U.S. maritime strategy, see Tom Stefanick, *Strategic Antisubmarine Warfare and Naval Strategy* (Lexington, Mass.: D. C. Heath, 1987), pp. 109–12.

28.   See Christopher N. Donnelly, "Soviet Operational Concepts in the 1980s," in *Strengthening Conventional Deterrence in Europe: Proposals for the 1980s*, Report of the European Security Study (New York: St. Martin's Press, 1983), pp. 105–36.

29.   An overview of U.S. and Soviet efforts in active defense is provided by Herbert F. York, "Strategic Defense from World War II to the Present," in *Strategic Defense and the Western Alliance*, ed. Sanford Lakoff and Randy Willoughby (Lexington, Mass.: D. C. Heath, 1987), pp. 15–32.

30.   Raymond L. Garthoff, "Mutual Deterrence, Parity and Strategic Arms Limitation in Soviet Policy," in *Soviet Military Thinking*, ed. Derek Leebaert (London: Allen and Unwin, 1981), pp. 92–124.

31.   Paul H. Nitze, "On the Road to a More Stable Peace," U.S. Department of State, *Current Policy* No. 657, February 20, 1985.

32.   On changes in Soviet doctrine, see John G. Hines, Phillip A. Petersen, and Notra Trulock III, "Soviet Military Theory from 1945–2000: Implications for NATO," *Washington Quarterly* 9 (Fall 1986): 117–37.

33.   Michael MccGwire, *Military Objectives in Soviet Foreign Policy* (Washington, D.C.: The Brookings Institution, 1987), Chapter 3. Counter-arguments with regard to the mid-1960s as a turning point appear in James M. McConnell, "SDI, the Soviet Investment Debate and Soviet Military Policy," *Strategic Review* 16 (Winter 1988): 47–62. McConnell suggests that the USSR under Gorbachev has favored preparedness for protracted conventional war, amid some controversy within the military and political establishment about investment priorities.

34.   "Soviet Arms Doctrine in Flux," New York *Times*, March 7, 1988, p. A1. The article quotes unnamed Pentagon officials, Western specialists on the Soviet Union, and Soviet sources. For skeptical counterpoint, see William F. Scott, "Another Look at the USSR's 'Defensive' Doctrine," *Air Force Magazine*, March 1988, pp. 48–52. Care must be taken to distinguish the different aspects of Soviet military doctrine described. Soviet military doctrine has both political and military-technical aspects. It is possible for the political component of Soviet military doctrine to be defensive while the operational-technical component remains offensive. This means that Soviet military planners would count on their political leadership to avert war if at all possible, but, once war seemed unavoidable, they would fight it with an offensive operational-strategic cast. See Stephen M. Meyer, "Soviet Perspectives on the Paths to Nuclear War," in Allison, Carnesale, and Nye, eds., *Hawks, Doves and Owls*, Chapter 7.

35.   Raymond L. Garthoff, *Detente and Confrontation: American-Soviet Relations from Nixon to Reagan* (Washington, D.C.: The Brookings Institution, 1985), pp. 776–80.

36.   John Hemsley, *Soviet Troop Control: The Role of Command Technology in the Soviet Military System* (Oxford: Brassey's, 1982).

37.   Joseph D. Douglass, Jr., *The Soviet Theater Nuclear Offensive*, Studies in Communist Affairs, Vol. 1 (Washington, D.C.: U.S. Government Printing Office, undated). Prepared for Office of Director of Defense Research and Engineering and Defense Nuclear Agency and published under the auspices of the U.S. Air Force. See also, Voroshilov Lectures, I, "Strategic Operations in a Continental Theater of Strategic Military Action," pp. 257–314 (Washington, D.C.: National Defense University Press, 1989).

38.   On pertinent technologies for active defense, see Gregory H. Canavan, "Defensive Technologies for Europe," in *Strategic Defense and the Western Alliance*, ed. Lakoff and Willoughby, pp. 33–52.

39.   On the Soviet view of command and control, see Stephen J. Cimbala, ed., *Soviet C3* (Washington, D.C.: AFCEA International Press, 1987), for a collection of representative views.

40.   See Walter Darnell Jacobs, *Frunze: The Soviet Clausewitz, 1885–1925* (The Hague: Martinus Nijhoff, 1969).

41.   An authoritative account is John J. Dziak, *Chekisty: A History of the KGB* (Lexington, Mass.: D. C. Heath, 1988).

42.   For observations and background, see John Erickson, *The Soviet High Command, A Military-Political History, 1918–1941* (New York: St. Martin's Press, 1962), pp. 666–68 and *passim.*

43.   See Colonel M. P. Skirdo, *The People, the Army, the Commander* (Moscow, 1970), published under the auspices of the U.S. Air Force, translated by DGIS Multilingual Section, Secretary of State Department, Ottawa, Canada.

44.   On controversy surrounding Khrushchev's military policy, see Oleg Penkovskiy, *The Penkovskiy Papers*, trans. Peter Deriabin (New York: Doubleday, 1965), pp. 223–60.

45.   See MccGwire, *Military Objectives in Soviet Foreign Policy*, Chapter 2.

46.   There are many sources on the Cuban missile crisis. A definitive study among political scientists is Graham T. Allison, *Essence of Decision: Explaining the Cuban Missile Crisis* (Boston: Little, Brown, 1971).

47.   Irving Janis, *Groupthink* (Boston: Houghton Mifflin, 1982), pp. 132–58, argues that U.S. decision making in the Cuban missile crisis was an example of successfully avoiding "groupthink," a self-destructive consensus-seeking tendency among groups of policy makers.

48.   McGeorge Bundy, transcriber, and James G. Blight, ed., "October 27, 1962: Transcripts of the Meetings of the Ex Comm," *International Security* 12 (Winter 1987–1988): 32–33.

49.   Ibid., p. 73.

50.   An indication of Kennedy's interest in the trading of U.S. missiles in Turkey for Soviet missiles in Cuba, even after most of his advisors bypassed that option, appears in ibid., p. 85.

51.   The case is made by Allison, *Essence of Decision, passim*. Allison develops three conceptual models of the crisis decision making based on very clear indications about U.S. decision making, but evidence for the explanatory power of those models with regard to Soviet decision making is more ambiguous. See Garthoff, *Reflections on the Cuban Missile Crisis* (Washington, D.C.: The Brookings Institution, 1989), revised.

52.   The U.S. in 1961 publicly announced that there was no "missile gap" in favor of the Soviet Union, as had been previously thought. Deputy Secretary of Defense Roswell Gilpatrick said as much in a speech cleared at the highest levels and U.S. NATO allies were briefed on the assumption that the same information would then leak to Soviet intelligence. The purpose of both overt and covert dissuasion was to deter Soviet pressure on Berlin. The decision was made "in the full knowledge that the information that the United States knew the true situation would alarm the Soviets and compel them to take some form of countermeasure." See Roger Hilsman, *The Politics of Policymaking in Defense and Foreign Affairs* (Englewood Cliffs, N.J.: Prentice-Hall, 1987), pp. 4–5.

53.   Strobe Talbott, ed. and trans., *Khrushchev Remembers* (Boston: Little, Brown, 1970), pp. 488–505.

54.   Colonel David M. Glantz, *Deep Attack: The Soviet Conduct of Operational Maneuver* (Fort Leavenworth, Kansas: Soviet Army Studies Office, U.S. Army Command and General Staff College, April 1987).

Selected Bibliography

This bibliography emphasizes primary sources and a minority of secondary sources that are repeatedly cited or are of special value for reference. Other important sources are cited in chapter notes.

Akhromeev, Marshal of the Soviet Union Sergei. "Doktrina predotvrashcheniya voyny zashchity mira i sotsializma." *Problemy Mira i Sotsializma* 12 (December 1987): 26–27.

Anureyev, Major General I. "Determining the Correlation of Forces in Terms of Nuclear Weapons." *Voyennaya mysl'* 7 (July 1968), FPD 0112/68, August 11, 1968, p. 38.

Bracken, Paul. *The Command and Control of Nuclear Forces.* New Haven: Yale University Press, 1983.

Byely, Colonel B., et al. *Marxism-Leninism on War and Army.* Moscow: Progress Publishers, 1972. U.S. Air Force Soviet Military Thought Series.

Cimbala, Stephen J., ed. *Soviet C3.* Washington, D.C.: AFCEA International Press, 1987.

Clausewitz, Carl von. *Vom Kriege* [On War]. Edited and translated by Michael Howard and Peter Paret. Princeton: Princeton University Press, 1976.

Davis, Paul K., and Peter J. E. Stan. *Concepts and Models of Escalation.* Santa Monica, Calif.: Rand Corporation, May 1984.

Donnelly, Christopher N. "Soviet Operational Concepts in the 1980s," in *Strengthening Conventional Deterrence in Europe: Proposals for the 1980s,* pp. 10–36. Report of the European Security Study. New York: St. Martin's Press, 1983.

Douglas, Joseph D., Jr. *The Soviet Theater Nuclear Offensive*, Vol. 1. Prepared for Office of Director of Defense Research and Engineering and Defense Nuclear Agency and published under the auspices of the U.S. Air Force. Washington, D.C.: U.S. Government Printing Office, undated.

Druzhinin, V. V., and D. S. Kontorov, *Ideya, algoritm, resheniye*. Moscow: Voyenizdat, 1972. Published in U.S. Air Force Soviet Military Thought Series as *Concept, Algorithm, Decision*. Washington, D.C.: U.S. Government Printing Office, undated.

Gareyev, Colonel General M. A. *M. V. Frunze — voyennyy teoretik*. Moscow: Voyenizdat, 1985.

Garthoff, Raymond L. *Detente and Confrontation*. Washington, D.C.: The Brookings Institution, 1985.

Glantz, David M. *August Storm: The Soviet 1945 Strategic Offensive in Manchuria*. Fort Leavenworth, Kansas: U.S. Army Command and General Staff College, February 1983.

Glazunov, N. K., and N. S. Nitikin. *Operatsiya i boy*. Moscow: Voyenizdat, 1983.

Gorbachev, M. "Speech to the Twenty-Seventh CPSU Congress." *Pravda*, February 26, 1986; "Speech to the Moscow Peace Forum." *Pravda*, February 17, 1987; "Rech' tovarischa M. S. Gorbacheva." *Krasnaya zvezda*, October 2, 1987, pp. 1–3.

Gray, Colin S. *Maritime Strategy, Geopolitics, and the Defense of the West*. New York: National Strategy Information Center, 1986.

Grechko, Marshal A. *Vooruzhennye sily sovetskogo gosudarstva*. Moscow: Voyenizdat, 1974.

Gribkov, General. "Opyt upravleniya koalitsionnymi gruppirovkame voysk." *Voenno-istoricheskiy Zhurnal* 3 (March 1984).

Hemsley, John. *Soviet Troop Control*. New York: Brassey's, 1982.

Hines, John G., Phillip A. Petersen, and Notra Trulock III. "Soviet Military Theory: 1945–2000: Implications for NATO." *Washington Quarterly*, Fall 1986, pp. 117–37.

Kir'yan, General M. M. *Voyenno-tekhnicheskiy progress i vooruzhennye sily SSSR*. Moscow: Voyenizdat, 1982.

Komer, Robert W. *Maritime Strategy or Coalition Defense?* Cambridge, Mass.: Abt Books, 1984.

Kozlov, General-Major S. N. *The Officer's Handbook*. Moscow: 1971. U.S. Air Force Soviet Military Thought Series.

Kulikov, V. "Strategicheskoe rukovodstovo vooruzhennymi silami." *Voyenno-istoricheskiy Zhurnal* 6 (June 1975).

Laschenko, General P. "Sovershenstvovaniye sposobev okruzheniya i unichtozeniya krupnykh gruppirovoka protivnika po opytu velikoy otechestvennoy voyny." *Voyenno-istoricheskiy Zhurnal* 2 (February 1985).

Lee, Wiliam T., and Richard F. Staar. *Soviet Military Policy since World War II.* Stanford, Calif.: Hoover Institution, 1986.

Lushev, General P. "High Combat Readiness of the Soviet Armed Forces — An Important Factor in the Defense of Socialism." *Voyenno-istoricheskiy Zhurnal* 6 (June 1987): 8.

Luttwak, Edward N. *The Pentagon and the Art of War.* New York: Simon and Schuster, 1984.

Mayorov, General A. M. "Strategicheskoye rukovodstovo v velikoy otechestvennoy voyne." *Voyenno-istoricheskiy Zhurnal* 5 (May 1985).

MccGwire, Michael, *Military Objectives in Soviet Foreign Policy.* Washington, D.C.: The Brookings Institution, 1987.

McConnell, James M. *The Soviet Shift Towards and Away from Nuclear Warwaging.* Working Paper No. 84–0690, Center for Naval Analyses, pp. 112–14.

Meyer, Stephen M. *Soviet Theater Nuclear Forces, Part II: Capabilities and Implications.* London: International Institute for Strategic Studies, Adelphi Papers No. 188, Winter 1983–1984.

Musial, Colonel (docent) Aleksander. "Character i znaczenie operacji powietrznych we wspolczesnych dzialanizch wojennych" [Character and Importance of Air Operations in Modern Warfare]. *Przeglad wojsk lotniczych i wojsk obrony powietrznej kraju* [Polish Air Forces and Air Defense Review] 3 (1982).

Ogarkov, Marshal N. V. *Istoriya uchit bditel'nosti.* Moscow: Voyenizdat, 1985.

_____. *Vsegda v gotovnosti k zashchite Otechestva.* Moscow: Voyenizdat, 1982.

Ol'shtynskiy, L. I. *Vzaimodeystviye armii i flota.* Moscow: Voyenizdat, 1983.

Panov, B. V., et al. *Istoriya voyennogo iskusstva.* Moscow: Voyenizdat, 1984.

Papp, Daniel S. *Soviet Policies toward the Developing World during the 1980s: The Dilemmas of Power and Presence.* Maxwell Air Force Base, Alabama: Air University Press, December 1986.

Sarkesian, Sam C. *The New Battlefield: The United States and Unconventional Conflicts.* New York: Greenwood Press, 1986.

Simonyan, Major General R. "Teatry voyennykh deystviy v plannakh NATO." *Krasnaya zvezda,* July 27, August 8 and 10, 1979.

Skirdo, Colonel M. P. *Narod, armiya, polkovodets.* Moscow: Voyenizdat, 1970.

Sokolovskiy, V. D. *Voyennaya strategiya.* Moscow: Voyenizdat, 1962, 1963, 1968.

Sovetskaya voyennaya entsiklopediya [Soviet Military Encyclopedia], Vols. 6 and 7. Moscow, 1979.

U.S. Department of Defense. *Soviet Military Power: 1988.* Washington, D.C.: U.S. Government Printing Office, 1988.

Vasendin, Major General N., and Colonel N. Kuznetsov. "Modern Warfare and Surprise Attack." *Voyennaya mysl'* 6 (June 1968), FPD 0015/69, January 16, 1969, p. 22.

Vigor, P. H. *Soviet Blitzkrieg Theory.* New York: St. Martin's Press, 1983.

Voroshilov Lecture Materials. Lectures from the Voroshilov Military Academy of the USSR General Staff, various years.

Voyennyy entsiklopedicheskiy slovar'. Moscow: Voyenizdat, 1983.

Yazov, General D. T. "Voyennaya doktrina Varshavskogo Dogovora — doktrina zashchity mira i sotsializma." *Krasnaya zvezda,* July 28, 1987, p. 2.

Yurechko, John J. "Command and Control for Coalitional Warfare: The Soviet Approach." *Signal,* December 1985, pp. 34–39, reprinted in Stephen J. Combala, ed. *Soviet C3* (Washington, D.C.: AFCEA International Press, 1987), pp. 17–34.

Zhilin, General P. *Istoriya voyennogo iskusstva.* Moscow: Voyenizdat, 1986.

Zhurkin, V., S. Karaganov, and A. Kortunov. "Vyzovy bezopastnosti — staryye i novyye." *Kommunist* 1 (1988): 42–50.

Zimin, Marshall of Aviation G. *Razvitiye protovoyozdushnoy oborony.* Moscow: Voyenizdat, 1976.

Index

About the Contributors

Daniel Gouré is Director of Soviet Studies, SRS Technologies, Inc., Arlington, Virginia. He was previously director of threat analysis, pilot architecture study, Strategic Defense Initiative Organization (SDIO). His contributions to the literature of national security studies include works on Soviet counter-measures to SDI, Soviet nuclear straregy and force planning, military conflict in space, and active defenses in Soviet policy and strategy. Gouré's current research includes analysis of trends in Soviet theater defense force structure and planning.

Colin S. Gray is President, National Institute for Public Policy, Fairfax, Virginia, and an Adjunct Professor of National Security Studies at Georgetown University. He has served on the President's General Advisory Committee on Arms Control and Disarmament and on advisory panels for the Office of Technology Assessment and for the various departments of the U.S. military services. Gray has published many books and articles about nationl security studies, strategy, arms control, deterrence, and maritime strategy.

Roger Hamburg is Professor of Political Science at Indiana University, South Bend. He is a Soviet area studies specialist who has published on the nature of Soviet military doctrine, Soviet approaches to low-intensity conflict, and other politico-military aspects of Soviet defense and foreign policy. Hamburg also has research interests in the Soviet economy and in the implications of Soviet economic trends for military decision making and operational planning. He is active in many professional associations in political science and military studies and has been the recipient of numerous grants and awards for his research.

John G. Hines was a senior analyst in the Army Intelligence Agency, senior analyst for Soviet assessments in the Office of Net Assessment, U.S. Department of Defense, Office of the Secretary of Defense, and an analyst in the Defense Intelligence Agency. He is now a senior analyst at the Rand Corporation. Hines has written and lectured extensively in the areas of Soviet strategy, operations, and control.

Lawrence J. Korb is Director of the Center for Public Policy Education, The Brookings Institution, Washington, D.C. He was Dean of the Graduate School of Public and International Affairs, University of Pittsburgh, before joining Brookings. During the first five years of the Reagan administration, Korb served as Assistant Secretary of Defense for Manpower, Reserve Affairs, Installations, and Logistics. He also served as Vice President for Corporate Operations at the Raytheon Company and Director of Defense Policy Studies at the American Enterprise Institute. Korb served on active duty as a naval flight officer for four years and retired from the navy reserve with the rank of captain. He is the author of about 100 books, monographs, and articles on national security issues.

Carnes Lord was Director of International Studies at the National Institue for Public Policy, Fairfx, Virginia, before joining the staff of Vice President Dan Quayle as principal national security advisor. Lord holds two Ph.D.s and has taught political science at the University of Virginia. From 1981–1984 he served on the staff of the National Security Council. Lord has contributed to the literature on strategy, arms control, and U.S. defense policy.

Phillip A. Petersen is Assistant for Europe in the Policy Support Program of the Deputy Under Secretary of Defense for Policy. He has served as a research analyst for the Library of Congress and the Defense Intelligence Agency. Petersen has contributed to scholarly journals, books, and other publications on Soviet, U.S., and West European military affairs.

Sam C. Sarkesian is Professor of Political Science at Loyola University of Chicago and Chairman of the Research Committee of the National Strategy Forum. He served as Chairman of the Inter-University Seminar on Armed Forces and Society from 1980–1987. Sarkesian has published numerous books and articles about national security studies, low-intensity conflict, and the national security policy-making process. He served for more than 20 years as an enlisted man and officer in the U.S. Army in Germany, Korea, and Vietnam, including duty in the Special Forces, Airborne, and Infantry units.

John E. Starron, Jr., is Professor of Political Science at the National Defense University and Director of Project HOMER, an ongoing study of global resources and national security policies. Starron teaches courses in public policy, the politics of resources, and mobilization. In 1985 he was exchange professor at the Korean National Defense College. Starron is coeditor of *Economic Basis of Pacific Security and Maritime Resources of the Indian/Pacific Oceans,* published in 1982 and 1983.

Colonel James E. Toth, USMC, has served with Fleet Marine Forces in various command and staff assignments since 1959, including expeditionary service in the Dominican Republic and the Republic of Vietnam. In addition to various operational planning assignments at tactical, theater, and national levels, he has participated in two national strategy reviews. Toth is currently teaching at the Industrial College of the Armed Forces and the National War College. He is a graduate of the Marine Corps Amphibious Warfare School, the Army Command and General Staff College, and the Air War College.

John Allen Williams is Associate Professor of Political Science at Loyola University of Chicago, where he teaches courses in U.S. politics and U.S. foreign and defense policy. He previously taught at the U.S. Naval Academy and the University of Pennsylvania. He is Vice Chairman, Executive Director, and a Fellow of the Inter-University Seminar on Armed Forces and Society and is general editor of the book series, "IUS Special Editions on Armed Forces and Society." He is a member of the governing council of the Section on Military Studies, International Studies Association.

About the Editor

Stephen J. Cimbala is Professor of Political Science at Pennsylvania State University, Delaware County Campus. His numerous previous works include *National Security Strategy* (Praeger, 1984).